Shelley In England

SHELLEY IN ENGLAND

Percy Bysshe Shelley
From the miniature at Irvington
by the Duc de Montpensier

SHELLEY
IN ENGLAND

NEW FACTS AND LETTERS
FROM THE SHELLEY WHITTON PAPERS

BY

ROGER INGPEN
EDITOR OF "THE LETTERS OF PERCY BYSSHE SHELLEY"

WITH ILLUSTRATIONS AND FACSIMILES

VOLUME I

BOSTON AND NEW YORK
HOUGHTON MIFFLIN COMPANY
1917

SHELLEY
IN ENGLAND

NEW FACTS AND LETTERS
FROM THE SHELLEY-WHITTON PAPERS

BY

ROGER INGPEN

EDITOR OF " THE LETTERS OF PERCY BYSSHE SHELLEY "

WITH ILLUSTRATIONS AND FACSIMILES

VOLUME I

BOSTON AND NEW YORK
HOUGHTON MIFFLIN COMPANY
1917

PRINTED IN GREAT BRITAIN

PREFACE

AN explanation may be necessary for adding yet
another biography to the already extensive list of
books on Shelley. It is now some years since an
important discovery relating to Shelley was made
by Mr. Charles Withall, of Messrs. Withall & Withall,
the successors to Mr. William Whitton, who was
entrusted more than a century ago with the legal
business of Sir Bysshe and Sir Timothy Shelley.
Mr. Charles Withall happened to find, among the
papers preserved in his offices, some letters of Percy
Bysshe Shelley, and also some pamphlets, including
copies of *A Necessity of Atheism* and *An Address to the
Irish People.* This discovery encouraged Mr. Withall
to make a further search, which resulted in bringing
to light other letters of the poet, besides a mass of
correspondence, including numerous letters from
various members of the Shelley family, as well as a
large number of legal documents, pedigrees, Mr.
Whitton's letter book and diaries and other papers.
Mr. Withall caused copies to be made of most of
this material, and, after arranging it in chronological
order, he submitted the result of his labours to Sir

Shelley in England

John C. E. Shelley of Avington Park and Field Place. The papers were subsequently shown to the publishers of the present volume, who asked me to undertake the work of editing them. Many of the documents related to the estates of the Michells and the Shelleys, and they threw some light on the history of those families. The first of the poet's letters, twenty-nine in number and all unpublished, is dated February 6, 1810, the last January 31, 1818; from the earlier date to the poet's death and afterwards to the death of the poet's son, Sir Percy Florence Shelley, there are numerous documents, and letters written by Sir Bysshe Shelley, Sir Timothy Shelley, William Whitton, Mary Shelley, T. L. Peacock, and many others, including two unpublished letters of Lord Byron. The most satisfactory manner of utilising this material appeared to be that of retelling the story of Shelley's early years, the portion of his life that he passed in England, especially as many new facts have been brought to light since the publication of Professor Dowden's monumental biography of the poet.

In writing these pages I have refrained from moralising, or attempting any detailed criticism of Shelley's literary work. As a youth he was charming and irresistible to his friends, but he had many faults, and these faults, which to-day may appear to have been mere eccentricities, did not show themselves in that light to his father. Shelley undoubtedly desired a reconciliation with his father, whose nervous

Preface

fears, however, a result chiefly of his solicitor's advice, were subsequently developed into an inflexible attitude towards his son.

The new letters of the poet throw some light on his relations with his father in regard to his life at Oxford, his expulsion from the University, his elopement and marriage with Harriet Westbrook. The fact that Shelley was actually married in Edinburgh is now revealed for the first time, with the date of the ceremony and the name of the officiating minister. That Shelley was arrested on two separate occasions for debt and that he appeared on the boards of the Windsor theatre as an actor in Shakespearian drama, are incidents in his life that hitherto have not been disclosed. The discovery by Mr. Charles Withall, while this book was in the press, of the Coroner's documents relating to the inquest on Harriet Shelley's body, has cleared up certain doubtful points in regard to her death. I have been able to tell something about the fate of Harriet's two children, as also about the life of Sir Percy Shelley, the poet's son by his second wife, and to give some particulars concerning Mary Shelley after the death of her husband.

The manuscript note-book of the poet, of which many pages are reproduced in reduced facsimile at the end of this volume, appears to have been found, after she was salvaged, in the *Ariel,* the ill-fated boat from which Shelley was drowned. Some sand from the Mediterranean Sea still clings to the original book, the pages of which long remained stuck together by the brine in which it had been soaked. The book contains a first draft of a portion of *Adonais* and the preface to that poem, besides the lines to Emelia Viviani and some verses in Italian, also a fair copy of a substantial part of *A Defence of Poetry*. The late Dr. Richard Garnett had evidently seen a portion of this book, as he printed, in his *Relics of Shelley*, a few passages from the draft of the preface to *Adonais*.

My acknowledgments are primarily due to Sir John Shelley, who has given his sanction to the publication of the Shelley-Whitton papers and permitted me to make use of many documents connected with his family. Sir John, moreover, has given his ready consent to the reproduction of the Shelley note-book in his possession, and has allowed his family portraits to be included among the illustrations. The miniature portrait of Shelley as a boy, by the Duc de Montpensier, which forms the frontispiece, is reproduced for the first time in photogravure from the original at Avington. Much of the beauty of this picture was lost in the engraving by J. G. Stodart which appears in Professor's Dowden's book, and the pencil drawing by Reginald Easton, now in the Bodleian, cannot be accepted as a faithful copy of the original. I have also to acknowledge the courtesy of Miss Shelley for reading the proofs.

To Mr. Charles Withall I owe a heavy debt of gratitude for his arrangement of the Shelley-Whitton

Preface

papers, in itself a formidable task, which considerably lightened my labours as it enabled me to view the material in chronological sequence. Mr. Charles Withall has likewise constantly advised me on difficult and doubtful points, has carefully collated the documents, and placed at my disposal the copies of the papers relating to the inquest on Harriet Shelley and to her burial, the discovery of the originals of which is due to his industrious research.

His brother Mr. Walter Withall has kindly allowed me to use his photograph of Sir Percy Shelley, and he has supplied me with some interesting recollections of, and facts relating to, him and Jane, Lady Shelley. I have to thank Dr. W. Shirley Arundell for allowing me to reproduce the portrait of William Whitton which is in his possession; and Mr. R. F. Grimley and Nobile Donna Zella Opezzo for the use of the photograph of her great-grandfather, Thomas Medwin. Mrs. Brodie Clark gave me some interesting information with respect to Shelley's first school at Brentford. Mr. Richard Edgcumbe allowed me to print a portion of Sir Walter Scott's letter to Shelley. Mr. Thomas J. Wise related to me some particulars concerning Miss Hitchener. I have again made use of Mary Shelley's letter to Leigh Hunt which Miss Alice Bird kindly allowed me to include in my collection of Shelley's correspondence.

I have to thank Professor Thomas Seccombe and Mr. Arthur Reynolds for reading proofs; Mr. V. C.

Shelley in England

Turnbull for help in deciphering the contents of
Shelley's manuscript book; and Mr. R. A. Streatfeild
for transcribing and translating the Italian poems in
the same book; also Mr. W. H. Helm and Mr. Walter
H. Whitear for suggestions.

R. I.

July 1916.

Contents

Illustrations

SHELLEY IN ENGLAND

CHAPTER I

THE SHELLEYS

Early history—The Shelley and Michelgrove estates—John Shelley—Edward Shelley of Worminghurst—Timothy Shelley and his American wife—Bysshe Shelley : his birth, education, and marriage—The Michells and Field Place—Bysshe Shelley's second marriage—The Duke of Norfolk—Sir Bysshe's declining years—Castle Goring.

THE Shelley family has long been settled in Sussex, where the name is not uncommon. Genealogists, an habitually sanguine class, have traced the poet's line from an ancient origin. The roll of Battle Abbey contains the name of a Shelley who tradition says came to these shores with the Conqueror. There were Shelleys in the past who held high offices and otherwise distinguished themselves by valiant deeds. Formerly they were staunch adherents to the ancient faith, and one of the name was punished by death for conspiring against Protestant Elizabeth in order to release Catholic Mary Queen of Scots.

The family to which the poet owed his descent

A

claimed to have derived its name from the Manor of
Shelley, which with Schottis in Knockholt and other
lands in Kent was held by Thomas Shelley in the reign
of Edward the First. This Manor of Shelley was sold
in 1537, but not before a John Shelley had acquired
the estates of Michelgrove in Sussex, by his marriage
with the daughter of John Michelgrove; and the
descendants of this John Shelley now hold the two
Shelley baronetcies. His eldest son, Sir William
Shelley, Knight, was one of the Justices of the Court
of Common Pleas, and grandfather of the John Shelley
who was among the earliest to be created a baronet in
1611, the year in which James the First instituted the
dignity of baronets. Edward Shelley of Worminghurst, who died in 1588, brother of the above-named
Sir William, was the ancestor of Bysshe Shelley (made
a baronet in 1806), and of his grandson Percy Bysshe
Shelley, whose name alone confers a distinction on that
branch of the family which otherwise is not conspicuous.

The poet's great-great-grandfather, John Shelley of
Fen Place, Worth, Sussex (born January 27, 1666;
married, in 1692, Hellen, one of the co-heirs of Roger
Bysshe of Fen Place, Sussex), had five sons. Timothy
his third son was born in 1700, and having only a
remote chance of succeeding to the family property,
like the cadet of many a family of good position, went

SIR WILLIAM SHELLEY

*After the picture attributed to Hans Holbein,
in the possession of Sir John Shelley, Bart.*

forth to make his way in the North American colonies, where he married Mrs. Johanna Plum, a widow of New York. The dates of his emigration, marriage, and return to England have not been identified, but he appears to have settled in Newark, New England, where his two sons, John and Bysshe, were baptized at Christ Church in 1729 and 1731 respectively. The Church archives, however, which might have supplied the date of his marriage and other particulars, were burnt by the British troops in the war of independence.[1]

At Guildford, which is closely connected with Newark, entries exist from 1632 onwards, of the births, marriages, and burials of a number of persons bearing the name of Shelley. But the only substantial record that has been brought to light of Timothy Shelley's sojourn in America is a *post-obit* document dated 1735, and filed among the deeds in New York City, in which he describes himself as a " Merchant of Newark in America," and promises to pay the sum of £100 so soon as he shall be possessed of an estate of the value of £200 a year which belonged to his father, " John Shelley of Fen Place, in the County of Sussex, in Great Brittain, Esq."

It would seem, therefore, that Timothy did not find the fortune in America that he sought. Although

---

[1] See " The Search for Shelley's American Ancestor," by John Malone. *Century Magazine*, August 1892.

described as a merchant, Medwin states, but for the truth of the story he says he "cannot vouch," that Timothy's younger son, Bysshe, exercised in America the calling of quack doctor, and married the widow of a miller. If there is any foundation for the legend, it must relate to Timothy Shelley, the great-grandfather of the poet, and not to his grandfather Bysshe, who could have been no more than a child when he came to England.

Timothy Shelley's eldest brother, Bysshe, died unmarried in 1733, and ten years later his brother John, the second son, was declared insane. Timothy may have returned to England some time before 1739, the year of his father's death. In 1738, his father, John Shelley, executed his will, and gave to his wife certain freehold hereditaments in Sussex for life, and after her death he gave the same to his son Timothy and the heirs male of his body. To his grandson Bysshe, then a boy of eight, he devised, by a codicil dated 1739, certain copyholds held of the Manor of Streatham in fee, and bequeathed to him a sum of £2000 and all his jewels, rings, plate, linen, books and things lately belonging to his *son* Bysshe. By the death of his uncle, Edward Shelley, in March 1748–49, Timothy inherited Field Place, on condition that he should re-settle all the property derived from his father, on his eldest son John, and after his death on Bysshe.

4

JOHN SHELLEY

*After the picture by Thomas Gainsborough, R.A.,
in the possession of Sir John Shelley, Bart.*

The Shelleys

Stolid John Shelley[1] therefore was, in the ordinary course of things, heir to the estates. His grandfather, John, left to him a legacy of £100; to his brother Piercy £500, and from the bequest of the copyholds at Streatham it would seem that the old gentleman had some knowledge of and a liking for his grandson Bysshe, and especially desired to provide for him.

Young Bysshe, a brown-eyed bright lad with good looks and engaging manners, was also a favourite with his grandmother, Hellen Shelley, who in her will executed in 1740 (she died two years later) gave him some of her personal treasures, namely, her walnut-tree cabinet, and her small cabinet inlaid with ivory, all her ready money, mortgages, bonds, bills, notes, plate, diamonds, rings, pearl-necklace, and half her best linen, and she devised to him her freehold land near Willett's Bridge, in East Grinstead. She furthermore " ordered her executor to bring up and educate her said grandson in an handsome manner, and with a scholastick and gentleman like education,

---

[1] The portraits of John Shelley and his brother Bysshe, both taken in their declining years, offer a striking contrast. There is nothing remarkable in the face of the elder man. It is typical of many a squire in the county who loved good living and the solid comforts of a country gentleman in easy circumstances. As a matter of fact he added nothing by his own exertions to the family estates and died childless. The face of the younger might be that of a diplomatist, of one who thoroughly understood the game of life and who played his cards successfully. As boys one would expect John to be stolid and dull, and Bysshe handsome and vivacious.

5

so that he may be fitten to be bred up or put to the Law or some other gentleman like science or employment. And she ordered and did thereby fully direct that her trustees thereafter named take special care that her said grandson should not be sent or putt to sea on any account or pretence whatsoever, or by any persons whomsoever." Although Mrs. Shelley appointed her son Timothy as one of the two trustees and guardians of Bysshe, her bequests to this grandson and the specific injunctions as to his upbringing would seem to show disapproval of Timothy Shelley's American wanderings, and to reflect on his occupation and colonial manners, which evidently were to her mind unworthy of Bysshe. She does not appear to have been concerned about the education of her elder grandson John, and only bequeathed him a legacy of £100.

Bysshe Shelley grew up a remarkably handsome man, fully six feet in height, polished in manners and address, and with a small fortune of his own which he took an early opportunity of increasing by marrying an heiress. In connection with this marriage, Medwin speaks of him as possessing " the *prestige* that never fails to attach itself to the travelled man." Perhaps the tour of Europe was a part of the early training provided for by his thoughtful grandmother. At any rate, at the age of twenty-one, in 1751, he captured the heart of Miss Mary Catherine Michell, a girl of sixteen,[1] the orphan daughter of the Rev. Theobald Michell of Horsham, who died in May 1737.

The frequent occurrence of the name of Michell in connection with that of Shelley has led to some confusion, and one of the most frequent errors is that Field Place, the birthplace of the poet, came into the possession of the Shelley family through the marriage of Bysshe Shelley with Mary Michell. As a matter of fact, she never possessed the house, and it did not fall into Bysshe Shelley's hands until many years after her death.

We find the first mention of the house in the will of Richard Mychell the elder, of Warnham, in 1524, who gave his wife the choice " whether she dwelt at Stamerh'm, or at ffelde place." After this date, for more than two hundred years, Field Place remained Michell property, and it passed into the Shelley family in the following manner. Timothy Shelley of Champneys married, in 1664, Katherine, daughter of Edward Michell of Stamerham, by whom he had a son, John Shelley—the poet's great-great-grandfather referred to

---

[1] In the settlement relating to the estates derived by Miss Mary Catherine Michell from her father and mother, and dated 22nd July 1754, where she is stated to be nineteen years of age, it was agreed between Bysshe Shelley and his wife Mary Catherine that, within three months of her attaining the age of twenty-one, these estates should be settled on Bysshe for life, with remainder to his wife for life, with remainder to the first and every other son of Bysshe and Mary Catherine Shelley in tail male.

above. Timothy Shelley's second wife was Mary Cheale, who bore him a son, Edward, in 1670. On the death of Timothy Shelley, his widow, Mary Shelley, was married a second time to John Michell of Field Place. This John Michell had by his wife three sons, none of whom left issue, and Field Place thereupon devolved on his daughter Ann, afterwards Mrs. Slyford, the mother of four daughters, from whom the property, having first been mortgaged to, was purchased in June 1729 by the Edward Shelley before mentioned, whose Michell grandparents had held these estates. Edward Shelley was a barrister of the Middle Temple, who lived to a ripe age, and died a bachelor in 1747–48; by his will dated 1746 he devised his estates, including Field Place, to his nephew Timothy (son of the John Shelley mentioned above), and after his death to John, eldest son of Timothy, and if he died without issue, which event happened, to Bysshe for life, with remainder to his second son Timothy in tail male. And he provided that if the said John or Bysshe should marry before twenty-three, or should not conform to the rites or ceremonies of the Church of England, and thus continue the exercise of the Protestant religion, then in either of said cases the estates to them respectively devised should cease.[1]

[1] Percy Bysshe Shelley was descended from Edward Michell of Stamerham (who was married in 1640) in three lines, as great-great-great-

The Shelleys

To return to Bysshe Shelley's matrimonial project, we find that it did not run smoothly, for Miss Michell's guardian refused to countenance the match. She was, however, undaunted by this opposition and eloped with her handsome suitor to London, where they were married at the chapel of Alexander Keith, the shady Mayfair parson; Bysshe, ignoring the provision in his uncle's will, married at twenty-two. Keith is generally credited as having solemnized the much discussed marriage of the fair Quaker, Hannah Lightfoot, with a mysterious personage supposed to be none other than the son of Frederick, Prince of Wales, young Prince George, afterwards George III. In the early years of the eighteenth century Fleet marriages were a byword, and hardly less notorious were the marriages at Keith's chapel : the parson himself was only second in popularity to the blacksmith of Gretna Green in the estimation of couples bent on contracting clandestine unions. Keith's chapel stood near the present one in Curzon Street, and its incumbent paid just as much attention as suited him to the forms of the legal ceremony. Later, Keith was excommunicated for celebrating marriages without banns or licence, and he was finally imprisoned in the Fleet. Here for some years

great-grandson through his father Timothy Shelley, and as great-great-great-grandson through Bysshe's marriage with Mary Catherine Michell, and the same relationship through his father's marriage with Miss Pilfold.

9

Shelley in England

he enjoyed considerable prosperity, but the Marriage Act put an end to his practices; he fell on evil times and died poverty-stricken in prison.

Altogether, Keith and his four priests are said to have "solemnized" upwards of four thousand weddings. Some biographers have stated that Bysshe Shelley was married in the Fleet, but the Shelley pedigree at the College of Arms states that the marriage took place at "Keith's Chapel, Mayfair, in 1752." Keith, however, could not himself have performed the ceremony, as he was at that date safely lodged in the Fleet.

Bysshe Shelley and his bride left London soon after the marriage for Paris, where, on their arrival, Mrs. Bysshe was attacked with smallpox, from which she was not at the time expected to recover. She lived, however, to become the mother of three children, two daughters and a son Timothy, the poet's father, but she died in 1760 at the early age of twenty-five.

After nine years of widowerhood, Bysshe Shelley married (and is said also to have eloped with) another heiress, namely, Elizabeth Jane Sidney, the daughter of William Perry of Penshurst, and a collateral descendant through her mother, Elizabeth Sidney, of Sir Philip Sidney. His eldest son by this union, John Shelley-Sidney of Penshurst, was made a baronet in 1818, and the baronet's son[1] was created

[1] Philip Charles Sidney, the second baronet; he married Lady Sophia FitzClarence, daughter of King William IV by Mrs. Jordan.

SIR BYSSHE SHELLEY, BART.

*After the picture by Sir William Beechey, R.A.,
in the possession of Sir John Shelley, Bart.*

Baron De L'Isle and Dudley in 1835. From a worldly point of view, therefore, Bysshe Shelley continued to prosper, for he inherited the Shelley family estates in 1790 on the death, without issue, of his elder brother, John Shelley of Field Place. From his early days it was Bysshe Shelley's desire to found a great house, and to retain for his family by entail the fortune he had amassed. He attained his object by making two wealthy marriages, and by luck which favoured him in his undertakings. As a younger son of a younger son, born far from England in a small country town of the American colonies, Bysshe Shelley's prospects of inheriting the family estates must at one time have seemed remote, and it was only by a chain of fortuitous events that they ultimately reached him. Yet this clever, ambitious man lived to become one of the wealthiest landowners in the county of Sussex. He was not the kind of man to neglect anyone who was likely to be of use to him, and he was careful to cultivate the friendship of Charles, eleventh Duke of Norfolk. A firm supporter he was of the Whig party as represented by the Duke, who, for services in the past and perhaps as a security of his devotion in the future, in 1806 secured a baronetcy for Bysshe Shelley.

Except an intelligent face, and great worldly possessions, there was little to attract either in the character or person of " Jockey of Norfolk," as the Duke was familiarly termed. As a youth he did not trouble himself with book-learning, and as a young man he turned Protestant for political reasons. A sensualist, glutton, drunkard and gambler, despite his enormous size, he loved to travel at break-neck pace all over the kingdom, from Greystoke, his place in Cumberland, to Holme Tracey and Arundel Castle. When in London he was habitually to be found at the gaming clubs in St. James's Street, and he pursued his innumerable amours to the end. Many stories are told of his hard drinking, his gargantuan appetite for beefsteaks, his lack of personal cleanliness, and his unwieldiness. Shortly before his death he was subject to lethargy. Charles Morris, in *The Clubs of London*, relates that towards the evening the Duke would become immovable in his chair. " He would then request the bell to be rung three times ; this was a signal for bringing in a kind of easy litter, consisting of four equidistant belts, fastened together by a transverse one, which four domestics placed under him, and thus removed his enormous bulk, with a gentle swinging motion, up to his apartment. Upon these occasions the Duke would say nothing, but the whole thing was managed with great system and in perfect silence." Such was the man into whose hands Sir Bysshe and his son entrusted their honour.

Like his father, Sir Bysshe is said to have actually

The Shelleys

practised medicine in London in partnership with Dr. Graham, notorious for his Temple of Health, at which Emma Hart (afterwards Lady Hamilton) assisted, but the story is discredited. His grandson, the poet, assured Hogg he had heard on good authority that Sir Bysshe, with whom he was acquainted, had lent the Doctor money to enable him to set up a purple chariot.

Medwin's recollections of Sir Bysshe Shelley in his declining years are by no means edifying. He is described as having a noble and aristocratic bearing ; the portrait of him by Beechey, at Avington, shows him to have been decidedly handsome, and there is some likeness traceable in the upper part of his features to those of his illustrious grandson. Age, however, had brought no influence to mellow his selfish and acquisitive nature : he was hard-headed and headstrong to the last.

For his children he probably felt little affection, and he certainly showed none ; two of his daughters by the second marriage led such miserable existences under his roof that they married without his consent rather than endure his temper ; he retaliated by making a scanty provision for them in his will.

His eldest son and heir, Timothy, lived in dread of him, but managed to avoid an open quarrel with his sire. He received every morning, so Medwin assures us, a bulletin of the old man's health, hardly, however, it may be presumed, as an act of filial piety.

In his grandson, Percy, Sir Bysshe is said to have shown an interest, and he even went so far as to pay the bills of the Horsham and Worthing printers who put into type some of the boy's earliest efforts at writing, which apparently are no longer extant. Hogg, who says that Shelley used to speak of his grandfather without love or hate, but with contemptuous indifference, suggests a certain indistinct sympathy as existing between these two natures, so opposite and antagonistic, on the common ground that they both disliked Timothy Shelley, whom the old man first taught his grandson to curse. Shelley told Hogg that whenever he went " with his father to visit Sir Bysshe he always received him with a tremendous oath, and continued to heap curses on his head as long as he remained in the room." [1] Speculative opinions had no attraction for the baronet, whose matter-of-fact mind allowed him to treat with toleration, born of indifference, those subjects that delighted his grandson and so greatly scared his son.

Shelley's regard for his grandfather, if it ever existed,

---

[1] "Sir Bysshe being Ogygian, gouty, and bed-ridden, the poor old baronet had become excessively testy and irritable ; and a request for money instantly aggravated and inflamed every symptom, moved his choler, and stirred up his bile, impelling him irresistibly to alleviate his sufferings by the roundest oaths " (Hogg, i. 139).

did not survive his youth, for in January 1812 he wrote to Miss Hitchener, " I hear from my uncle that Sir B. Shelley is not likely to live long—that he will die soon. He is a complete atheist, and builds all his hopes on annihilation. He has acted very ill to three wives. He is a bad man. I never had respect for him : I always regarded him as a curse upon society. I shall not grieve at his death. I will not attend his funeral. I shall think of his departure as that of a hard-hearted reprobate." I do not know whether Sir Bysshe could claim to have married thrice, but he certainly did not pine for the want of feminine society, as in his will, in which he disregards the just claims of some of his lawfully begotten issue, he does not forget to provide for several of his children born out of wedlock.

Towards the end of the eighteenth century Sir Bysshe Shelley began to build, on a part of the settled estates, comprised in the settlement of 1791, his great mansion, Castle Goring, which is said to have cost him upwards of eighty thousand pounds. The house, which stands on rising ground surrounded by about 130 acres of land, commands an extensive view of the English Channel, is of an extraordinary design and a substantial proof of Sir Bysshe's eccentric character. This ambitious mansion is really composed of a pair of buildings joined in the centre, having two distinct styles of architecture which were also carried out in the interior decorations. The south-west front was designed by Biagio Rebecca, the Italian decorative painter, in the Palladian style from a villa in the vicinity of Rome. The north-east façade, described as " Modern Gothic," is a reduced copy of a portion of Arundel Castle. Among the apartments on the ground floor was one which Sir Bysshe designed for a " Justice Room," but the house was still unfinished at his death, and soon afterwards (on August 21, 1816) was put up for sale by auction, but failed to find a purchaser. It is not surprising, for in an order of the Court of Chancery of January 16, 1819, concerning the property, the house is described as in an unfinished and uninhabitable state.

In consequence of want of attention it had become infested with dry-rot, which had already made great ravages, and, if it were suffered to remain much longer without repair, there would not have been an inch of sound timber on the premises. The only alternative was to pull down the building and dispose of the materials, which would have produced several thousand pounds. But no such power existed under the settlement of 1791; it was therefore suggested that the difficulty might be overcome by an Act of Parliament. Nothing, however, was done, for, in December 1824, Sir Timothy Shelley leased the house to Captain George Richard Pechell for fourteen years at a yearly rent of £20. Modest as this sum appears,

NORTH-EAST FRONT

SOUTH-WEST FRONT

CASTLE GORING

the lessee covenanted for the tenant to put the place in repair within two years at his own cost, and to insure the building against fire for £12,000. And it much needed a hand to arrest the decay into which it was crumbling from dry-rot. The floorings of some of the rooms had fallen in, 165 large squares of glass besides smaller ones were wanting, the woodwork was rotting, the plastering was injured by damp, and handles, locks, and keys were wanting. So much was required to be done to the building, that Captain Pechell was not required to repair certain portions of it, nor to complete the fittings of a space intended for the library.

The house with the land and buildings, including a farm, the whole comprising 139 acres, was sold in 1845 for £11,250 to Captain Pechell, then in occupation, by the poet's widow, Mary Shelley, and her son, Sir Percy F. Shelley.

Sir Bysshe as an old man was eccentric and penurious. He spent a fortune in building Castle Goring, and never completed it for his occupation, but passed the last years of his life at Arun House, a small place near the town-hall at Horsham overlooking the river Arun, where he practised the strictest economy and was attended by an old servant, " as great a curiosity as his master." According to one authority [1] he was

---

[1] The unidentified newspaper editor, who in his Reminiscences—*Fraser's Magazine*, June 1841—says of Sir Bysshe, to whom he had been introduced by his grandson the poet, that, according to the current gossip of the place

Shelley in England

as indifferent to his personal appearance as he was to his style of living. He wore a round frock, and one of his diversions was a daily visit to the taproom of a humble tavern in the town, "not drinking" but as a silent auditor of the local gossip. At the time of his death in 1815, at the age of eighty-four, besides the will and its elaborate accompaniment of legal documents, there were found in his room, according to Medwin, bank-notes to the amount of ten thousand pounds, some between the leaves of the few books he possessed, while others were discovered in the folds of the sofa, or sewn into the lining of his dressing-gown. Sir Bysshe's habit of hoarding money in his house is exemplified by some extracts from his trustees' accounts, with which I have been furnished. The value of the bank-notes discovered in the baronet's house was actually £12,816.

in which he resided, he "had in his youth either been crossed in love, or had in a fit of passion committed some act of violence which had left a strong and melancholy impression on his mind. He had become what some persons would call eccentric, but he always struck me as having a dash of insanity."

CHAPTER II

CHILDHOOD

EITHER the education of Timothy, Sir Bysshe's eldest son, was sadly neglected, or the recipient failed to derive much advantage from it. It was intended that he should enter Sidney Sussex College, Cambridge,[1] which was founded by Lady Frances Sidney, Countess of Sussex, and in which the family of his stepmother had interests. But he eventually went to University College, Oxford, at which college Robert Dudley, Earl of Leicester, founded two scholars' places, and the Sidneys as the heirs of Earl of Leicester had the right of nominating these two scholars. After the usual course of studies he made the Grand Tour of Europe, but the only benefit that he derived from his travels was a smattering of French and a bad picture of Vesuvius in eruption, " if we except a certain *air* miscalled that of the old school, which he could put on or off as

---

[1] Medwin, vol. i. p. 10. Cf. also *University College, Oxford*, by G. M. Edwards, p. 210.

the occasion served." He did not possess the force of character of his father, who was a cynic, a materialist, and latterly a miser ; he had a kinder heart, though he made the fatal mistake of trusting his weak head to rule his heart.[1] His well-meant intentions were often misdirected : he had a passion, but little aptitude, for managing people, and he treated his servants well. For outward forms and conventions he was a great stickler : a church-goer, a reader of Paley's theology (whose chief arguments he claimed to have originated), he was a fussy, somewhat commonplace type of the squire of his day. Notwithstanding the fact that his literary preferences inclined to La Rochefoucauld and Lord Chesterfield, he did not shine as a letter-writer : as Member of Parliament for the Rape of Bramber, he failed to make any figure in the House, but was merely a consistent supporter of his own party.

Sir Bysshe had established a precedent for his family on the all-important question of marriage ; one may therefore be sure that the grand opportunity of Timothy Shelley's life was watched by his father with very critical eyes, and as one who had grown up with the tradition before him, if he did not marry money, his choice fell upon a gentlewoman of birth equal to his own. Timothy Shelley had engaged himself before he

---

[1] " He was slight of figure, tall, very fair, with the Shelley blue eyes " (Dowden, *Life of Shelley*, vol. i. p. 4).

Childhood

set out on his European travels to Elizabeth, a distant cousin, and daughter of Charles Pilfold of Effingham Place, and was married to her in October 1791 at West Grinstead. She was a great beauty, and had been brought up by her aunt, Lady Ferdinand Pool, the wife of the father of the turf. Mrs. Timothy Shelley was narrow-minded, mild and tolerant, a good letter-writer, but no reader of books; it was greatly to her disappointment that her son showed little disposition to take part in the field-sports of a country-gentleman. Timothy Shelley settled at Field Place, which, Miss R. C. Travers[1] says, seems to have been nearly always a secondary or dower house. Sir Bysshe, having other estates in Sussex and elsewhere, gave up his life interest to his son Timothy, in Field Place, which had come into his possession in 1790 by the death of his brother, and in this now historic house Timothy's first child and son, Percy Bysshe Shelley, came into the world on Saturday, August 4, 1792.[2] Field Place House, which is situated

---

[1] In the following description of Shelley's birthplace I have made liberal use, and in some cases have adopted the phrasing, of an interesting and valuable illustrated description of Field Place by Miss R. C. Travers, now Mrs. H. M. Hyndman (her father, Major Travers, at one time occupied the house), which appeared in the *English Illustrated Magazine* under the title of "The Youth of Shelley."

[2] Medwin states (vol. i. p. 1) that Shelley derived the name of Percy from "an aunt who was distantly connected with the Northumberland family."

Shelley in England

in the parish of Warnham, about two and a half miles west of Horsham, stands in well-wooded grounds some distance from the road, in a slight hollow surrounded by trees, and is approached by a drive from the south. The ffelde place mentioned in 1524 by Richard Mychell in his will, which is probably the core of the present building, was a timbered Sussex farmhouse, with the magnificent kitchen and the many little old rooms still remaining. In 1678 the Michells built the new front of Field Place, and a stone carving of their coat of arms with this date appeared under the central gable of the house until a recent tenant removed it. The stone was rescued by a local tradesman, who built it face inwards into the walls of a modern cottage near Broadbridge Heath, where it may still be found. The Field Place of to-day is a comfortable gabled structure "roofed with great slabs of Horsham stone"; the pillared portico, or verandah, in front of the building which joins the two wings is a modern addition, put up in 1846 by Sir James Duke, a former tenant of the house. The front door in Shelley's time stood under the central gable, but it has since been removed and its place filled by a plaster relief of the nine muses, which was known as "Shelley's ladies" during Major Travers' occupation. The house remains much as Shelley knew it: the fine old oak staircase must often have echoed with his footsteps and those of his

Drawn by D. Collins

FIELD PLACE

AS IT WAS IN SHELLEY'S TIME

Childhood

sisters, but one cannot say to what extent the grounds may have changed since his time. His great-uncle, John Shelley, who, like his grandfather Bysshe, was born in America, rebuilt the stables, and it has been suggested that he planted the fine rhododendrons in the American garden.

On the ground floor in the south wing there is a room off the drawing-room formerly known by the young people as "Confusion Hall," and over it on the next floor is the room in which Shelley was born. From the windows of this quiet and pleasant chamber he first took his view of the world—the south meadow, the lawn, and the great trees. Above the fireplace there is a brass tablet, put up by Sir Percy Shelley, inscribed with the date of the poet's birth and the following quatrain by Dr. Richard Garnett:

> " Shrine of the dawning speech and thought
> Of Shelley ! Sacred be
> To all who bow where Time has brought
> Gifts to Eternity."

Six other children were born to Timothy Shelley on the following dates: Elizabeth, May 10, 1794; Hellen, January 29, 1796, and who died four months later; Mary, June 9, 1797; another daughter also named Hellen, September 26, 1799; Margaret, January 20, 1801; and John, the youngest, March 15, 1806. The daughters were all remarkable for their beauty; Hogg says it was often observed that "very few families can boast of four such handsome girls." And Bysshe (as he was always called in the family) was as good-looking as his sisters : a slight figure, with beautiful hands, white skin, and fair ringlets ; his eyes are described as very dark blue. Miss Hellen Shelley, who has preserved, from recollection or from hearsay, most of the stories of Shelley's childhood, was only about twelve when Shelley left home for good. She is, however, our chief authority ; in writing of her brother's personal appearance, she remembered that "his figure was slight and beautiful ; his hands were models," and she referred to the "fixed beauty" of his eyes. On another occasion she says : "The engraved portraits of Bysshe, which have hitherto been published, are frightful pictures for a spiritual-looking being like a poet. Yet I do not expect that my ideal will ever be created, because he must have altered from boy to man. His forehead was white, the eyes deep blue— darker than [his brother] John's. He had an eccentric quantity of hair in those days, when he came by stealth to Field Place ; and Elizabeth, on one occasion, made him sit down to have it cut, and be made to look like a Christian." The written records of Bysshe's appearance as a child are borne out in the beautiful miniature portrait by the Duc de Montpensier now at Avington, which forms the frontispiece to the present volume.

Childhood

Bysshe's brother John was so much his junior that he hardly enters into his life, but Miss Hellen Shelley recollected seeing the two boys at play together in the grounds at Field Place under the fir trees on the lawn, Bysshe, then from Eton on holiday, gently pushing down his little brother in petticoats, to let him rise and beg for a repetition of such falls, rolling with laughing glee on the grass, and then wheeling the child along quickly in a little cart and upsetting him in the strawberry bed.

Bysshe spent his early days at Field Place, where he was brought up with his sisters, to whom his good temper remained a pleasant memory, and Miss Hellen Shelley could not recall a single instance of the reverse towards any of them. He was an imaginative boy, and was fond of inventing wonderful stories for his sisters' entertainment, stories in the truth of which he himself would believe later. These tales were listened to eagerly evening after evening when the little girls were admitted to the dining-room for dessert. They would sit on his knees, and he would tell them about the great Tortoise which lived in Warnham pond,[1] a tale probably founded on an ancient local legend of a

[1] Medwin tells us (vol. i. p. 123) that Mr. Timothy Shelley kept a boat "at Warnham pond, a lake of considerable extent, or rather two (lakes) connected by a drawbridge, which led to a pleasure-garden and a boat-house." There is a reference to the pond in the following letter, the earliest extant of Shelley's voluminous correspondence, which was

Shelley in England

Great Old Snake that haunted the neighbourhood : also with another veteran, " a snake of unusual magnitude," that had frequented the gardens of Field Place, according to tradition, for three hundred years ; it was accidentally killed by the carelessness of a gardener with his scythe while mowing the grass.

The spacious garret under the roof of Field Place was made the fancied habitation of an old grey alchemist with a long beard whom Bysshe promised his sisters that they should see " some day."

His amusements were not, however, always of such a harmless character. He had a passion for playing with fire, and one of his tricks was to fill a portable stove with some inflammable liquid and carry it flaming through the kitchen to the back door. His cousin, John Grove, says that " in one of his experiments

written a few days before his eleventh birthday, and three years earlier than the birth of his brother John : .

Monday, July 18, 1803.

DEAR KATE,—We have proposed a day at the pond next Wednesday ; and, if you will come to-morrow morning, I would be much obliged to you ; and if you could anyhow bring Tom over to stay all night, I would thank you. We are to have a cold dinner over at the pond, and come home to eat a bit of roast chicken and peas at about nine o'clock. Mama depends upon your bringing Tom over to-morrow, and if you don't we shall be very much disappointed. Tell the bearer not to forget to bring me a fairing—which is some ginger-bread, sweetmeat, hunting-nuts, and a pocket-book. Now I end.—I am not, Your obedient servant,   P. B. SHELLEY.

MISS KATE,
HORSHAM, SUSSEX.

Free, P. B. SHELLEY.

28

Childhood

he set fire to the butler, Laker, and then soused him with a pail of water."

On taking up the study of chemistry and electricity he became a terror to his sisters, especially when he offered to cure their chilblains by means of an electric battery. Miss Hellen Shelley relates an anecdote of her brother's kind thought for a sufferer from this painful complaint. One morning while she was seated with others in the little sitting-room at Field Place, a countryman was observed to pass the window with a truss of hay on a prong over his shoulders : the man when challenged proved to be Bysshe in a rustic garb, on his way to a young lady at Horsham who had been prescribed hay-tea for her chilblains. There is another story of his pranks at Field Place. He once applied to Colonel Sergison in good Sussex dialect for the post of gamekeeper's boy, and his suit was considered seriously, whereupon he gave vent to an explosion of boisterous laughter.

Sometimes he would take his sisters for long rambles, and when his short-cuts meant climbing fences and traversing muddy fields to the detriment of their shoes he would carry the little one of the party. Miss Hellen Shelley's stories of her brother show that he was full of pleasant attentions to children. His desire to adopt and educate a child was one that he cherished for some time. She says that he " often talked seriously of purchasing a little girl for that purpose : a tumbler, who came to the back door to display her wonderful feats, attracted him, and he thought she would be a good subject for the purpose, but all these wild fancies came to naught. He would take his pony and ride about the beautiful lanes and fields surrounding the house, and *talk* of his intention, but he did not consider that board and lodging would be indispensable, and this difficulty probably was quite sufficient to prevent the talk from becoming reality."

Once [1] when he was confined to the house with illness and not allowed to go out, he came to the window and kissed his sister, Margaret, through the pane of glass, and she remembered his face and lips pressed against the window. To continue his sister Hellen's recollections, she says that at a later period it was his habit to walk out alone at night ; the old servant of the family would follow him, and on returning say, " Master Bysshe only took a walk and came back." He was full of cheerful fun, and would amuse himself with writing verses ; there were some lines satirising the peculiarities of a French governess, who unfortunately happened to see them, to the consternation of her pupils. On another occasion he wrote a play with his eldest sister, and sent it to Matthews, but it was re-

[1] In 1806.

Childhood

turned as unsuitable for acting.[1]   These early effusions
have perished, but the following lines, which are probably Shelley's earliest efforts in verse that have been
preserved, are worth quoting.   The date given to them
in Mr. Thomas Hutchinson's edition of Shelley's poems
is 1800.   The sheet upon which they were copied by
his sister is headed with the drawing of a tabby-cat :

> " A cat in distress,
>   Nothing more, nor less,
> Good folks, I must faithfully tell ye,
>   As I am a sinner,
>   It waits for some dinner
> To stuff out its own little belly.
>
>   You would not easily guess
>   All the modes of distress
> Which torture the tenants of earth ;
>   And the various evils,
>   Which, like so many devils,
> Attend the poor souls from their birth.
>
>   Some a living require,
>   And others desire
> An old fellow out of the way ;

---

[1] This failure, however, did not deter him from his desire to become
a writer for the stage, for in an unpublished letter, of uncertain date,
but probably anterior to 1811, written from Field Place to Graham,
Shelley promised to write some songs to be set to music by Woelff
(Graham's music master) whom he desired to compose an overture for
a farce. He also inquired for the addresses of the manager of the
Lyceum and Covent Garden Theatres, as he had a farce and a tragedy
that he wished to offer them. " The tragedy," he adds, " is not yet
finished."

Shelley in England

And which is the best
I leave to be guessed,
For I cannot pretend to say.

One wants society,
Another variety,
Others a tranquil life;
Some want food,
Others, as good,
Only want a wife.

But this poor little cat
Only wanted a rat,
To stuff out its own little maw;
And it were as good
Some people had such food,
To make them *hold their jaw!* "

Shelley's memory was always remarkable, and, even when he was a small child, very retentive; as an instance, his sister says she had frequently heard from her mother that he repeated word for word Gray's verses on the " cat drowned in a tub of gold fishes " after once reading them, and he would at his father's bidding recite long Latin quotations. As a young child he shared the same education as his sisters, but at six he went daily to learn Latin at the house of the Rev. Mr. Edwards, the Vicar of Warnham, whom Medwin describes as " of only limited intellect," and with a pronounced Welsh accent.

Except for his holidays, Shelley spent very little

Childhood

time at Field Place after his tenth year, when he left
home for boarding-school.

One direct reference only in Shelley's verse to the
days of his childhood has been preserved in the fragment printed among the poems written in 1816 :

> " Dear Home, thou scene of earliest hopes and joys,
>   The least of which wronged Memory ever makes
>   Bitterer than all thine unremembered tears."

The following lines in *Zastrozzi* may also be reminis-
cent :

" . . . that ecstatic, that calm and serene delight only experienced by the innocent and which is excited by a return to the
place where we have spent our days of infancy."

CHAPTER III

SCHOOLDAYS

Shelley goes to school at Syon House Academy—His cousin,
Tom Medwin—Description of the schoolhouse—Dr. Greenlaw—Sir
John Rennie—Petty tyranny of the boys—Shelley's joke—His
friend—His miscellaneous reading—Adam Walker—Astronomy—
Dancing lessons—Leaves Syon House School.

WHEN Shelley reached the age of ten, in 1802, he was
sent as a boarder to Syon House Academy, Isleworth,
near Brentford, presided over by the Rev. Dr. Greenlaw, where his cousin, Tom Medwin,[1] son of the Horsham lawyer, had preceded him. Syon Park House,
as it is now called, is situated on the London Road
nearly opposite the lane that leads to Syon Park. It
is enclosed by high walls, but can be easily identified
by the Gazebo, or summer-house, which surmounts
the wall on the public road. The house is a solid
structure and has been standing for more than three

---

[1] Concerning his relationship with Shelley, Medwin says, "Miss
Michell, Sir Bysshe's first wife, was my grandfather's first cousin, and
my mother bore the same degree of consanguinity to Miss Pilfold
[Shelley's mother]." Although Medwin was Shelley's senior he does not
appear to have protected him at school. In later life, at least, he was
devoted to Shelley, and his biography of the poet was written in terms
of eulogy. He, Medwin, however, failed to make the best use of his
facilities for writing the life of Shelley, whom he had known as a boy,
and also during the last year of his life.

34

Schooldays

centuries, the family of its present owner, Colonel Brodie Clark, having held it for over a hundred years. It formerly belonged to, and it may have been built for, Dr. John King, who in 1611 became Bishop of London. Mrs. Brodie Clark tells me that the American heroine, Princess Pocahontas, visited the Bishop at this house during her brief sojourn in England. This must have been between 1616 and 1617, for she landed during the earlier year, and died off Gravesend in the following March immediately after having embarked for Virginia. The Bishop, who wrote verses himself, was father of a poet, Henry King, afterwards Bishop of Chichester. The old house, therefore, is associated with more than one poet : the pious writer of " The Exequy " and the author of " Adonais."

The precise position of Shelley's school at Brentford had latterly been lost sight of, even Professor Dowden was without definite knowledge of its exact position when he wrote his Life of Shelley, and it remained for Mr. Fred Turner of the Brentford Public Library to identify it. Since Shelley's time it has undergone some changes, and a modern addition has been made to the building at the eastern end. The schoolroom has disappeared ; it extended to the high road and was probably at one time the old banqueting-hall. The exact position of the playground can no longer be located, although in the garden there remained till recently an old stump with some staples attached to it, which is supposed to have been a relic of the Bell tree, an elm so called from its having suspended from its branches the "odious bell whose din," says Medwin, "when I think of it, yet jars in my ears."

Just inside the high walls that surrounded the house, and which gave it a somewhat gloomy appearance, there were excellent gardens and a playground, which Medwin describes as of very limited dimensions —a few hundred yards—and surrounded by four stone walls. The situation was open and healthy, and the total number of boys about fifty, ranging from eight to sixteen years of age. They were well fed and taken care of by Mrs. Greenlaw and her sister, Miss Hodgkins. The eldest daughter, Miss Greenlaw, taught the youngest boys their letters, whilst the doctor and his assistants devoted themselves to the others, the subjects comprising chiefly the classics, writing, arithmetic, French, and occasionally geography and astronomy.[1]

Dr. Greenlaw, a Scotch clerical Doctor of Laws, was in old age "of a sanguinary complexion; he indulged in an inordinate quantity of snuff from his Scotch mull, and he usually wore his spectacles above his bushy eyebrows. Though not wanting in good qualities he possessed a choleric and capricious temper, which was

[1] Rennie.

Schooldays

influenced by the daily occurrences of a domestic life not the most harmonious, and of which his face was the barometer and his hand the index." [1]

He was a tolerable Greek and Latin scholar, but he seems to have had his limitations and prejudices, and he did not engender in Shelley his love of the classics. " He acquired his knowledge of them, as it were, intuitively, and seemingly without study, for during school hours he was wont to gaze at the passing clouds, all that could be seen from the lofty windows which his desk fronted, or watch the swallows as they flitted past, with longing for their wings ; or would scrawl in his school-books—a habit he always continued—rude drawings of pines and cedars, in memory of those on the lawn of his native home. On these occasions, our master would sometimes peep over his shoulder, and greet his ears with no pleasing salutation." [2] When Dr. Greenlaw was in one of his good humours he indulged in what he termed *facetiae*, and to Shelley's disgust but to the amusement of the school he would on such occasions relate a coarse joke.

Syon House Academy evidently did not make such

[1] *Cf.* Medwin. Hogg says that, in walking to Bishopsgate from London with Shelley, " he pointed out to me, more than once, a gloomy brick-house, as being this school. He spoke of the master, Dr. Greenlaw, not without respect, saying ' he was a hard-headed Scotchman, and a man of rather liberal opinions.' Of this period of his life he never *gave me* an account."

[2] Medwin.

Shelley in England

a favourable impression on Medwin as on his school-fellow, Sir John Rennie, the engineer, who included a brief account of his schooldays in his autobiography. It was not a " Do-the-boys Hall," but the unappetising food provided at Syon House school was prepared and distributed with true Scotch frugality to the pupils, who were mostly the sons of London shopkeepers of rude habits and coarse manners. To Shelley the school was a perfect hell, where he " passed as a strange unsociable being " ; [1] his slender figure, girlish gestures, and his lack of interest in the games of the other boys singled him out as " fair sport " or a butt. Although fagging as it is practised at our large public schools was not in vogue at Dr. Greenlaw's academy, there was enough petty tyranny to render Shelley's life at times un-bearable. When maddened by the persecution of his schoolfellows he would give way to furious paroxysms of rage, and seize any object at hand, even a small boy, to hurl at his tormentors. He knew, however, how to play a joke on his schoolfellows, as the following story shows. A boy [2] in a class below Shelley was one day trying to compose a Latin nonsense verse to be written down for the scanning, when Shelley came along and asked what he was doing. On being

[1] Medwin.
[2] The late Mr. W. C. Gellibrand, who died in his ninety-third year on April 20, 1884. The story was contributed, in Mr. Gellibrand's words, to the *Athenæum* for May 3, 1884, by Mr. Augustine Birrell.

SYON PARK HOUSE, ISLEWORTH

FORMERLY SYON HOUSE ACADEMY

informed he said, " Give me your slate and I will do it for you." The boy went off to play, and when he returned he had hardly time to look at what Shelley had written on the slate, much less copy it afresh, so he handed it to the master, who called him up and asked if he had written the verse. The lad foolishly replied " yes," whereupon he was asked to construe it, and to his horror he found that it ran :

"Hos ego versiculos scripsi, sed non ego feci."

The boy was duly flogged, but he afterwards had the satisfaction of giving Shelley a pommelling. The narrator of this story said that Shelley looked like a girl in boy's clothes, and that he fought with open hands. He used to roll on the floor when flogged, not from the pain, but from a sense of indignity.

Shelley was, however, capable of great warmth of friendship for those whom he liked, and, "if treated with kindness, he was very amiable, noble, high-spirited and generous." [1] Among his papers after his death was found the following fragment, which is said to have been written not long before that event. It will find an appropriate place here, when speaking of the friendship that he formed at Syon House, to which period of his schooldays it probably relates,

[1] Rennie.

as he mentions that his age was about eleven or twelve :

"I once had a friend whom an inextricable multitude of circumstances has forced me to treat with apparent neglect. To him I dedicate this essay. If he finds my own words condemn me, will he not forgive ?

"The nature of love and friendship is very little understood, and the distinctions between them ill-established. This latter feeling—at least, a profound and sentimental attachment to one of the same sex, often precedes the former. It is not right to say, merely, that friendship is exempt from the smallest alloy of sensuality. It rejects, with disdain, all thoughts but those of an elevated and imaginative character. I remember forming an attachment of this kind at school. I cannot recall to my memory the precise epoch at which this took place ; but I imagine it must have been at the age of eleven or twelve.

"The object of these sentiments was a boy about my own age, of a character eminently generous, brave and gentle ; and the elements of human feeling seemed to have been, from his birth, genially compounded within him. There was a delicacy and a simplicity in his manners, inexpressibly attractive. It has never been my fortune to meet with him since my schoolboy days ; but either I confound my present recollections with the delusions of past feelings, or he is now a source of honour and utility to every one around him. The tones of his voice were so soft and winning, that every word pierced into my heart ; and their pathos was so deep, that in listening to him the tears have involuntarily gushed from my eyes. Such was the being for whom I first experienced the sacred sentiments of friendship. I remember in my simplicity writing to my mother a long account of his admirable qualities and my own devoted attachment. I suppose she thought me out of my wits, for she returned no answer to my letter. I remember we used to walk the whole play-hours up and down by some moss-covered palings, pouring out our hearts in youthful talk. We used to speak of the ladies, with whom we were in love, and I remember that our usual practice was to confirm each other in the everlasting fidelity, in which we had bound ourselves towards them, and towards each other. I recollect thinking my friend exquisitely beautiful. Every night, when we parted to go to bed, we kissed each other like children, as we still were ! "

The name of Shelley's friend is not known ; he could hardly have been Medwin, who was Shelley's senior by some four years, although he tells us that he was the only one in the school with whom Shelley could communicate his sufferings or exchange ideas.

On holidays, when the other boys were playing within the narrow limits of the playground, Shelley would pace backwards and forwards with Medwin along the southern wall, indulging in various vague and undefined ideas, and pour out his sorrows to his friend, " with observations far beyond his years, which according to his after ideas seem to have sprung from

an ante-natal life." In other words we may suppose
that he talked above the head of Tom Medwin. The
familiar passage in the dedication to " The Revolt of
Islam," in which Shelley recalls a resolution of his
schooldays, seems to relate to Syon House rather than
to Eton, where there was no grass.

" Thoughts of great deeds were mine, dear Friend, when first
  The clouds which wrap this world from youth did pass.
I do remember well the hour which burst
  My spirit's sleep : a fresh May-dawn it was,
  When I walked forth upon the glittering grass,
And wept, I knew not why : until there rose,
  From the near schoolroom, voices, that alas !
  Were but one echo from a world of woes—
The harsh and grating strife of tyrants and of foes.

And then I clasped my hands and looked around—
  —But none was near to mock my streaming eyes,
Which poured their warm drops on the sunny ground—
  So without shame, I spoke : ' I will be wise,
  And just, and free, and mild, if in me lies
Such power, for I grow weary to behold
  The selfish and the strong still tyrannise
  Without reproach or check.' I then controlled
My tears, my heart grew calm, and I was meek and bold.

And from that hour did I with earnest thought
  Heap knowledge from forbidden mines of lore,
Yet nothing that my tyrants knew or taught
  I cared to learn, but from that secret store
  Wrought linked armour for my soul, before

44

Schooldays

It might walk forth to war among mankind ;
   Thus power and hope were strengthened more and more
   Within me, till there came upon my mind
A sense of loneliness, a thirst with which I pined."

The set tasks of the school gave Shelley no trouble ;
with a memory so tenacious that he never forgot a
word after once having turned it up in his dictionary,
he soon outstripped his classmates. "He was fond of
reading," says Medwin, "and he greedily devoured all
the books which were brought to the school after the
holidays ; these were mostly *blue* books. Who does
not know what blue books mean ? but if there should
be any ignorant enough not to know what those darling
volumes, so designated from their covers, contain, be it
known, that they were bought for sixpence, and embodied stories of haunted castles, bandits, murderers,
and other grim personages—a most exciting and interesting sort of food for boys' minds; among those of
larger calibre was one which I have never seen since,
but I still remember with a *recherché* delight. It was
Peter Wilkins. How much Shelley wished for a
winged wife and little winged cherubs of children ! "
The Minerva Press of Lane [1] in Leadenhall Street was

[1] "Lane made a large fortune by the immense quantity of trashy novels
which he sent forth from his Minerva Press. I perfectly remember the
splendid carriage in which he used to ride, and his footmen with their
cockades and gold-headed canes" (*Recollections of the Table-talk of Samuel
Rogers*, 1856, p. 138).
Hughes of Ludgate Street, and Lee of Half-Moon Street, Bishopsgate,

one of the chief purveyors of this class of literature.

When this stock was exhausted, Shelley would haunt the circulating library of Mr. P. Norbury in Brentford High Street. This enterprising librarian also carried on the business of a printer and publisher of the same kind of extravagant fiction to which Shelley was addicted. In an advertisement at the end of W. Helme's *Evenings Rationally Employed*, which he issued in 1803, he announced his intention of publishing *The Watch Tower ; or, The Sons of Ulthona*, an historical romance in 5 vols. by T. J. Horsley Curteis, author of *Ethelwina, Ancient Records*, and *The Scottish Legend ;* also *Murray House*, in 3 vols., by Mrs. Parsons, author of *The Mysterious Visit, The Peasant of Ardenne Forest, The Miser and his Family*, &c.

The actual shop of Norbury is now occupied by the stationery and printing works of Mr. Stutters, and is still much in the same condition as in Shelley's time. Mr. Fred Turner, who looked at a few of the books that were in circulation at the library, found nothing

were other publishers of the same class who in the early years of the nineteenth century issued sixpenny books with the following titles: " *The Midnight Groan ; or, the Spectre of the Chapel : involving an Exposure of the Horrible Secrets of the Nocturnal Assembly : a Gothic Romance" ; "Florian de Videmont, Chieftain of the Blue Castle ; or, Lorenzo the Starving Prisoner, and the Saviour of Almagro and his two Daughters from the Horrors of the Red Chamber" ; "Lucretia ; or, the Robbers of the Hyrcanean Forest" ; " Algehira ; or, Mystic Captives : a romantic Fragment.*"

specially indicative of Shelley's literary predilections. Apart from "blue books," the volumes that most delighted Shelley at this time were the romances of Anne Radcliffe, "Monk" Lewis, and Charlotte Dacre, better known as "Rosa Matilda," whose *Zofloya; or, The Moor* (the last named was published after Shelley left Brentford), is especially named as a favourite by Medwin, upon which he is said by the same authority to have based his two novels—*Zastrozzi*, and *St. Irvyne; or, The Rosicrusian.*

It is hardly surprising that, after supping on the horrors of the Minerva Press, he should have been subject to strange and sometimes frightful dreams. Medwin did not sleep in Shelley's dormitory, but he said that he could never forget seeing him walk into his room one moonlight night. His eyes were open and he advanced with slow steps towards the open window ; the sleep-walker was waked by his arm being seized by Medwin, who led him back with difficulty to his bed, but it was some time before his disquietude was allayed.

During Shelley's second or third year at Syon House, Adam Walker, the self-taught natural philosopher, was summoned to the school to deliver a course of lectures on Astronomy to the boys in the great room of the Academy, and he displayed his Orrery.

Shelley in England

Walker had spent many years in lecturing, and among the public schools that he had visited were Eton and Winchester. The pursuits of his varied career had ranged from an ushership in a school at the age of fifteen, to that of a hermit on one of the islands on Winandermere. He had engaged in trade, and was responsible for some inventions, but lecturing was the occupation that he found most profitable.[1]

Astronomy proved an entirely new sphere to Shelley, and Walker's lectures opened to him a fresh field for his speculations ; the idea of a plurality of worlds especially delighted him. Walker's lectures concluded with a demonstration of the powers of the solar microscope, which excited Shelley's curiosity, though not to the same extent as the lectures on Astronomy. In after years Shelley became the possessor of a microscope, which Hogg relates he pawned in London in order to alleviate the distress of an old man. He afterwards recovered this instrument

[1] Some idea of the lectures to which Shelley was an attentive listener may be gathered from Walker's publications. That they were sufficiently comprehensive is shown by the title-page of the " *Analysis of a Course of Lectures on Natural and Experimental Philosophy*, viz. Magnetism, Mechanics, Chemistry, Pneumatics, Hydrostatics, Electricity, Fortification Optics, use of the Globes, &c., Astronomy, by A. Walker, M.D.S., Lecturer on Philosophy to His Royal Highness the Duke of Gloucester ; *Eton* and *Winchester* Colleges, &c." This little book, which contains a mass of information more or less correct, went through many editions. Of the planets he says, " Who can doubt therefore but they are inhabited, as well as all the worlds of the other system ? How much too big is this idea for the human imagination ! "

and retained it for several years, long after he had parted with all the rest of his philosophical apparatus.

" If Shelley abominated one task more than another," says Medwin,[1] " it was a dancing lesson. At a ball at Willis's rooms, where, among other pupils of Sala, I made one, an aunt of mine asked the dancing-master why Bysshe was not present, to which he replied in his broken English : ' Mon Dieu, madam, what should he do here ? Master Shelley will not learn any ting— he is so *gauche*.' In fact, he continued to abscond as often as possible from the dancing lessons, and, when forced to attend, suffered inexpressibly."

The Rev. C. H. Grove, in recalling some recollections of his cousin, says : " The first time I saw Bysshe was when (I was) at Harrow—I nine years old ; my brother George, ten. We took him up at Brentford, where he was at school, at Dr. Greenlaw's, a servant of my father's taking care of us all. He accompanied us to Town, and spent the Easter holidays there. The only circumstance I can recollect to mention in connection with that visit was, that Bysshe, who was some few years older than we were, thought it would be good service to play carpenters, and, under his auspices, we got carpenter's axes, and cut down some of my father's young fir-trees in the park :

[1] Medwin, i. 28.

my father often used to remind me of that circumstance." [1] This happened when Shelley was twelve,
in 1804, the year when he left Syon House School.

[1] Rev. H. C. Grove's letter, dated February 16, 1857, to Miss Hellen
Shelley, from Professor Dowden's corrected copy of Hogg's *Life of Shelley*.
It is noticeable that Hogg prints Ferne (Mr. T. Grove's Wiltshire seat)
instead of Town.

CHAPTER IV

ETON

IN the year 1804 Shelley left Syon House School for Eton, but for him it was hardly a change for the better. Instead of sixty schoolfellows, he found himself among five hundred boys, and a corresponding increase in the number of his tormentors. He signed his name on 29th July in the books of the head-master, Dr. Goodall, a courteous, dignified, bewigged gentleman, and a scholar, but one who lacked the sterner qualities of the disciplinarian.

The lower school was ruled during most of Shelley's time with firmer hands than those of the mild Dr. Goodall, by Dr. John Keate, who succeeded to the head-mastership in 1809. Short and thickset, Keate was " little more (if more at all) than five feet in height, and not very great in girth, but in this space was concentrated the pluck of ten battalions." [1] As a

[1] Kinglake's *Eōthen*, ch. xviii.

young man he had been a resolute fighter, as an older man he was " tremendously fierce." [1]

"The very sight of the cocked hat he always wore, placed frontways on his head like that of Napoleon, struck terror in the hearts of all offenders." [2] His dress was grotesque, and the flowing black gown on his squat figure suggested a little widow-woman. Dr. Keate's face was of a ruddy hue ; his red, shaggy eyebrows were very prominent, and he had the peculiar knack of using them for the purpose of pointing out any object towards which he wished to direct attention. The rest of his features, which were strikingly original, and easily lent themselves to caricature, resembled those of a bull-dog; indeed it was believed in the school that he possessed the bull-dog's power of pinning a bull with his teeth. His stentorian voice he could modulate with skill, "but he also had the power of quacking like an angry duck in order to inspire respect" : [3] his habitual severity he judged as fitting for a head-master.

Keate was the embodiment of honour and rectitude, an excellent scholar, and famed for his Latin verse. On succeeding to the head-mastership on Dr. Goodall's becoming Provost, he at once took steps

[1] Kinglake's *Eōthen*, ch. xviii.
[2] Gronow's *Recollections*.
[3] Kinglake's *Eōthen*, ch. xviii.

to introduce very severe measures in dealing with
the slackness prevalent in the school during his pre-
decessor's *régime*, and for some time his efforts were
met with the most determined opposition on the part
of the boys. As a disciplinarian Keate showed no
moderation in the use of the rod, having on one
memorable occasion flogged eighty boys into submission, a task that occupied him till past midnight.
Despite his blustering manner, Keate is said to have
been not altogether devoid of kindness, and he
was, on the whole, a popular head-master, but his
rough and despotic character could hardly have
appeared otherwise than brutal to a boy of Shelley's
nature.

Shelley first lodged at the house of Mr. Hexter,
an Eton writing-master and a " dame." He afterwards boarded at the house of the Rev. George Bethell,[1]
a good-humoured, noisy, jolly-looking old fellow ; but
regarded as the dullest man in the school. " Botch "
Bethell, as they nicknamed him on account of the
dreadful botches that he made in altering the boys'
verses, was remembered for his verbose sermons, and

[1] " This Mr. Bethell was, to boys, famous for inefficiency as a classical
teacher ; but he was a true gentleman, a cadet of a good Yorkshire
family ; he was known *to men* as a modest but steadfast vindicator of ' the
statutable rights of scholars ' of Eton College against the iniquitous usurpa-
tions of the Provost and Fellows. He was a just and also a courteous
man" (William Cory, in *The Notebook of the Shelley Society*, 1888,
p. 15, Part i.).

Shelley in England

his fatuous comments on the boys' tasks by the following couplet in which he was ridiculed :

> " Didactic, dry, declamatory, dull,
>   Big, blustering Bethell bellows like a bull."

On entering this school, says Dowden, Shelley was placed in the upper fourth form ; in 1805 he was in the remove ; in 1808 in the upper fifth ; and when leaving, in 1810, in the sixth form.

Bethell's house, which was taken down in 1863, " was," says William Cory,[1] " next door to a shop well known fifty years back—a shop kept by some elderly women called Spire or Spires. At the end of the village of Eton in which the schoolboys lived, there was at the same time a shop kept by people named Towers. I dare say Shelley may, like me, have heard Gray's line quoted thus : ' Ye ancient Spires, ye distant Towers.' " Shelley did not forget Spires, if Gronow is to be trusted, for in his Recollections, when describing how he came across Shelley for the last time on the seashore at Genoa in 1822, " the poet was making a true poet's meal of bread and fruit. He at once recognised me, jumped up, and appearing greatly delighted, exclaimed, ' Here you see me at my old Eton habits, but instead of the green fields for a couch I have the shores of the Mediterranean.

[1] *The Notebook of the Shelley Society*, 1888, p. 15, Part i.

54

Eton

It is very grand, and very romantic. I only wish I had some of the excellent brown bread and butter we used to get at Spires'; but I was never very fastidious in my diet.' Then he continued in a wild and eccentric manner : 'Gronow, do you remember the beautiful Martha, the Hebe of Spires's ? She was the loveliest girl I ever saw, and I loved her to distraction.'"[1] While Gronow sat by Shelley's side " he asked many questions about myself and many of our schoolfellows "; which shows that he did remember his friends at Eton, although the contrary has been asserted.

The practice at Eton of making indiscriminate presents of handsomely bound books among classmates on leaving the school was in vogue in Shelley's time, and he possessed at Oxford an unusual number of such books, Greek and Latin classics, each inscribed with the name of the donor. Hogg says that these volumes were a proof of Shelley's popularity with his schoolfellows, and many of them " who were at Oxford frequently called at his rooms, but he did not encourage their visits as they interrupted his favourite studies."[2]

Although Shelley did not care to share the amuse-

[1] *Reminiscences and Recollections of Captain Gronow*, vol. i. p. 155, 1900.

[2] Hogg's *Life of Shelley*, vol. i. p. 124.

ments of other boys, preferring to wander alone, generally with a book, for the hour together, he made some close friends. He could not, however, have been a popular boy, for according to Mrs. Shelley " he was disliked by the masters, and hated by his superiors in age, but he was adored by his equals. He was all passion—passionate in his resistance to injury, passionate in his love. Kindness could win his own soul, and the idea of self never for a moment tarnished the purity of his sentiments."

These friendships were in after years remembered both by himself and by his companions. Edward Leslie, afterwards Rector of Dromore, possessed several volumes presented to him at Eton, each inscribed with his name " from his affectionate friend, Percy Bysshe Shelley." Mr. Leslie's son, the Rev. Robert J. Leslie of Holbeach, informed Professor Dowden [1] that he supposed his father was " Shelley's best and dearest friend; the one that appreciated his genius more than any other boy except Charles Ball . . . they were in the same house, as were also Ball and Lord Howe." Shelley and Leslie were generally credited with putting a bull-dog into Dr. Keate's desk, but another boy afterwards assumed the sole responsibility for this prank. Mr. Leslie related that Shelley used to compose poems and dramas, which

[1] Dowden's *Life of Shelley*, vol. i. p. 26.

the boys, with a display of mock interest, would invite him to rehearse, and that when he thought his audience was enraptured they would burst into laughter. The trick was frequently played on him, but he could easily be persuaded to incur its repetition. Leslie often tried to console him, and his son "heard him speak with tears of 'Poor dear Shelley! it was no wonder that he went wrong.'" Andrew Amos, who became an eminent lawyer and a county court judge, boarded at Hexter's with Shelley; he remembered composing plays with him and acting them before the lower boys.

Charles William Packe was a pupil of Bethell's and in 1808 sat near Shelley in school. He was afterwards M.P. for South Leicestershire, and Colonel of the Leicestershire Yeomanry. Among other recollections of his friend, he says: "Shelley was too peculiar in his genius and his habits to be 'the hare with many friends'; but the few who knew him loved him, and, if I may judge from myself, remember with affectionate regret that his schooldays were more adventurous than happy."

Gronow tells us that Shelley was his friend and associate at Eton, but he may not have known him very intimately as he was Shelley's junior by two years. He describes him, however, as a "boy of studious and meditative habits, averse to all games and sports, and a great reader of novels and romances. He was a thin, slight lad, with remarkably lustrous eyes, fine hair, and a very peculiar shrill voice and laugh." Gronow adds that Shelley's "most intimate friend at Eton was a boy named Price, who was considered one of the best classical scholars amongst us."

One of Shelley's closest friends was Walter S. Halliday, who embodied some recollections of him in a charming letter printed by Hogg.[1] He said that he loved Shelley for his kindliness and affectionate ways, and added that "he was not made to endure the rough and boisterous pastime at Eton, and his shy gentle nature was glad to escape far away to muse over strange fancies, for his mind was reflective and teeming with deep thought." Shelley's love of nature was intense, and not caring for the games of the school he was glad of any opportunity to escape and wander for hours with Halliday about Clewer, Frogmore, the Park at Windsor, Stoke Park, and Gray's churchyard, while he related " his marvellous stories of fairyland, of apparitions, spirits, and haunted ground, and his speculations were then (for his mind was far more developed than mine) of the world beyond the grave."

Halliday, however, was mistaken when he stated

[1] Hogg's *Life of Shelley*, vol. i. p. 43.

that his friend never went out in a boat on the river. Shelley informed Medwin that the greatest delight he experienced at Eton was the boating. And Medwin himself had been present at a regatta in 1809 at Eton, when Shelley assisted and seemed to enjoy it. But his love of the Thames began at Brentford where he more than once played the truant with Medwin and rowed to Kew, and once to Richmond, to see Mrs. Jordan in *The Country Girl*, at the theatre there, the first he ever visited. Allowances being made for the fact that one's schooldays are generally more agreeable when viewed in retrospect, he recalled with evident pleasure, in 1821, the summer evenings at Eton spent on the river, in his poem "The Boat on the Serchio":

> . . . " Those bottles of warm tea—
> (Give me some straw)—must be stowed tenderly ;
> Such as we used, in summer after six,
> To cram in great-coat pockets, and to mix
> Hard eggs and radishes and rolls at Eton,
> And, couched on stolen hay in those green harbours
> Farmers call ' gaps,' and we school-boys called ' arbours,'
> Would feast till eight."

Mr. Henry Wagner, whose father was at Eton, and of Shelley's age, told me he had heard him relate that the nickname "Mad Shelley" was generally known in the school. It was perhaps owing to this epithet that he and other boys avoided Shelley. At Eton he was also called "Shelley the atheist," which, according to Hogg, was used in the classical sense meaning Antitheist, an opposer and contemner of the gods, and not one who denies their existence. " At Eton," he says, " but at no other school that I ever heard of, they had the name and office of atheist; but this usually was not full, it demanded extraordinary daring to attain to it; it was commonly in commission, as it were, and the youths of the greatest hardihood might be considered as boys commissioners for executing the office of Lord High Atheist." [1]

Shelley's eccentric habits, the odd carelessness of his dress, and his indifference to the school sports, made him a conspicuous figure, and the boys soon found out that much amusement could be devised by goading him into a rage. Professor Dowden has described what was known as a Shelley-bait, in which the unfortunate lad was surrounded by a jeering throng of boys, and reduced to a state of frenzy by his tormentors, who would disperse when his pent-up passion burst in all its fury.

Sir John Taylor Coleridge was of Shelley's standing at Eton: he afterwards became a judge, and was at one time a contributor to, and later editor of, the *Quarterly Review*, in which periodical he " cut up " Shelley's " Revolt of Islam " in the most merciless manner. " Coleridge," relates William Cory, " used to say that

---

[1] *Life of Shelley*, vol. i. p. 137.

Eton

he never joined in teasing Shelley, but he did not know anyone else that did not tease him : there used to be a 'Shelley-bait' every day about noon : the boys hunted Shelley up the street : he was known for not wearing strings to his shoes. I believe that boys suffer more from mortification than from rough usage, and that a life may be poisoned by insulting notice taken of deficiencies of dress. I consider the shoe-strings in this case not to have been trifles."[1] Another writer whose recollections of Sir John Coleridge deserve attention gives a different version of his attitude to Shelley. Mr. Stephen Coleridge says : " My two grandfathers were at Eton together, and I have at different times heard each of them speak of Shelley, who was there at the same time. My grandfather, the Judge, like other boys, had not much sympathy for the eccentricities of genius at that age, and I am afraid he did not exert himself to prevent a diversion known as a 'Shelley-hunt,' in which the poet was chivied about, and any handy missile thrown at him. My other grandfather, my mother's father, Mr. Seymour, once told me that he was some way from Eton up the river one day, and came upon Shelley, who had been out duck-spearing, but that the poet had somehow speared his own leg instead of any duck, and was lying quite helpless, unable to walk.

[1] *The Shelley Notebook*, p. 14 (Shelley Society's publications).

Shelley in England

Whereupon my grandfather hoisted him upon his back and carried him all the way back to school." [1]

Shelley used to relate the story of stabbing an upper boy with a fork, " as an almost involuntary act, done on the spur of anguish, and he made the stab as the boy was going out of the room." [2] But Shelley's storms of passion, though dangerous while they lasted, were invariably due to some aggravation, and they were not of long duration. He would frequently show his sympathy for the younger boys by assisting a dullard with his tasks. Shelley was the very opposite to a bully, he was hot-tempered but far from ill-tempered, his friends all testified to his generous and open-hearted nature.

It has been stated that Shelley stood alone at Eton, but, when he attempted the bold task of resisting the fagging system, it is hardly to be wondered at. From the boys in the upper forms, who were fagmasters, he naturally got no support, and his own classmates and juniors were not courageous enough to join him. There seems to be a considerable doubt if he really tried to abolish fagging, but he rebelled single-handed at what he regarded as a tyranny and refused to obey his fagmaster. [3] To defy such a deeply rooted custom

[1] From *Memories*, by the Hon. Stephen Coleridge. (John Lane, 1913.)
[2] Mrs. Shelley to Leigh Hunt, April 8, 1825.
[3] Henry Matthews, who afterwards became a judge, was author of *The Diary of an Invalid*—a popular book of travel in its day.

of the school denoted considerable pluck. Halliday said, when perhaps bearing in mind Shelley's attitude towards fagging, that he "had great moral courage, and feared nothing but what was base and low."

It is not perhaps possible to place reliance on all of the stories told of Shelley's schooldays, though many of them seem to be well attested.

Much as the poet disliked fighting for fighting's sake, Captain Gronow stated in his *Recollections* that Shelley once engaged in a fight at Eton against Sir Thomas Styles. Gronow could not recollect what cause induced Shelley to enter the ring, but he witnessed the contest, and stated that the combatants met in the playing-fields, and that a ring was formed with seconds and bottle-holders. The tall, lank figure of the poet towered above the thickset little baronet, and Shelley's confidence increased after a successful round. He then "spouted in Greek one of the defiant addresses usual with Homer's heroes when about to commence single combat, to the no small amusement of the boys," whereupon Styles went to work in earnest and soon knocked out his opponent, who, in defiance of the rules, broke through the ring and escaped.

Shelley did not venture again to enter the pugilistic arena, but passed much of his leisure in the study

Shelley in England

of the occult sciences, natural philosophy, and chemistry; his pocket money was spent on books "relative to these pursuits, on chemical apparatus and materials," and many of the books treated of magic and witchcraft. In his second letter to Godwin, in which he related the chief events of his boyhood, he said: "Ancient books of Chemistry and magic were perused with an enthusiasm of wonder, almost amounting to belief. My sentiments were unrestrained by anything within me; external impediments were numerous and strongly applied; their effect was merely temporary." He would watch the livelong nights for ghosts, and while at home he had endeavoured to obtain admission to the vaults of Warnham Church, where he might sit all night in expectation of seeing one. At Eton he consulted books on the grim subject of raising a ghost, and once at midnight he stole from the Dame's house with the object of putting his knowledge to the test. He took with him a skull—the prescribed implement for an incantation—and crossing a field, among the long grass, was alarmed to hear it rustle as if the evil one followed behind him. His fears somewhat abated when he had passed over the field, as he could no longer hear the pursuer. At length he reached a small stream, when he stood with one foot on either side of it, and repeated an incantation and drank thrice from the skull, but no ghost appeared,

Eton

probably because he had failed to repeat the correct formula of the charm.[1]

He recalled these pursuits in his " Hymn to Intellectual Beauty " in the often quoted lines :

" While yet a boy I sought for ghosts, and sped
    Through many a listening chamber, cave and ruin,
    And starlight wood, with fearful steps pursuing
Hopes of high talk with the departed dead.
I called on poisonous names with which our youth is fed :
    I was not heard : I saw them not :
    When musing deeply on the lot
Of life, at that sweet time when winds are wooing
    All vital things that wake to bring
    News of birds and blossoming,
    Sudden thy shadow fell on me :
I shrieked, and clasped my hands in ecstasy :
I vowed that I would dedicate my powers
    To thee and thine : have I not kept the vow ?
    With beating heart and streaming eyes, even now
    I call the phantoms of a thousand hours
    Each from his voiceless grave. . . ."

The study of physical science apparently was discouraged at Eton in Shelley's days, for in a note that Timothy Shelley wrote to Medwin senior (from whom Shelley had borrowed a volume) he said : " I have returned the book on chemistry as it is a forbidden thing at Eton."[2] Chemical experiments were certainly pro-

---

[1] Hogg's *Life of Shelley*, vol. i. pp. 33–34.

[2] Miss Hellen Shelley recollected seeing her brother's face and hands burned and blackened by some badly managed experiment, probably at Eton, with *lunar caustic*. The white frocks of his sisters, in some mysterious manner, were found stained with black marks, the result, no doubt, of frequent visits to the Hall Chamber, Bysshe's room at Field Place.

hibited in the boys' rooms, but one day when Shelley was engaged in the production of "a blue flame" his tutor, Bethell, caught him in the act and angrily asked him what he was doing. Shelley jocularly replied that he was "raising the devil." Mr. Bethell seized hold of a mysterious implement on the table, and in an instant was thrown against the wall, having grasped a highly charged electrical machine. Of course, the young experimentalist paid dearly for this unfortunate occurrence."[1] William Cory, who gives a variation of this legend in his paper "Shelley at Eton," tells us that Shelley was "amusing his companions with a frictional electric machine in his own room, and charging the door handle failed in his dutiful attempt to warn his tutor, Mr. Bethell, against opening the door when he came to stop the noise caused by the electric shocks."[2]

On one occasion he is said to have set fire to a tree by means of gunpowder and a burning-glass,[3] and at

[1] *Shelley Memorials*, p. 6.

[2] "Shelley at Eton," *Shelley Society's Notebook*, 1886, Pt. i. p., 14. Medwin mentions that Bysshe, who as a boy was fond of flying kites at Field Place, made an electrical one, borrowing the idea from Franklin, with the object of drawing lightning from the clouds.

[3] William Cory (*ibid.*) states that one day when he was in South Meadow—a field adjoining the well-known Brocas, and used in winter for football and hurdle races by the Eton boys—with Mr. Edward Coleridge (brother of Sir John Coleridge), he pointed out to him a wretched pollard willow with only half a trunk and black inside, and said, "This is the tree that Shelley blew up with gunpowder: that was his last bit of naughtiness at school."

another time he employed a travelling tinker to assist him in constructing a steam engine, which, however, burst, and very nearly blew him and the unfortunate Mr. Bethell and his family into the air. Besides Shelley's love of experimental chemistry and electricity, his interest in astronomy was again aroused by Adam Walker, who came on a lecturing visit to Eton. Shelley once more turned his eyes to the heavens, and, in the words of one of his schoolfellows, " night was his jubilee." [1]

But he probably received some solid assistance and encouragement in his studies in chemistry and astronomy, and his Eton days were brightened by the friendship of Dr. James Lind. When Shelley met him this amiable old man was well past seventy ; he had been settled for many years at Windsor as physician to the Royal household, and was devoted to the King.[2] He was an eccentric character—as thin as a lath. He had travelled in China, the Hebrides and Iceland, and possessed a collection of Indian and other curiosities picked up on his travels. Miss Burney described him, in her diary of 1785, as too fond of tricks, conundrums, and queer things to maintain the confidence

---

[1] Dowden, i. p. 29.

[2] Hogg believed that Shelley had learnt to curse the King and his father from Dr. Lind, but he appears to have been convinced subsequently that Shelley had hoaxed him, and that he intended to expunge the statement from his book in a second edition. See Dowden, i. pp. 32-33.

of his patients, but Shelley held him in the highest estimation and never mentioned his name except in terms of the tenderest respect. He regarded him as "exactly what an old man should be, free, calm-spirited, full of benevolence and even of youthful ardour; his eyes seemed to burn with supernatural spirit beneath his brow, shaded by his venerable locks; he was tall, vigorous and healthy in his body; tempered, as it had ever been, by his amiable mind. I owe to that man far, ah! far more than I owe to my father; he loved me, and I shall never forget our long talks where he breathed the spirit of the kindest tolerance and the finest wisdom."

Shelley used to relate how, when he was recovering from a severe fever at Field Place during the holidays, he was warned by a servant that his father had been overheard while consulting about sending him to a private madhouse.[1] Being master of three pounds, with the servants' help he contrived to send for Dr. Lind. "He came," says Shelley, "and I shall never forget his manner on that occasion. His profession gave him authority; his love for me ardour. He dared my father to execute his purpose, and his menaces had the desired effect." The story was told by Mrs. Shelley, in what she declared were Shelley's

---

[1] This story is related by Medwin in his *Life of Shelley*, also in *The Diary of Polidon*, though not so circumstantially.

own words, spoken to her on the night that decided her destiny, and Hogg had heard him speak more than once of the incident, but he believed that Shelley's "recollections were those of a person not quite recovered from a fever which attacked his brain, and still disturbed by the horrors of the disease." Dr. Lind died at the age of seventy-six in 1812, the year after Shelley left Oxford, but he never forgot his old friend, and had him in his mind when he described in "The Revolt of Islam" the hermit who released Laon from prison in Cantos iii. and iv., as he believed he had been delivered by Dr. Lind from pressing danger during his illness at Field Place.

He was "an old man . . . stately and beautiful," he says, who

> ". . . had spent his livelong age
> In converse with the dead, who leave the stamp
> Of ever-burning thoughts on many a page,
> When they are gone into the senseless damp
> Of graves ;—his spirit thus became a lamp
> Of splendour, like to those on which it fed :
> Through peopled haunts, the City and the Camp,
> Deep thirst for knowledge had his footsteps led,
> And all the ways of men among mankind he read,"

—and Dr. Lind was also the "original" of Zonoras, the aged instructor of Prince Athanase, his

> ". . . one beloved friend,
> An old, old man, with hair of silver white
> And lips where heavenly smiles would hang and blend
> With his wise words ; and eyes whose arrowy light

Shelley in England

Shone like the reflex of a thousand minds.
He was the last whom superstition's blight
Had spared in Greece. . . ."

Shelley's studies at Eton were chiefly of his own choosing. His friend Halliday tells us that "his lessons were child's play to him, and his powers of versification remarkable, although the making of Latin verse was not to his liking. He read Lucretius and was fascinated, and he translated several books of Pliny's *Natural History*, including the chapter "De Deo," which, according to Medwin, was "the first germ of his ideas respecting the Nature of God." It was his intention to make a complete version of this book, but he stopped short at the chapter on Astronomy, on learning from Dr. Lind that it baffled the best of scholars. In his second letter to Godwin, he told him that at Eton he made his first acquaintance with *Political Justice*. This book, which was destined to work such a potent influence on his life and character, he borrowed from Dr. Lind.[1]

Shelley's appearance, however, was not always one of unkempt carelessness, as some of the descriptions given above would lead us to suppose. We get a glimpse of him during these schooldays as he appeared to the eyes of his sister Hellen, who in her recollections of her brother says, that "he ordered clothes to his

---

[1] Hogg's *Life of Shelley*, ch. xvi.

own fancy at Eton, and the beautifully fitting silk pantaloons, as he stood as almost all men and boys do, with their coat tails near the fire, excited my silent, though excessive admiration." And when he took part in the Montem processions of the years 1805 and 1809, he appeared in the former year as pole-bearer in the uniform of a midshipman, with a blue jacket, white trousers, silk stockings and pumps; on the second occasion he walked as full corporal, attended by his pole-bearers.

The following interesting reference to Shelley was written down in 1848 by Lord Monson:[1] "Among the more celebrated names at Eton in my time I have a slight recollection of Shelley. He was captain of the Oppidans, I think, in 1810—a fair lad, who, I think, boarded at Bethell's. I remember many odd freaks recorded of him. He bought a large brass cannon at an auction at Windsor, and harnessed many lower boys to draw it down into college. It was captured, I think, by one of the tutors, and kept till the holidays at Hexter's."

[1] "Reminiscences of Eton," by William John, sixth Lord Monson, *Nineteenth Century*, April 1909. It is hardly necessary to say that there is nothing to support Lord Monson's supposition that Shelley was captain of the Oppidans.

CHAPTER V

FIRST ATTEMPTS AT AUTHORSHIP

Shelley as a sportsman—Literary projects—*The School of Terror*
—"The Wandering Jew"—Correspondence with Walter Scott—
Gessner—The publication of *Zastrossi*—Pouching the reviewers—
St. Irvyne—Shelley's ignorance of German—The Newspaper Editor's
reminiscences—Shelley goes up to Oxford—The Easter vacation
—Harriet Grove—*Original Poetry by Victor and Cazire.*

SHELLEY returned to Field Place in the December of
1809 for his Christmas vacation, and his companion
was Medwin, who recalled in after years the walks
that they took together on this occasion. Sir Timothy
was a keen sportsman, and Shelley, who was himself
an excellent shot, often carried a gun on his shoulder
in his father's preserves. Medwin tells us an amazing
story of Shelley " killing, at three successive shots,
three snipe at the tail of the pond in front of Field
Place." But the country gentleman's pleasure in killing was not deeply rooted in Shelley, and, long before
he found it abhorrent,[1] he was content to let the game-

---

[1] *Cf.* " Alastor," lines 13-17 :

" If no bright bird, insect or gentle beast
I consciously have injured, but still loved
And cherished these my kindred ; then forgive
This boast, beloved brethren, and withdraw
No portion of your wonted favour now ! "

72

First Attempts at Authorship

keeper slay the birds (which were afterwards taken to his mother) while he sat immersed in his book. The statement, however, that Shelley was a good shot was undoubtedly true, and he was later fond of pistol practice and indulged in it as one of his favourite amusements at Oxford, Marlow, and in Italy.

Shelley's mind in the winter of 1809–10 was full of literary projects, and " he had," as Medwin tells us, " begun to have a longing for authorship—a dim presentiment of his future fame—an ambition of making a name in the world." [1] His earliest efforts proclaimed him " a romanticist." The Gothic movement which in the latter part of the eighteenth century had grown out of Walpole's *Castle of Otranto*, Clara Reeve's *Old English Baron*, the novels of Mrs. Radcliffe, the metrical *Tales of Wonder* and other horrors of " Monk " Lewis, with a host of even more worthless imitations, still found favour with the reading public when Shelley was beginning to take an interest in reading. He was attracted by the work of *The School of Terror*, although its popularity was on the wane, for those who were tired of "Gothic horrors" were finding enjoyment in the gentle satire of Miss Austen [2] and Miss Edgeworth, and the romantic narrative poems of Walter Scott.

[1] Medwin, vol. i. p. 53.

[2] Miss Austen ridicules the taste of her day for *The School of Terror* in *Northanger Abbey*, ch. iv. :

" When you have finished *Udolpho*, we will read *The Italian* together ;

Shelley in England

During Shelley's schooldays we have seen that he "was haunted with a possession of the wildest and most extravagant romances," and that much of his time was spent in wandering alone with the companionship of a book. "From a reader," he says, "I became a writer of romances; before the age of seventeen I had published two, *St. Irvyne* and *Zastrozzi*."[1] Medwin tells us that he wrote with him in the winter of 1809–10, in alternate chapters, the commencement of a wild, extraordinary romance, in which a hideous witch played a part. About the same time, Shelley projected and Medwin joined him in an ambitious literary undertaking, no less than a long narrative poem in the metre of Scott's popular metrical romances on the subject of "The Wandering Jew." Shelley or Medwin had "picked up, dirty and torn, in Lincoln's Inn Fields" a fragment of a translation of Schubart's poem "The Wandering Jew," a portion of the *German*

and I have made out a list of ten or twelve more of the same kind for you."

"Have you, indeed? How glad I am! What are they all?"

"I will read you their names directly; here they are in my pocket-book: *Castle of Wolfenbach, Clermont, Mysterious Warnings, Necromancer of the Black Forest, Midnight Bell, Orphan of the Rhine,* and *Horrid Mysteries.* These will last us some time."

"Yes, pretty well; but are they all horrid? Are you sure they are all horrid?"

"Yes, quite sure."

[1] Shelley's second letter to Godwin, January 10, 1812. The statement as to his age is incorrect, as he was apparently between seventeen and eighteen when he wrote *Zastrozzi*.

First Attempts at Authorship

Museum, 1802, vol. 3, and this story suggested the idea for the poem. Medwin, whose account of the transaction is far from convincing, claimed to have written almost entirely himself the first three cantos,[1] save a few additions and alterations. The vision in the third canto he confessed to have taken from Lewis's "Monk," and with equal candour he declared the Crucifixion scene to be a plagiarism from a volume of Cambridge prize poems.[2] "After seven or eight cantos were perpetrated, Shelley sent them to Campbell for his opinions on their merits with a view to publication. The author of *The Pleasures of Hope* returned the MS. with the remark that 'there were only two good lines in it,' namely:

> " It seemed as if some angel's sigh
> Had breathed the plaintive symphony."

" This criticism gave the death-blow to our hopes of immortality."[3]   He does not tell us, and perhaps he was not aware, that Shelley sent the poem to the publishers of Walter Scott's poems, Ballantyne & Co., who replied on September 24, 1810, from Edinburgh:

" We are extremely sorry at length, after the most mature deliberation, to be under the necessity of

---

[1] In *The Shelley Papers*, 1833, Medwin says that he was responsible for the first four cantos, and that six or seven cantos were written.

[2] Probably the Seatonian poem for 1765 on the Crucifixion by Thomas Zouch. As Mr. Dobell points out, the Crucifixion scene in "The Wandering Jew" as we have it shows no evidence of plagiarism.

[3] Medwin, vol. i. p. 53.

declining the honour of being the publishers of the present poem ; not that we doubt its success, but that it is perhaps better suited to the character and liberal feelings of the English than the bigoted spirit which yet pervades many cultivated minds in this country. Even Walter Scott is assailed on all hands, at present, by our Scotch spiritual and evangelical magazines and instructors, for having promulgated atheistical doctrines in ' The Lady of the Lake.'"

It would be difficult to detect anything of a heterodox character in such a poem as "The Lady of the Lake," which was at that time selling in thousands, and for many years was a favourite prize in girls' schools ; John Ballantyne, therefore, in declining to publish Shelley's poem, probably invented an excuse at the expense of his friend, Walter Scott.

Shelley made another attempt to find a publisher for "The Wandering Jew," and offered it in a letter dated September 28, 1810, to John Joseph Stockdale,[1] a publisher in Pall Mall, who made a business of issuing from his shop in Pall Mall volumes of minor poetry and romances, often, no doubt, at the authors' risk. There is nothing in Shelley's published letters to show what was Stockdale's decision, nor is there any evidence of its having appeared in book form. Four cantos of the poem, however, were printed in *The Edinburgh Literary Journal* for the year 1829, with

[1] John Stockdale.

First Attempts at Authorship

Shelley's preface dated January 1811, and his dedication: "To Sir Francis Burdett, Bart., M.P., in consideration of the active virtues by which both his public and private life is so eminently distinguished, the following poem is inscribed by the author." The editor of this periodical states that when Shelley visited Edinburgh in 1811 he brought the poem with him, and that the MS. had since been in the custody of a literary gentleman of that town to whom it was offered for publication. The MS. is more likely to have been that which he offered in 1810 (with the preface post-dated) in his letter quoted above to Ballantyne, who requested Shelley to advise him how to return it. The four cantos of "The Wandering Jew" were also published in *Fraser's Magazine*, three years after its appearance in *The Edinburgh Literary Journal* in 1831, as "an unpublished poem," with the sanction of Mrs. Shelley. This version of the poem, which varies considerably from that published in *The Edinburgh Literary Journal*, contains neither the dedication nor the preface, and must have been printed from another—possibly an earlier—copy, and perhaps the identical MS. which Shelley sent to Stockdale. The poem, on its appearance in *Fraser's Magazine*, was introduced by a long article from the pen of either W. Maginn, or Father Mahoney, under the initials O. Y. of the pseudonym, Oliver Yorke. Medwin printed in his *Life of Shelley* some portions of a preface which he tells us Shelley intended for the poem, but no portion of these extracts resembles the preface printed in *The Edinburgh Literary Journal*.

"The Wandering Jew" is excluded from more important editions of Shelley's poetical works, owing to Medwin's claim to have participated in its composition. I agree with Mr. Dobell [1] in the opinion that Shelley wrote, if not the whole of the poem as we now have it, considerably more than Medwin. It is more animated than Medwin's acknowledged poems, and it was evidently composed with the same enthusiasm which enabled Shelley to produce his two novels. The poem, in fact, is not as Medwin says, "a sort of thing such as boys write," but what one might have expected from the author of *Zastrozzi* and *St. Irvyne*. Shelley, moreover, acknowledged the poem as his, without reference to his alleged coadjutor, in offering it to Stockdale, and apparently he sent it as his own work to the firm of Ballantyne. In the preface as printed in *The Edinburgh Literary Journal* he uses the first-person singular, and the dedication quoted above is written in the third person and he uses the word "author." Shelley also quoted passages

[1] Mr. Bertram Dobell, who was the first to call attention to the publication of "The Wandering Jew" in *The Edinburgh Literary Journal*, edited an excellent edition of the poem, which was issued by the Shelley Society in 1887.

First Attempts at Authorship

from "The Wandering Jew" at the heads of two chapters of *St. Irvyne*. At the time of writing his *Life of Shelley*, Medwin tells us he had retained the MS. of his portion of the poem and that he could have identified easily Shelley's contributions, which he admits were far the better. Perhaps Medwin's chief part of the work consisted in supplying the material, while Shelley held the pen, or it may have been that Shelley dictated the poem to Medwin. If Shelley ceased to take an interest in the poem when he failed to induce either the Ballantynes or Stockdale to publish it, he returned to the subject of " The Wandering Jew " when writing "Queen Mab," and included the fragment by Schubart among the notes. In 1823, ten years after "Queen Mab" was printed, a poem by Medwin was published with the title of "Ahasuerus the Wanderer," but it is curious to observe that no influences of the earlier poem are discernible in this work.

Shelley was not at all diffident when he desired the opinion of anyone with whom he was personally unacquainted. He took the bold step of writing a letter without waiting for an introduction, a practice which he had learnt at Eton from Dr. Lind.[1] In this manner he addressed some letters to Felicia Dorothea Browne (afterwards Mrs. Hemans), whose juvenile poems, composed at the age of twelve, had appeared in 1808,

[1] Hogg's *Life of Shelley*, vol. i. p. 270.

but her mother wrote to Medwin's father and begged him to use his influence with Shelley to stop the correspondence.[1] We have seen that he also wrote to Campbell for an opinion of his poem on " The Wandering Jew," and later to Byron, Moore, and Godwin. He probably wrote to other authors, but his letters, if they have survived, have not yet come to light. He addressed at least one letter to Walter Scott, whose most interesting reply is given in the last volume of the *Diary of Frances Lady Shelley*, edited by Mr. Richard Edgcumbe. Shelley had asked an opinion of his poetry. No date is printed with Scott's reply, but it evidently relates to an early period of Shelley's life, and probably before he went up to Oxford. The following are some of the most interesting passages :

" Sir,—I am honoured with your letter, which, in terms far too flattering for the proverbial vanity of an author, invites me to a task which in general I have made it a positive rule to decline, being repeated in so many shapes that, besides the risk of giving pain, it became a real encroachment upon the time which I must necessarily devote to very unpoetical labours. In your case, however, sir, a blunt refusal to give an opinion asked in so polite a manner, and with so many unnecessary apologies, would be rude and unhandsome.

[1] " I believe I mentioned to you the extraordinary letters with which I was once persecuted by (Mr. Shelley) ; he, with whom ' Queen Mab hath been ' " (Mrs. Hemans, in a letter dated November 15, 1822). Medwin states that in later years she became an admirer of Shelley's poetry, and " in some measure ' modelled her style after his."

First Attempts at Authorship

I have only to caution you against relying very much upon it. The friends who know me best, and to whose judgment I am myself in the constant habit of trusting, reckon me a very capricious and uncertain judge of poetry, and I have had repeated occasion to observe that I often failed in anticipating the reception of the poetry from the public."

Scott then goes on to give some very sound advice to his correspondent, and the following is characteristic :

" No good man can ever be happy when he is unfit for the career of simple and commonplace duty, and I need not add how many melancholy instances there are of extravagance and profligacy being resorted to, under the pretence of contempt for the common rules of life. Cultivate then, sir, your taste for poetry, and the belles-lettres, as an elegant and most interesting amusement, but combine it with studies of a more serious and solid cast, such as are most intimately connected with your prospects in future life, whatever those may be. In the words of Solomon, ' My son, get knowledge, and with all thy getting, get understanding.' . . . With respect to the idylls of which you have favoured me with copies, they seem to me to have all the merits, and most of the faults of juvenile compositions. They are fanciful, tender and elegant, and exhibit both command of language and luxuriance of imagination.

" On the other hand, they are a little too wordy, and there is too much the air to make the most of everything : too many epithets, and too laboured an attempt to describe minute circumstances. . . . Upon the whole, I think your specimen augurs very favourably of your talents, and that you have not any cause for the apprehensive dejection you have experienced, and which I confess I do not think the worst symptom of your powers. But I do not greatly admire your model. Gessner's ' Arcadia ' is too ideal for my taste and sympathy, or perhaps I am too old to relish it. Besides, I dislike the measured prose, which has all the stiffness and pedantry of blank verse, without its rhythm and harmony. I think you have a greater chance of making more progress by chusing a more severe and classical model. But, above all, be in no hurry to publish. A name in poetry is soon lost, but it is very difficult to regain it." . . .

It would appear that a translation of Solomon Gessner's *Idylls* had fallen in Shelley's way, and that the specimens he had sent to Scott for his criticism were acknowledged to be imitations of the Swiss writer's " Death of Abel " and other works by the mediocre Gessner which were written in a kind of poetical prose, in their day very popular, not only in Switzerland and Germany, but in French and English translations. There is no work of this writer bearing the title of " Arcadia," and Scott seems to use the word in the sense of the Arcadian fancy of Gessner's *Idylls*.

It was during his last term at Eton, in April 1810, that Shelley experienced for the first time the pride of authorship, for early in that month his novel *Zastrozzi* was ushered into a not very sympathetic world under the auspices of G. Wilkie and J. Robinson, the Paternoster Row publishers. About a year earlier, on May 7, 1809, Shelley had written from Eton to Messrs. Longman & Co., stating that he intended to finish and publish a romance, and offering to send them the MS. Messrs. Longmans appear to have replied that they would be happy to see the novel when finished. They did not, as we have seen, publish *Zastrozzi*, which it is possible, though not certain, is the romance referred to in this letter; on the other hand, it may have been some earlier work from Shelley's fertile pen. Packe believed that Shelley received a sum of £40 for *Zastrozzi*, and " with a part of the proceeds he gave a most magnificent banquet to eight of his friends," of whom Packe was one. Medwin, apparently relying on hearsay, speaks of a " breakfast party," and puts down the cost at £50.

Zastrozzi gained for its author a new kind of notoriety at Eton, and Lord Monson was among those who remembered that Shelley had written " a small book in one volume in which he collected together all the horrors he could think of. It was a farrago of what in those days we called pamphlets, little sixpenny books of romance, which the boys in want of reading used to purchase," and he adds, " I quite forget the name of this work of Shelley's, nor have I ever met with it in after life."

It has been stated that Shelley had sold his novel to

his publisher, but he showed his solicitude in its welfare in writing from Eton on April 1st to Graham, and complaining that Robinson would "take no trouble about the reviews; let everything proper be done about the venal villains," he said, "and I will settle with you when we meet at Easter. We will all go in a posse to the booksellers in Mr. Grove's barouche and four—show them that we are no Grub Street garretteers. . . . We will not be cheated again—let us come over Jock (probably J. Robinson), for if he will not give me a devil of a price for my poem and at least £60 for my new Romance in three volumes, the dog shall not have them. Pouch the reviewers—£10 will be sufficient, I should suppose, and that I can with greatest ease repay when we meet at Passion week. Send the reviews in which *Zastrozzi* is mentioned to Field Place, the *British Review* is the hardest, let that be pouched well. My note of hand if for any larger sum is quite at your service, as it is of consequence in fiction to establish your name as high as you can in the literary lists. Let me hear how you proceed in the business of reviewing."

Although Shelley displayed in this letter a precocious knowledge of the practices of the reviewers, his efforts met with no marked results. The venal villains, if "pouched," did not respond to the bribe : the book which is quoted in the *British Critic* for April

First Attempts at Authorship

1810, among the publications of the month, was advertised in the *Times* of the 5th and 12th of June, and reviewed unfavourably in the *Critical Review* for November 1810.

The new novel to which Shelley refers above was probably *St. Irvyne*. Messrs. Longmans, whom he had approached in regard to *Zastrozzi*, had issued a romance which he much admired entitled *Zofloya, or the Moor*, by Mrs. Byron or Charlotte Dacre, better known under her pseudonym of "Rosa Matilda," and Medwin stated [1] this romance was the model both for *Zastrozzi* and *St. Irvyne*. *Zofloya* is a very scarce book, but Swinburne discovered a copy many years ago and described it in a curious letter which I have read through the courtesy of Mr. W. M. Rossetti, to whom it was addressed. The book is not in the British Museum ; M. A. Koszul, however, found it on the shelves of the Bodleian Library, and he is convinced that both of Shelley's novels were derived from this weird work of fiction, which confirms Medwin's statement, although Medwin says elsewhere that *St. Irvyne* was suggested by Godwin's novel, *St. Leon*, which he "wonderfully admired." [2]

It is evident that Shelley's mind was saturated with the romantic fiction of the day, and he was able with

---

[1] *Life of Shelley*, vol. i. p. 30.
[2] *Ibid.*, p. 69.

his tenacious memory to reproduce the artificial phrases and sentiments of these romances without exercising any creative faculty that he may have possessed of his own.

It has been suggested that Shelley's two novels were translations from the German, and this supposition seems to be based on the authority of Medwin and on the statement of the unknown " Newspaper Editor "[1] whose Reminiscences of Shelley appeared in *Fraser's Magazine* for June 1841. This writer, who was, generally speaking, well-informed, was introduced by Edward Graham to Shelley during his short career at Oxford. On one occasion Shelley came up to London and spent three days with this acquaintance, who says : " At this time he was without a guinea, and had even one day recourse to my own slenderly furnished purse for a small sum, which he repaid on the morrow out of a very small balance which he had received from a bookseller. On this visit to the metropolis he had brought with him the MS. of three tales, one original, the other two translations from the German, which were written in a common school ciphering book. He offered them to three or four booksellers for ten pounds, but could not find a purchaser. On the evening which

---

[1] Mr. H. Buxton Forman has suggested that the " Newspaper Editor " was William Henry Merle, author of "Costança, a Poem," and some novels. But Dr. Richard Garnett informed Mr. W. M. Rossetti, apparently with assurance, that he was Gibbons Neale.

First Attempts at Authorship

preceded my departure (from London to take up a position on a provincial journal) he insisted upon my accepting them as a token for remembrance. They were of a very wild and romantic description, but full of energy. I kept them until about the year 1822, when I lent them for perusal to a friend who held an official situation in the Tower. When I applied for them at the end of some months, I had the mortification of hearing that they had been lost. Two years ago, taking up by chance a paper called the *Novelist*, I saw in it one of those tales as a reprint. How it obtained publication I know not. I am quite sure from the style of the MS. presented to me, that it was not a copy of a paper of which Shelley had preserved the original ; I am equally certain that my friend did not deceive me when he informed me that he had lost the book in which it was written."

The " Newspaper Editor " fails to mention and seems to be unaware that two of Shelley's novels had been published during his lifetime. Both of these romances were reprinted in *The Romancist and Novelist's Library*, and he must have seen one, probably the earlier of these novels. Hogg, however, who knew Shelley's mind pretty thoroughly during his Oxford days, emphatically denies that Shelley possessed any acquaintance with German. In the account of his first actual meeting with

Shelley in England

Shelley at dinner in hall at University College, their conversation practically opened with an animated discussion on the relative merits of German and Italian literature. Shelley expressed an enthusiastic admiration for the poetical and imaginative works of the former school, while Hogg supported the claims of the latter. Later in the evening Shelley confessed that he was not qualified to maintain the discussion, " for he was alike ignorant of Italian and German and had only read the works of the Germans in translations, and but little Italian poetry, even at second hand." Hogg also admitted that he knew nothing of German and but little of Italian.[1] And he is equally emphatic in another statement regarding Shelley's want of knowledge of German. In mentioning the fragment of Schubart's " Wandering Jew," to which reference has already been made, Hogg says that, " if it had been in German, Shelley could not have translated it at that time (1809–10), for he did not know a word of German. The study of that tongue—both being equally ignorant of it—we commenced together in 1815."[2] Medwin, however, thought Hogg was mistaken in this respect, for, when the former met Shelley at Oxford in November 1810, he showed him " a volume of tales which he had himself translated from

[1] Hogg's *Life of Shelley*, vol. i. p. 53.
[2] *Ibid.*, vol. i. pp. 193–4.

88

First Attempts at Authorship

the original " (German). Medwin spent the whole day with him, and for half an hour he perused these MSS., and formed a very low idea of the literature of the country then almost unknown in England. It is evident that the books that had fallen into his hands were from the pens of very inferior writers, and I told him he had lost his time and labour in clothing them in his own language, and that I thought he could write much better things himself." It is certainly a curious fact that both the " Newspaper Editor " and Medwin state that they had seen a MS. volume of tales of Shelley purporting to be from the German. As far as I am aware, there is no other statement or any evidence in his letters that Shelley had a knowledge of German, at this date. He was, we know, interested in German literature through translations—Burger's *Lenore* he had studied in the translation with Lady Diana Beauclerc's illustrations ; as an admirer of the works of " Monk " Lewis he is sure to have been acquainted with his translation of *The Bravo of Venice*, and from the recently published letter of Walter Scott to Shelley, mentioned above, it appears he admired some work, probably the *Idylls*, of Solomon Gessner.

Early in April 1810, Shelley went up to Oxford, and on the 10th of that month he signed his name as a student in the books of University College. He had been given what is known as the Leicester Exhibition at that College on the nomination of his uncle, John Shelley-Sidney, Esq., by inheritance from Robert Dudley, Earl of Leicester. After matriculating he returned to Field Place for the Easter holidays. His sister, Elizabeth, was at home, but the two younger girls, Mary and Hellen, were at Church House, Miss Fenning's school, which formerly stood on the north side of Clapham Common, near the Old Town, and directly facing Trinity Church. Shelley, in anticipation of a visit to London, and in the throes of composing his novel *St. Irvyne*, addressed with the aid of Elizabeth the following mad letter[1] to their friend Graham on Easter Monday :

FIELD PLACE,
Monday (April 23, 1810).

" MY DEAR GRAHAM,—At half after twelve do you be walking up and down the avenue of trees near Clapham Church, and when you see a Post Chaise stop at Mrs. Fenning's door, do you advance towards it, and without observing who are inside of it speak to them— An eventful and terrific mystery hangs over it—you are to change your name from Edward Fergus Graham to William Grove—prepare therefore for something extraordinary. There is more in a cucumber than you are aware of—in two cucumbers indeed ; they are now almost 2s. 6d. apiece—reflect well upon that ! ! !—All

---

[1] The original is in the collection of Mrs. Alfred Morrison.

MARGARET SHELLEY   HELLEN SHELLEY

After a picture in the possession of Sir John Shelley, Bart.

this is to be done on Tuesday (April 24), neither Eisbh. or myself cares what else you have to do.

> "If Satan had never fallen,
> Hell had been made for thee!"[1]

"Send two 'Zastrozzis' to Sir J. Dashwood in Harley Street, directed to F. Dashwood, Esq.—Send one to Ransom Morland's to be directed to Mr. Chenevix.—I remain, yours devotedly,

P. B. SHELLEY.

"N.B.—The Avenue is composed of vegetable substances moulded in the form of trees called by the multitude Elm trees. Elizabeth calls them so, but they all lean as if the wind had given them a box on the ear, you therefore will know them—Stalk along the road towards them—and mind and keep yourself concealed as my Mother brings a blood-stained stiletto which she purposes to make you bathe in the life-blood of her enemy.

"Never mind the Death-demons, and skeletons dripping with the putrefaction of the grave, that occasionally may blast your straining eye-ball.—Persevere even though Hell and destruction should yawn beneath your feet.

"Think of all this at the frightful hour of midnight, when the Hell-demon leans over your sleeping form and inspires those thoughts which eventually will lead you to the gates of destruction.

(signed by) ELIZABETH SHELLEY."

[1] This couplet is quoted by Shelley from "The Revenge" as a motto for chapter ix. of *St. Irvyne.*

Shelley in England

" DEAR GRAHAM,

ELIZA. SHELLEY.

The fiend of the Sussex solitudes shrieked in the wilderness at midnight—he thirsts for thy detestable gore, impious Fergus.—But the day of retribution will arrive.

H +D means Hell Devil.

(*Written by Elizabeth Shelley*.)

" DEAR GRAHAM,—We really expect you to meet us at Clapham in the way described by the *Fiendmonger* : should you not be able to be there in time we will call at Miller's Hotel in hopes you will be able to meet us there, but we hope to meet you at Clapham, as Vine Street is so far out of our way to L(incoln's Inn) Fields, and we wish to see you.—Your sincere Friend,

E. SHELLEY.

DEATH +HELL +DESTRUCTION if you fail.

" Mind and come for we shall seriously expect your arrival, I think the trees are on the left hand of the Church.—P. B. S."

[Addressed outside]
    "EDWARD FERGUS H+D+GRAHAM, Esq.
        "Vine Street, Piccadilly, London."

The writers of this curious invitation seem to have had some misgivings whether Graham would take it seriously, hence the more rational postscripts.

After the Easter vacation, Shelley returned to Eton, and on July 30th he pronounced his speech of Cicero

First Attempts at Authorship

against Catiline and finished his schooldays.[1] He then returned home for the midsummer holidays, and spent probably what was one of the happiest periods of his life. It was the occasion of his second meeting with his cousin, Charles Henry Grove, who had just left the Navy, and who recalled in a letter to Miss Hellen Shelley this visit to Field Place with his father, mother, and his sisters Charlotte and Harriet. "Bysshe," he says, "was more attached to my sister Harriet than I can express, and I recollect well the moonlight walks we four had at Strode, and also at St. Irving's:[2] the name, I think, of the place, then the Duke of Norfolk's, at Horsham. That was in the year 1810. After our visit to Field Place, we went to my brother John's house in Lincoln's Inn Fields, where my mother, Bysshe, and Elizabeth joined us and a very happy month we spent. Bysshe full of life and spirits, and very well pleased with his successful devotion to my sister. In the course of that summer to the best of my recollection, after we had retired into Wiltshire, a continual correspondence was going on, as, I believe, there had also been before, between Bysshe and my sister Harriet."

[1] Dowden's *Life of Shelley*.

[2] "St. Irving's Hills, a beautiful place, on the right-hand side as you go from Horsham to Field Place, laid out by the famous Capability Brown, and full of magnificent forest trees, waterfalls, and rustic seats. The house was Elizabethan. All has been destroyed."—Hogg's note.

Shelley in England

Thomas Grove, Shelley's uncle by his marriage in 1781 with Charlotte Pilfold, sister of Shelley's mother, lived at Ferne House, Donhead, Wiltshire, near Shaftesbury. He was also the proprietor of Cwm Elan, an estate of ten thousand acres situated five miles east of Rhayader in Radnorshire. The house in a beautiful valley, praised by W. L. Bowles in his poem "Coombe Ellen," can no longer be seen, as it was destroyed towards 1894 in a water-supply scheme for Birmingham. Thomas Grove was the father of a large family of five sons and three daughters, of whom the following come into Shelley's story : Thomas, the eldest, lived at Lincoln's Inn Fields, and later occupied the Welsh estate; John was a surgeon, who on his father's death succeeded to the estates ; Charles Henry was successively an officer in the Navy, a surgeon, and a clergyman. Harriet Grove was born in 1791, but, as she and Bysshe lived in counties far apart from one another, they had not met since childhood until the year 1808, when she was a girl of seventeen and he a year younger. Medwin seems to refer to 1810 in describing this meeting, but there are reasons for assigning the earlier date, as Shelley speaks of " two years of speechless bliss " in the " Melody to a scene of Former Times "—undoubtedly a serious poem addressed to Harriet Grove—with which he concludes his otherwise frivolous "Posthumous Fragments of

First Attempts at Authorship

Margaret Nicholson "—published in the latter part of 1810.

All those who mention her refer to the rare beauty of Harriet Grove, and Medwin knew none that surpassed or could compete with her ; he compared her to one of Shakespeare's women, or to some Madonna of Raphael. A strong family likeness to Harriet Grove was noticeable in Bysshe :

> " She was like him in lineaments—her eyes,
>   Her hair, her features, they said were like to his,
>   But softened all and tempered into beauty."

And this resemblance could not have been unknown to Shelley, who had her in mind when he wrote in 1820 of the love of " Fiordispina and Cosimo " :

> " They were two cousins almost like to twins,
>   Except that from the catalogue of sins
>   Nature had rased their love—which could not be
>   But by dissevering their nativity."

In Romney's beautiful portrait of her mother, Mrs. Thomas Grove, one can trace this likeness.

Among the excursions taken during this happy summer was probably one to the school at Clapham Common to see his sisters, a visit which Miss Hellen Shelley remembered. " He came once," she said, " with the elders of the family, and Harriet Grove, his early love, was of the party : how fresh and pretty she was ! Her assistance was invoked to keep the wild boy quiet, for he was full of pranks, and upset the port wine in the tray cloth, for our school-mistress was hospitable, and had offered refreshments ; then we all walked into the garden, and there was much ado to calm the spirits of the wild boy." [1]

During this summer Bysshe made a selection of his verses for publication, to which his sister Elizabeth contributed three or four poems. This little collection, his first poetical publication, comprising a total of seventeen pieces, he put into the hands of C. & W. Phillips, a firm of Worthing printers, and then called on Stockdale, the Pall Mall publisher, to whom he afterwards submitted his poem " The Wandering Jew." At Shelley's request, to extricate him from a pecuniary difficulty with his printer, Stockdale, who consented to publish the volume, on September 17th received 1480 copies in sheets of a slender pamphlet of sixty-four pages with the title, *Original Poetry by Victor and Cazire*, Victor standing for Bysshe, and Cazire for his sister. Shelley, anticipating a considerable demand for the book, had ordered an edition of 1500 copies (twenty of which were retained by the author), and it was duly advertised as " published this day, price 4s. in boards," in the *Morning Post* of September 19th. The sole reference to the volume in

---

[1] Hogg, vol. i. p. 18.

First Attempts at Authorship

Shelley's printed correspondence, besides his notes to Stockdale, is to be found in an undated letter to his friend Edward Graham, of whom he asks, " What think you of our Poetry ? What is said of it ?—No flattery, remember." Little time, however, was given for the book to " circulate "—as not long after it was announced Stockdale happened to examine its contents, and he recognised one of the poems in the volume entitled " St. Edmond's Eve " to be the work of Matthew Gregory Lewis. *The Tales of Terror,*[1] in which this poem originally appeared, under the title of " The Black Canon of Elmham ; or, St. Edmond's Eve," is a book with which one would have expected the young authors of Field Place to have been familiar, and as a matter of fact Cazire " lifted " the ballad from the volume in its entirety. It is somewhat surprising that Victor did not himself detect the peculation. Stockdale, however, was not slow in communicating his discovery to Shelley, " when, with the ardour natural to his character, he expressed the warmest resentment at the imposition practised upon him by his coadjutor, and he instructed me to destroy all the copies, of which about one hundred had been put into circulation " by himself and the author. Probably

[1] Miss Hellen Shelley says that " Monk " Lewis's poems had a great attraction for her brother, " and any tale of Spirits, fiends, &c., seemed congenial to his taste at an early age " (Hogg's *Life of Shelley,* vol. i. p. 15).

few, if any, were sold, and the majority sent out found their way to the reviewers' waste-paper baskets. But among those to whom copies were presented by the authors was Harriet Grove, who wrote in her diary on September 17, 1810 : " Received the Poetry by Victor and Cazire. C. offended, and with reason. I think they have done very wrong in publishing what they have of her." C. stands for Harriet's sister Charlotte Grove, whose name may probably be filled with the first blank in the lines :

"So . . . is going to . . . you say,
I hope that success her great efforts will pay
That . . . will see her, be dazzled outright,
And declare he can't bear to be out of her sight,"

of the epistle " To Miss [Harriet Grove]. From Miss [Elizabeth Shelley] " which is the second piece in the book.

Miss Hellen Shelley states (Hogg, i. 16) that Bysshe had some of her verses printed, but that when she saw her name on the title-page, " H-ll-n Sh-ll-y," she " felt more frightened than pleased. As soon as the publication was seen by my superiors it was bought up and destroyed." Perhaps Miss Hellen had a confused idea that she was also a contributor to the " Victor and Cazire " volume. Her age in 1810 was only eleven.

The *Original Poetry by Victor and Cazire* was noticed in two periodicals—perhaps only two—namely,

First Attempts at Authorship

The British Critic for April 1811, and *The Poetical Register and Repository of Fugitive Poetry* for 1810 and 1811, but this last was not issued till 1814, when Shelley had long ceased to be interested in the welfare of the book. Poor as are the verses which it criticises, the review that follows is no better :

" There is no ' original poetry ' in this volume ; there is nothing in it but downright scribble. It is really annoying to see the waste of paper which is made by such persons as the putters together of these sixty-four pages. There is, however, one consolation for the critics, who are obliged to read all this sort of trash. It is, that the crime of publishing is generally followed by condign punishment, in the shape of bills from the stationer and printer, and in the chilling tones of the bookseller, when, to the questions of the anxious rhymer, how the book sells, he answers that not more than half a dozen copies have been sold."

In his introduction to the " Fitzboodle Papers,"[1] Mr. George Saintsbury has pointed out a curious resemblance which he observes between the " Willow Songs " of " Ottilia " and Shelley's song (No. 12) in the " Victor and Cazire " volume, beginning " Fierce roars the midnight storm." The late Dr. Garnett, to whom he pointed this out, acknowledged the resemblance, but thought it impossible that Thackeray could have

---

[1] *The Oxford Thackeray*, 1908, vol. iv.

seen the poem. Although " the likeness of rhythm and spirit " is curious, it is more reasonable to suppose, as Dr. Garnett suggests, that Thackeray recalled some romantic ballad of M. G. Lewis or by a writer of his period.

CHAPTER VI

OXFORD

EARLY in October 1810, at the beginning of the Michaelmas term, Shelley returned to Oxford and entered into residence at University College. His rooms, which were situated on the first floor, over the door in the corner of the quadrangle, next to the Hall, are now in use as the junior common-room of the College. Mr. Timothy Shelley, who had been at the same College, probably accompanied Bysshe to Oxford on this occasion, but, not liking the accommodation of an inn, he repaired to a house in the High Street bearing the sign of a leaden horse, at which he had lodged when he was at the University. It was then occupied by Mr. J. Slatter, a plumber, the son of his former landlord, another son of whom was at the time going into partnership with Munday, the Oxford bookseller and printer. Mr. Shelley called at Munday's shop, where

he told Bysshe (who was with him) to get his supplies
of books and stationery. Then turning to the bookseller he said, with parental pride, " My son here has
a literary turn, he is already an author, and do pray
indulge him in his printing freaks." If Mr. Shelley
ever remembered this advice he probably regretted it,
as in a very short time he was to look upon his son's
" printing freaks " as anything but to be indulged.
But Bysshe's literary works, to which his father
alluded, were at this time comparatively harmless.
He had published his novel *Zastrozzi*, and was joint-
author of the abortive collection of *Original Poetry by
Victor and Cazire*, so promptly suppressed on account
of his coadjutor's indiscretion, which had robbed it
of any claim to originality it might otherwise have
possessed. Bysshe also had with him the completed
MS. of his second novel *St. Irvyne*, the publication of which had been undertaken by Stockdale at
the author's expense, of which more hereafter.

It is not possible to write of Shelley's residence at
Oxford without reference to his intimate friend and
biographer, Thomas Jefferson Hogg. The eldest son
of a barrister and a Tory, Hogg was born at Norton,
co. Durham, on May 24, 1792, and was, consequently,
Shelley's senior by a little more than two months.
Hogg was intelligent, fond of study and of literature,
and although he did not share all his enthusiasms, he

was devoted to Shelley and apparently his only friend at Oxford. Hogg's inimitable description of Shelley's short career at the University is practically our only source of information of the poet's life at that period, and in the following account I have drawn on his biography, often using his own words.

In January 1810, Hogg went to University College, and at the commencement of Michaelmas term—that is, at the end of October in the same year, he "happened one day to sit next to a freshman at dinner." It was Shelley's first appearance in hall. "His figure was slight, and his aspect remarkably youthful, even at our table, where all were very young. He seemed thoughtful and absent. He ate little, and had no acquaintance with anyone. I know not how it was that we fell into conversation, for such familiarity was unusual, and, strange to say, much reserve prevailed in a society where there could not possibly be occasion for any. We have often endeavoured in vain to recollect in what manner our discourse began, and especially by what transition it passed to a subject sufficiently remote from all the associations we were able to trace. The stranger had expressed an admiration for poetical and imaginative works of the German school; I dissented from his criticisms. He upheld the originality of the German writings; I asserted their want of nature. 'What modern literature,' said he, 'will you compare to theirs?' I named the Italian. This roused all his impetuosity; and few, as I soon discovered, were more impetuous in argumentative conversation. So eager was our dispute that, when the servants came in to clear the tables, we were not aware that we had been left alone. I remarked that it was time to quit the hall, and I invited the stranger to finish the discussion at my rooms. He eagerly assented. He lost the thread of his discourse in the transit, and the whole of his enthusiasm in the cause of Germany; for, as soon as he arrived at my rooms, and whilst I was lighting the candles, he said calmly, and to my great surprise, that he was not qualified to maintain such a discussion, for he was alike ignorant of Italian and German, and had only read the works of the Germans in translations, and but little of Italian poetry, even at second hand. For my part I confessed, with equal ingenuousness, that I knew nothing of German, and but little of Italian; that I had spoken only through others, and, like him, had hitherto seen by the glimmering light of translations."

While Shelley was thus engaged in an animated discourse on his favourite study chemistry, in which his companion felt but a slight interest, Hogg had leisure to examine, and indeed to admire the appearance of his very extraordinary guest. "It was," he said, " a sum of many contradictions. His figure was slight and fragile, and yet his bones and joints were large and strong. He was tall, but he stooped so much that he seemed of low stature. His clothes were expensive, and made according to the most approved mode of the day, but they were tumbled, rumpled, unbrushed. His gestures were abrupt and sometimes violent, occasionally even awkward, yet more frequently gentle and graceful. His complexion was delicate and almost feminine, of the purest red and white; yet he was tanned and freckled by exposure to the sun, having passed the autumn, as he said, in shooting. His features, his whole face, and particularly his head, were, in fact, unusually small; yet the last *appeared* of a remarkable bulk, for his hair was long and bushy, and in fits of absence and in the agonies (if I may use the word) of anxious thought, he often rubbed it fiercely with his hands, or passed his fingers quickly through his locks unconsciously, so that it was singularly wild and rough. In times when it was the mode to imitate stage-coachmen as closely as possible in costume, and when the hair was invariably cropped like that of our soldiers, this eccentricity was very striking. His features were not symmetrical (the mouth, perhaps, excepted), yet was the effect on the whole extremely powerful. They breathed an animation, a fire, an enthusiasm, a vivid and preternatural intelligence, that I never met with in any other countenance. Nor was the moral expression less beautiful than the intellectual; for there was a softness, a delicacy, a gentleness, and especially (though this will surprise many) that air of profound religious veneration that characterises the best works, and chiefly the frescoes (and into these they infused their whole souls) of the great masters of Florence and of Rome. I recognised the very peculiar expression in these wonderful productions long afterwards, and with a satisfaction mingled with much sorrow, for it was after the decease of him in whose countenance I had first observed it."

Hogg admired the enthusiasm of, and was drawn towards, his new acquaintance, who appeared to him to possess all those intellectual qualities that he had vainly expected to meet at the University. There was, however, one physical blemish, namely his voice, on account of which Hogg believed it would not be possible for him to endure his society. "It was intolerably shrill, harsh and discordant; of the most cruel intonation. It was perpetual and without remission; it excoriated the ear." Hazlitt and Lamb were both in later years repelled by Shelley's shrill voice. Hogg, however, became accustomed to it before long and its discordance ceased to trouble him. Peacock says that Shelley's voice was certainly a defect, but that it was chiefly noticeable when he spoke under excitement. It was not only dissonant like a jarring string, but he spoke in sharp fourths, the most unpleasing sequence of sound that can fall on the human ear. He seemed to have his voice under command when he spoke calmly or was reading, and it was then good in time and tone, low, soft, but clear, distinct and expressive. Peacock had heard him with pleasure read almost all Shakespeare's tragedies.[1]

At a quarter to seven Shelley announced to his newly made friend that it was time for him to attend a lecture on Mineralogy, from which he declared enthusiastically that he expected to derive much pleasure. Although the painful voice of his companion caused Hogg to hesitate in asking him to return to tea, he overcame his repugnance, and Shelley, gladly assenting, hurried out of the room, while his footsteps echoed as he ran through the silent quadrangle, and afterwards along the High Street.

But he came back to Hogg's rooms disillusioned, and determined that the lecturer on Geology should never see him again. He had stolen away before the discourse was finished, "for it was so stupid," he said, "and I was so cold, that my teeth chattered. He

[1] Shelley's cousin, Charles Grove, "had no unpleasant recollections of his harsh voice." He was not without an ear for music. Miss Hellen Shelley could remember how her brother used to sing to them: "he could not bear any turns or twists in music, but liked a tune played quite simply."

talked about nothing but stones, stones, stones, stones, nothing but stones, and so drily." The professor appeared to be displeased, for in trying to get out of the lecture-room without being observed, Shelley had struck his knee against a bench.

After supper Shelley talked of the wonders of chemistry, and asserted that it was the only science that deserved to be studied. While speaking of his own labours in this field, he suddenly started up and proposed that Hogg should go instantly with him to see his galvanic trough.

Anticipating some of the modern uses of chemistry and electricity, Shelley imagined " an unfruitful region being transmuted into a land of exuberant plenty ; the arid wastes of Africa refreshed by a copious supply of water." " It will," he said, " perhaps be possible at no very distant date to produce heat at will and to warm the most ungenial climates—as we now raise the temperature of our apartments to whatever degree we may deem agreeable or salutary. But if this be too much to anticipate, at any rate we may expect ' to provide ourselves cheaply with a fund of heat that will supersede our costly and inconvenient fuel, and will suffice to warm our habitations, for culinary purposes and for the various demands for the mechanical arts.' " It is curious to read of his forecast of the uses of electricity and aerial navigation. " What a mighty instrument would electricity be in the hands of him who knew how to wield it . . . by electrical kites we may draw down the lightning from heaven. The galvanic battery is a new engine . . . what will not an extraordinary combination of troughs of colossal magnitude, a well arranged system of hundreds of metallic plates effect ? The balloon has not yet received the perfection of which it is surely capable ; the art of navigating the air is in its first and most helpless infancy. It promises prodigious facilities for locomotion, and will enable us to traverse vast tracts with ease and rapidity, and to explore unknown countries without difficulty. Why are we still so ignorant of the interior of Africa ?—why do we not despatch intrepid aeronauts to cross it in every direction, and to survey the whole peninsula in a few weeks ? The shadow of the first balloon, which a vertical sun would project precisely underneath it, as it glides silently over that hitherto unhappy country, would virtually emancipate every slave, and would annihilate slavery for ever."

Of mathematics he declared he knew nothing, " and treated the notion of their paramount importance with contempt." But Metaphysics he, declared " in a solemn tone and with a mysterious air as ' a noble study indeed.' . . . Then, rising from his chair, he paced the room with prodigious strides and discoursed of souls, a future state, and of pre-existence. Until he suddenly remarked the fire was nearly out, and the candles were glimmering in their sockets, when he hastily apologised for remaining so long." Hogg promised to visit the chemist in his laboratory, on the following day, and lighting him down stairs with the stump of a candle he soon heard him running through the quiet quadrangle in the still night. "That sound became afterwards so familiar to my ear, that I still seem to hear Shelley's hasty steps."

It was nearly two o'clock before Hogg reached his friend's rooms. Shelley, who took no note of time, was amazed to learn that it was so late. He was cowering over the fire, his feet resting on the fender, in an attitude of dejection, the cause of which was a slight cold and the presence of a scout who had been tidying his room, and whose withdrawal as soon as Hogg made his appearance was a welcomed relief to his young master. Shelley's rooms presented a very curious appearance to his visitor. It was evident that they "had just been papered and painted ; the carpet, curtains, and furniture were quite new, but the general air of freshness was greatly obscured by the indescribable confusion in which the various objects were mixed. Books, boots, papers, shoes, philosophical instruments, clothes, pistols, linen, crockery, ammunition, and phials innumerable, with money, stockings, prints, crucibles, bags, and boxes, were scattered on the floor and in every place ; as if the young chemist, in order to analyse the mystery of creation, had endeavoured first to reconstruct the primeval chaos. The tables and especially the carpet were already stained with large spots of various hues, which frequently proclaimed the agency of fire. An electrical machine, an air-pump, the galvanic trough, a solar microscope, and large glass jars and receivers were conspicuous amidst the mass of matter. Upon the table by his side were some books lying open, several letters, a bundle of new pens, and a bottle of Japan ink, that served as an inkstand ; a piece of deal, lately part of the lid of a box, with many chips, and a handsome razor that had been used as a knife. There were bottles of soda-water, sugar, pieces of lemon, and the traces of an effervescent beverage. Two piles of books supported the tongs, and these upheld a small glass retort above an argand lamp. I had not been seated many minutes before the liquor in the vessel boiled over, adding fresh stains to the table, and rising in fumes with a most disagreeable odour. Shelley snatched the glass quickly and, dashing it in pieces among the ashes under the grate, increased the unpleasant and penetrating effluvium."

The evening was spent at Shelley's rooms, and he spoke on poetry with the same animation and glowing zeal that characterised his former discourses. Hogg, indeed, found his young friend a "'whole University in himself' in respect of the stimulus and incitement which his example afforded to my love of study." Hogg and Shelley almost invariably passed the afternoon and evening together; at first alternately at their respective rooms, but afterwards, when they had become more familiar, most frequently by far at Shelley's; sometimes one or two good and harmless men of their acquaintance were present, but they were usually alone. His rooms were preferred because there his philosophical apparatus was at hand, and he was able at any moment to ascertain by actual experiment the value of some new idea that rushed into his brain. He spent much of his time and money at this time in the assiduous cultivation of chemistry. These chemical operations seemed to an unskilful observer to promise nothing but disasters. His hands, his clothes, his books, and his furniture were stained and corroded by mineral acids. More than one hole in the carpet could elucidate the ultimate phenomenon of combustion; especially a formidable aperture in the middle of the room, where the floor also had been burnt by the spontaneous ignition caused by mixing ether with some other fluid in a crucible; and the honourable wound was speedily enlarged by rents, for the philosopher as he hastily crossed the room in pursuit of

Oxford

truth was frequently caught in it by the foot. Hogg feared with reason that his friend would poison himself, as the plates and glasses and his tea things were used indiscriminately with crucibles, retorts and recipients, to contain the most deleterious ingredients. Once, when Hogg was taking tea with Shelley by the fireside, his attention was attracted by a sound in the cup into which he was about to pour some tea, and on looking into it he found a seven-shilling piece partly dissolved by *aqua regia*. Although Shelley laughed at his caution, he used to speak with horror of the consequences of having inadvertently swallowed, through a similar accident, some mineral poisons—perhaps arsenic—at Eton, which he believed had not only "seriously injured his health, but that he feared he should never entirely recover from the shock it had inflicted on his constitution." Hogg, however, detected no serious or lasting injury in his youthful and healthy, although somewhat delicate, aspect.

To Hogg the study of the physical sciences offered no attraction, and he says that through his lack of sympathy Shelley's zeal, at first so ardent, gradually cooled. Nevertheless their intimacy increased rapidly, and they soon formed a habit of passing the greater part of their time together. If by chance Shelley saw Hogg at Chapel, he studiously avoided all communication, and, as soon as the doors were open, retreated hastily to his rooms. He often absented himself from dinner in the hall, which he disliked as he did all College meetings, and he would then lunch with Hogg at one, and take long country walks in the afternoon. Otherwise it was not their custom to meet before that hour, but the country walk was seldom omitted. Shelley usually furnished himself with a pair of duelling pistols and ammunition ; and when he came to a solitary spot he would pin up a card or fix some other mark on a tree or bank, and amuse himself by firing at it. He was a good shot, and his frequent success gave him much delight. But he handled his weapons so carelessly that at length he was induced to leave them at home, as Hogg often contrived secretly to abstract the flints or would purposely forget to bring the powder-flask or some other accessory.

During their rural excursions Shelley loved to walk in the woods, or to stroll on the banks of the Thames. Water had a perennial attraction for him. Hogg says he was a devoted worshipper of the water-nymphs ; for whenever he found a pool, or even a small puddle, he would loiter near it, and it was no easy task to get him to quit it. He specially mentions a pool in an old quarry at the foot of Shotover Hill, where his friend would linger until dusk, " gazing in silence on the water, repeating verses aloud or engage in earnest discussion. Sometimes he would hurl a big stone into the water, exult at the splash, and quietly watch the decreasing agitation until the last faint ring had disappeared on the surface." And he would split slaty stones, and when he had collected a sufficient number he would "gravely make ducks and drakes of them, counting with the utmost glee the number of bounds, as they flew along skimming the surface of the pond."

His passion for sailing paper boats he learnt later. It was his practice to screw up a scrap of paper into the semblance of a boat, and on committing it to the water would watch its fortunes. It generally sank, but very occasionally his frail bark would perform its journey and reach the other side of the water. Shelley derived much delight from this form of amusement, and Hogg, who seems to have shown exemplary patience in keeping him company, says that on one occasion only was he successful in prevailing on · him to abandon his favourite sport while "any timber remained in the dockyard." It was a bitterly cold Sunday afternoon early in the new year, the sun had set, and it threatened to snow. The poet, with swollen hands, blue with cold, was "creating a paper navy to be launched simultaneously," when Hogg said, "'Shelley, there is no use in talking to you; you are the Demiurgus of Plato!' He instantly caught up the whole flotilla, and bounding homewards with mighty strides, laughed aloud—laughed like a giant, as he used to say." As long as any paper remained available to Shelley, when he was engaged in this pursuit, he would continue to convert it into paper boats. After consuming any waste paper he might have with him, he would use the covers of letters, then the letters themselves, even the communications of valued correspondents would share the same fate. And the fly-leaves of books, for he seldom was without one, were used for the same purpose, though he never destroyed the text. Once, so a mythical legend goes, he found himself on the bank of the Serpentine (having exhausted his supplies at the round pond in Kensington Gardens), and the only scrap of paper that he could muster was a bank post-note for fifty pounds. After hesitating for some time, he yielded to temptation and, twisting it into a boat, he committed it to the waves; then he watched its fortunes with anxiety, and was gratified at recovering it on its arrival at the other side of the water.

On returning from their long afternoon rambles, Shelley would be overcome with extreme drowsiness, and sleep from two to four hours, often so soundly that his slumbers resembled a deep lethargy. "He lay occasionally on the sofa," but, as he was very sensitive to cold, "more commonly stretched upon the rug before a large fire, like a cat, and his little round head was exposed to such a fierce heat" that Hogg used to wonder how he could bear it. Sometimes his friend would interpose some shelter, but the sleeper usually contrived to turn himself round and to roll again into the spot where the fire glowed the brightest. "His torpor was generally profound, but he would sometimes discourse incoherently for a long while in his sleep. At six he would suddenly compose himself, even in the midst of a most animated narrative, or of earnest discussion ; and he would lie buried in entire forgetfulness, in a sweet and mighty oblivion, until ten, when he would suddenly start up, and rubbing his eyes with great violence, and passing his fingers swiftly through his long hair, would enter at once into a vehement argument, or begin to recite verses, either of his own composition or from the works of others, with a rapidity and an energy that was often quite painful." And, while Shelley slept, Hogg seized the opportunity of getting several uninterrupted hours for writing or reading.

As soon as he woke Shelley would be ready for his supper, after which his discourse was eminently brilliant. Although he was as unwilling to separate as Dr. Johnson, on the stroke of two Hogg would rise and depart, with promises to meet him on the morrow.

Before *St. Irvyne* was published, Shelley brought out another volume. He was quick to act on his father's hint to Munday the printer, who soon had a chance of indulging him in one of his printing freaks. It must have been on a morning early in November 1810, when his newly made friend, Hogg, called on Shelley at his rooms and found him so absorbed with correcting proofs that an hour passed before he broke silence. He then announced his intention of publishing some poems, the proofs of which he put into the hands of Hogg, who, after reading them through attentively twice, pronounced judgment. He thought that there were some good lines in the verses, but also many irregularities and incongruities. Shelley did not attempt to defend his work, but remarked that, as he was not proposing to issue the poems with his own name, its publication could not harm him. Hogg disagreed with this argument, and the matter was dropped until after dinner, when Shelley returned to the subject. He suggested correcting the defects, but Hogg pointed out that an alteration here and there would transform the verses into burlesque poetry. The poet was amused with the idea, but he gave up his intention of publishing the book. The proofs of the volume, however, lay about Shelley's rooms for some days, and he and Hogg employed themselves from time to time in altering and making the verses more and more ridiculous. Shelley enjoyed the joke, and, in order to give it an additional touch of absurdity, a title-page was devised in which the book was described as " Posthumous Fragments of Margaret Nicholson : being poems found among the papers of that noted female who attempted the life of the King in 1786. Edited by John FitzVictor." Hogg says that the story of Peg Nicholson, the mad washerwoman who tried to stab George the Third with a carving-knife outside his palace, was still in the memory of everyone. The woman was living, but as an inmate of Bedlam she was dead to the world, and it was supposed she could suffer no harm by imposing this sheaf of verse on the world as her posthumous works under the editorship of a fictitious nephew, by name FitzVictor, apparently a son of the Victor who had collaborated recently with Cazire. "The idea," said Hogg, " gave an object and purpose to our burlesque ; to ridicule the strange mixture of sentimentality with the murderous fury of revolutionists, that was so prevalent in the compositions of the day. When the bookseller called for the proof, Shelley told him he had changed his mind about issuing them, but showed him the altered verses. The man was so pleased with the whimsical conceit that he asked if he might publish the book on his own account— promising secrecy and as many *gratis* copies as might be required. The permission was given, and in a few hours the printed volume, ' a noble quarto,' appeared —consisting of a small number of pages printed in handsome type, in ink of a rich glossy black, on large, thick white drawing paper. Shelley had torn open a large square bundle of books before the printer's boy had quitted the room, and holding a copy in both hands he ran about in an ecstasy of delight, gazing at the superb title-page."

The book was advertised in the *Oxford Herald* for November 17 as just published, price 2s. Hogg says that the first poem, "a long one condemning war in the lump . . . had been confided to Shelley by some rhymester of the day." And in a letter to Graham from Oxford, dated November 30, Shelley speaks of another poem in the volume, namely, a part of the "Epithalamium," as being "the production of a friend's *mistress ;* it had been concluded there," he says, " but she thought it abrupt and added this [some extra lines] : it is omitted in numbers of the copies—that which I sent to my mother did not, of course, contain it—I shall possibly send you the above to-day, but I am afraid that they will not insert it— But you mistake ; the Epithalamium will make it sell like wildfire, and, as the *Nephew* is kept a profound secret, there can arise no danger from the indelicacy of the Aunt— It sells wonderfully here, and is become the fashionable subject of conversation— What particular subject do you mean, I cannot make out, I confess— Of course, to my Father, Peg is a profound secret ; he is better and recovering very fast."

Oxford

Hogg also says of the book, "nor was a certain success wanting, the remaining copies were rapidly sold in Oxford at the aristocratical price of half a crown for half a dozen pages. We used to meet gownsmen in High Street reading the goodly volume as they walked—indeed it was a kind of fashion to be seen reading it in public, as a mark of a nice discernment, of a delicate and fastidious taste in poetry, and the very criterion of a choice spirit." And although he adds that "nobody suspected, or could suspect, who was the author"; and "the thing passed off as the genuine production of the would-be regicide," the authorship was known to others in Oxford.

Charles Kirkpatrick Sharpe, in an amusing letter written from Christ Church on March 15, 1811, and published by Lady Charlotte Bury in her *Diary Illustrative of the Times of George the Fourth*, says : "Talking of books, we have lately had a literary Sun shine forth upon us here, before whom our former luminaries must hide their diminished heads—a Mr. Shelley, of University College, who lives upon arsenic, aqua-fortis, half an hour's sleep in the night, and is desperately in love with the memory of Margaret Nicholson. He has published what he terms the Posthumous Poems, printed for the benefit of Mr. Peter Finnerty, which I am grieved to say, though stuffed full of Treason, is extremely dull, but the Author is a great genius, and, if he be not clapped up in Bedlam or hanged, will certainly prove one of the sweetest swans on the tuneful margin of the Charwell. . . . Shelley's style is much like that of Moore burlesqued, for Frank is a very foul-mouthed fellow, and Charlotte, one of the most impudent brides that I ever met with in a book."

Another person at Oxford who was in the secret of the authorship was the partner of Munday, the printer of the volume, Henry Slatter, who contributed his recollections of Shelley to the fourth edition of Montgomery's *Oxford*. Slatter's statement that the " Posthumous Fragments of Margaret Nicholson " was " almost still-born" is more likely than Hogg's account of its success. It is curious that both Charles Kirkpatrick Sharpe and Slatter state that the profits of the " Fragments " were to be applied to Peter Finnerty.[1] Slatter also tells us with regard to this book that " the ease with which Shelley composed many of the stanzas therein contained is truly astonishing ; when surprised with a proof from the printers, in the morning, he would frequently start off his sofa, exclaiming, that that had been his only bed, and, on being informed that the men were waiting for more copy, he would sit down and write off a few stanzas, and send them to the press, without even revising or reading them— this I have myself witnessed." When one considers

[1] See page 149.

the quality of the verses, however, this literary activity does not appear very astonishing.

While " Peg Nicholson " was going through the press, Shelley was preparing *St. Irvyne*, his second novel, for the printers, after Stockdale, his publisher, had been over the manuscript. On November 14, he wrote to Stockdale from University College :

" I return you the Romance by this day's coach. I am much obligated by the trouble you have taken to fit it for the press. I am myself by no means a good hand at correction but I think I have obviated the principal objections which you allege.

"Ginotti, as you will see, did *not* die by Wolfstein's hand, but by the influence of that natural magic which, when the secret was imparted to the latter, destroyed him. Mountfort being a character of inferior import, I did not think it necessary to state the catastrophe of *him*, as at best it could be but uninteresting. Eloise and Fitzeustace are married and happy, I suppose, and Megalena ·dies by the same means as Wolfstein. I do not myself see any other explanation that is required. As to the method of publishing it, I think as it is a thing which almost *mechanically* sells to circulating libraries, &c., I would wish it to be published on my *own* account. . . . Shall you make this in one or two volumes ? "

Shelley wrote again about *St. Irvyne* to Stockdale, from Oxford on November 19, and expressed surprise " that the Romance would make but one small volume, it will at all events be larger than *Zastrozzi*." He was, however, mistaken, for his new novel was shorter. "What I mean," he continues, "as 'Rosicrucian' is the elixir of eternal life which Ginotti has obtained, Mr. Godwin's romance of 'St. Leon' turns upon that superstition ; I enveloped it in mystery for the greater excitement of interest, and on a re-examination you will perceive that Mountfort physically did kill Ginotti, which must appeal from the latter's paleness. . . . When do you suppose *St. Irvyne* will be out ? " This last question was again asked of Stockdale by the anxious young author in another letter from Oxford on December 2. By December 10 the novel, printed and bound, was in Shelley's hands, as on that date he presented a copy to his uncle, Mr. Robert Parker, with a note begging his acceptance of the romance, and adding, " Mr. Parker's initial opinion on the book would be regarded as an honour." [1] Stockdale advertised *St. Irvyne* in the *Times* for January 26, 1811, as " The University Romance.—This day is published, price only 5s. *St. Irvyne ; or, The Rosicrucian :* a Romance. By a

---

[1] This copy of *St. Irvyne* was sold at auction by Messrs. Sotheby on July 22, 1908, for £200. On December 18, 1810, Shelley requested Stockdale to send copies of the romance to Miss Marshall, Horsham, Sussex ; T. Medwin, Esq., Horsham ; T. J. Hogg, Esq., Rev. (———) Dayrell's, Lymington Dayrell, Buckinghamshire ; and six copies to himself. On January 11, 1811, he ordered a copy to be sent to Miss Harriet Westbrook, 10 Chapel Street, Grosvenor Square. He also sent a copy to Robert Southey.

Oxford

Gentleman of Oxford University. Printed for Stockdale Junior, 41, Pall Mall," and an earlier announcement probably in this form had caught the author's eye when he wrote to his publisher from Field Place, on December 18, "I saw your advertisement of the Romance, and approve of it highly; it is likely to excite curiosity." If any novel needed a magnetic influence to attract readers, *St. Irvyne* needed it, but, although the publisher continued to advertise the book, the public was not attracted. By January 11, Shelley may have had some misgivings as to its reception, and ingenuously asked his publisher, "Do you find that the public are captivated by the title-page?" Unless Stockdale equivocated, Shelley must have been disappointed; the public showed no signs of being "captivated," for the book, so far from selling "mechanically" at the circulating libraries, appears to have fallen practically unnoticed by the press. *The British Critic*,[1] however, said, "Would that this gentleman of Oxford had a taste for other and better pursuits; but, as we presume him to be a *young gentleman*, this may in due time happen."

Charles Kirkpatrick Sharpe was one of the very few of Shelley's contemporaries at Oxford who took an interest in his doings. In two of his letters, dated respectively on March 15 and October 1811, he speaks

[1] For January 1811.

of " Margaret Nicholson," " St. Irvyne," " The Necessity of Atheism," and a poem on the State of Public Affairs. Of the last two we shall have something to say later. In speaking of the novel he writes, " There appeared a monstrous romance in one volume, called *St. Irvyne ; or, The Rosicrucian.* Here is another pearl of great price ! All the heroes are confirmed robbers and causeless murderers, while the heroines glide *en chemise* through the streets of Geneva, tap at the palazzo doors of their sweethearts, and on being denied admittance leave no cards, but run home to their warm beds, and kill themselves. If your lordship would like to see this treasure I will send it." [1]

[1] *Diary Illustrative of the Times of George the Fourth*, by Lady Charlotte Bury, 1838.

CHAPTER VII

OXFORD (*continued*)

Further characteristics — Shelley's practical joke — His spare diet—Reading habits—Studies—Plato—Shelley's philosophical doubts—Stockdale warns Mr. Timothy Shelley of his son's views— Mr. Shelley's anger—Shelley's engagement with Harriet Grove cancelled—Elizabeth Shelley and Hogg—Shelley and Bird—*Leonora*— " A Poetical Essay on the Existing State of Things "—Peter Finnerty.

To the description of Shelley, as he appeared to Hogg on first making his acquaintance at Oxford, may be added some physical and mental characteristics from the same and other sources. In stature he was above middle height, being five feet ten, but his studious habits and shortness of sight had caused him to stoop from the shoulders. Leigh Hunt, who met him probably during these Oxford days, or shortly after, says " he was then a youth not come to his full height, very gentlemanly, earnest, gazing at every object that interested him, and quoting the Greek dramatists." His body was spare, but his bones large, and although he was strong, light, and active, with singular grace of movement, at times his gestures were almost awkward. Of ordinary mundane wisdom he possessed none, his

127

simplicity was infantine, the genuine simplicity of true genius ; and the purity of his life was most conspicuous. "In no individual," says Hogg, "was the moral sense more completely developed, and in no being was the perception of right and wrong more acute. Towards injustice of all kinds he was keenly sensitive, and his philanthropy was boundless. His generous sympathy on witnessing the infliction of pain was too vivid to allow him to consider the consequences of interfering. Hogg tells a story how he rescued a donkey that was being cruelly beaten by a lad in his efforts to force it to carry a burden beyond its strength. On another occasion Shelley procured some milk, and endeavoured to soothe a young and half-witted child, whom he had found, apparently deserted, in a country lane, suffering from exposure and hunger. These instances of his kindness of heart were due to that natural impulse for helping the suffering which, to the end of his life, was one of the most beautiful characteristics of his nature.

We are told that he was habitually grave and possessed an "invincible repugnance to the comic," yet the pranks of a schoolboy still lingered. "The metaphysician of eighteen actually attempted once or twice to electrify the son of his scout, a boy like a sheep, by name James, who roared aloud with ludicrous and stupid terror whenever Shelley affected to bring by stealth any part of his philosophical apparatus near to him." [1]

At Oxford, Shelley did not practise vegetarianism, but the plainness of his diet anticipated it, for he questioned even at that time the justification of slaying animals for food. Bread in his case was more than figuratively his staff of life : he could have made it his sole sustenance if compelled by necessity, and he would have been content to do so. When walking in the streets of London, if overcome with hunger he would make a sudden dart into a baker's shop and, purchasing a loaf, break it and offer half to his companion. He said with surprise one day to Hogg, " Do you know that such an one does not like bread ? Did you ever know a person who disliked bread ? " and he added that a friend had actually refused one of his spontaneous offers of half a loaf. In his pockets he generally carried a supply of his favourite food, and " a circle of crumbs on the floor often marked the place where he had sat at his studies, his face nearly in contact with his book, greedily devouring bread amidst his profound abstractions." Occasionally he would add, as a relish to his regimen of bread, common cooking raisins, or oranges and apples from the stalls. For drink he was content with cold water, of which he took frequent draughts, but tea he welcomed, and he

[1] Hogg, vol. i. p. 132.

would take cup after cup. He drank wine sometimes and diluted it largely with water: spirits he entirely eschewed.

His studies at Oxford were self-imposed, the curriculum of the University he could not or would not follow. He was always actively employed, and no student ever read more assiduously. At all hours he was to be found, book in hand, reading, in season and out of season, at table, in bed, and especially during his walks. Not only in the country lanes, but in the streets of Oxford and the most crowded thoroughfares of London did he pursue his studies. Stooping low with bent knees and outstretched neck, he pored earnestly over the volume before him, and he would elude, with his vast and quiet agility, any malignant interruptions.[1] Hogg, who gives this account of Shelley's reading habits, adds that he never beheld eyes that devoured the pages more voraciously than his, and he was convinced that two-thirds of the day and night were often employed in reading. His inextinguishable thirst for knowledge prompted him frequently to read for sixteen out of the twenty-four hours, when, his book laid open on the chimney-piece, as was his custom, Hogg found it difficult to rouse him from his abstractions to join in conversation.

[1] Hogg, vol. i. p. 125.

Oxford

The Oxford of Shelley's time differed little from that of the eighteenth century, when Gibbon spent there the most idle and unprofitable fourteen months of his whole life. Then, as formerly, the fellows enjoyed their emoluments, their food and wine, and troubled themselves little with reading, thinking, or supervising the studies of the place. " Their conversation," says Gibbon in the account of his life at Magdalen, " stagnated in a round of college business, Tory politics, personal anecdotes, and private scandal ; their dull and deep potations excused the brisk intemperance of youth."

Shelley, who readily met any friendly or sympathetic advances, was quickly repelled by the display of pretentious affectation which was the characteristic attitude of the dons.

A feeble attempt, but not of the kind likely to appeal to Shelley, was made by the authorities to direct his studies. Not long after he arrived at Oxford he was sent for one morning by a little man, presumably a college tutor, who said to him in an almost inaudible whisper, " You must read," and he repeated this injunction many times in his small voice. With Shelley's studious habits, the advice must have appeared welcome, and he replied that he had no objection. To satisfy his mentor, he told him that in his pocket he had some books which he began to take out. The little man stared at Shelley and remarked that that was not exactly what he meant, " You must read *Prometheus Vinctus*, and Demosthenes' *de Corona* and Euclid—and then he added, " You must begin with Aristotle's *Ethics* and go on with his other treatises." Although Shelley did not appreciate this counsel, he soon took very kindly to the scholastic logic of Oxford and " seized its distinctions with his accustomed quickness."

With Hogg " he exercised his ingenuity in long discussions respecting various questions in logic, and more frequently in metaphysical enquiries." They read much together, and their studies included Locke's *Essay concerning the Human Understanding*, Hume's *Essays*, and *Le Système de la Nature*. The authorship of this book, which has been ascribed both to Helvetius and to J. B. Mirabaud, was really the work of Baron d'Holbach, one of the French Encyclopædists. Shelley's curiosity may have been aroused by seeing Godwin's reference to *Le Système* in *Political Justice*. He was undoubtedly impressed, if not influenced by Holbach's book, and he refers to it in an early letter to Godwin (July 29, 1812) as " of uncommon powers, yet too obnoxious to accusations of sensuality and selfishness." A month later he expressed his intention of translating it, but, zealous champion as he was at that time of free-thought, he was unable to endorse entirely the theories of naturalism as set forth in *Le Système*, and he contented himself by quoting some extracts from the book in the notes to " Queen Mab."

They also read Plato, but in Dacier's translation, and in an English version. Shelley earnestly yearned for some vigorous mental exercise, and, although he would have found it then, as he did afterwards, in the study of Plato, he sought for this stimulant in those writers who assailed revealed religion. Hogg suggests that " to a soul loving excitement and change, destruction, so that it be on a grand scale, may sometimes prove hardly less inspiring than creation." Shelley's credulity was such that he " believed implicitly every assertion, so that it was improbable, and incredible, exulting in the success of his philosophic doubts, when like the calmest and most suspicious of analysts he refused to admit, without strict proof, propositions that many, who are not deficient in metaphysical prudence, account obvious and self-evident." But, whatever Hogg may say, Shelley was too intelligent to accept the hollow religious conventions practised and enjoined by his father.

The Shelleys were Whigs, and Bysshe was brought up in an environment in which Liberal ideas were at least nominally encouraged. The personal attitude of his grandfather, Sir Bysshe, towards religion was apparently one of supreme indifference. But Timothy

Shelley in England

Shelley observed the outward forms and teaching of the Church of England such as were in use in the eighteenth century. It was a respectable institution which it was the duty of every country gentleman to support. Professor Dowden stated that Timothy Shelley entered himself as a subscriber for two copies of the Unitarian Sermons of Dr. Sadler under the title "a friend of religious liberty," and said, "When Mr. Edwards [the Vicar of their parish] dies, I should like Mr. Sadler as our clergyman." Timothy Shelley possessed no gift for polemics, but he held to the arguments of Paley (he habitually called him Palley) and recommended his works to his doubting son. Bysshe, who said to Hogg, "my father will call him Palley; why does he call him so?" derived no satisfaction from the study of that divine. His attitude of mind may perhaps have been fostered by his mother, who, according to Bysshe, appears to have been far from orthodox. In a letter to Hogg he writes, "My mother is quite rational; she says, 'I think *prayer* and thanksgiving are of no use. If a man is a good man, philosopher or Christian, he will do very well in whatever state awaits us.' I call this liberality."[1]

Shelley's discussions with Hogg during his first term at Oxford had done much to confirm him in his scepticism. Mr. Lang and others speak of his atti-

[1] May 15, 1811.

Oxford

tude as a kind of pose, or boyish prank to tease the dons. But there is every evidence that, whatever Hogg may have been, Shelley, though biassed, was in deadly earnest, for he anxiously studied every book within his reach that was likely to support his views. On November 11, he asked Stockdale in a letter from Oxford to obtain for him " An Hebrew Essay demonstrating that the Christian religion is false," which a clergyman writing in the *Christian Observer* [1] had declared "as an unanswerable yet sophistical argument," and he added that, if it were translated into Greek, Latin, or any of the European languages, he would thank Stockdale to send it.

One can understand that such a book would have appealed to him, as among those with whom he was accustomed to correspond on religious matters were several clergymen.

So far from making a secret of his views, Shelley must have expressed them freely, for both he and Hogg enjoyed a reputation throughout the University for entertaining dangerous opinions.

Shelley was in London, about the middle of December, on his way from Oxford to Field Place, where he was to spend his Christmas holidays, and he probably paid his promised visit to Stockdale's shop to inquire

---

[1] Dr. Richard Garnett looked through this periodical, but could find no such article.

about the publication of *St. Irvyne*. Stockdale, who later earned notoriety as the publisher of a scandalous publication known as the *Memoirs of Harriette Wilson*, appears in 1810 to have been still susceptible of being shocked. He declared, in his recollections of Shelley written some years later,[1] that " not merely by slight hints, but constant allusions, personally and by letters," was he " rendered extremely uneasy respecting Mr. Shelley's religious, or indeed irreligious sentiments towards which all his conversations, reading, and pursuits clearly tended." Few people could withstand Shelley's frank enthusiasm, and he easily won Stockdale's warm regard. The bookseller's motives appear to have been well intentioned, but he was not entirely disinterested : it was reasonable that he may have expected to earn the gratitude of Mr. Timothy Shelley when he communicated to him his suspicions regarding Bysshe's views of religion. The only result of his meddling was that Mr. Shelley lost no time in calling on him at his shop. Stockdale thereupon enlarged on the dangers that threatened his son, and suggested as a remedy that some friend capable of entering into his feelings might endeavour to gain the young man's confidence. But the only friend at this

---

[1] In *Stockdale's Budget*, 1827. A copy of this curious publication is in the British Museum. Dr. Richard Garnett was the first to draw public attention to Stockdale's references to Shelley in his article, " Shelley in Pall Mall," *Macmillan's Magazine*, June 1860.

time who was capable of gaining Bysshe's confidence was Hogg, whom Stockdale seems to have suspected; to Hogg was imputed the blame of having led the poet astray. Smarting under the blow which had been administered by the well-meaning bookseller, Mr. Shelley at once wrote to his erring son, who was now at Field Place, one of his wildly furious letters, in which Hogg was probably made the subject of attack, and he appears to have threatened to withdraw Bysshe from college.

On Mr. Shelley's return home, he wrote on December 23 to thank Stockdale " for the very liberal and handsome manner in which you imparted to me the sentiments you held towards my son, and the open and friendly communication."

But what proved to be the last Christmas that Bysshe spent under his father's roof was anything but a peaceful one. Stockdale had betrayed him to his father and, as he wrote to Hogg on December 20, had " converted him to sanctity. He mentioned my name," he goes on to say, " as a supporter of sceptical principles. My father wrote to me, and I am now surrounded, environed by dangers, to which compared the devils who besieged St. Anthony were all inefficient. They attack me for my detestable principles : I am reckoned an outcast : yet I defy them, and I laugh at their ineffectual efforts. . . . My father wished to withdraw me from College: I would not consent to it. There lowers a terrific tempest, but I stand, as it were, on a pharos, and smile exultingly at the vain beating of the billows below . . ." "How can I fancy that I shall ever think you mad," he adds: "am I not the wildest, the most delirious of enthusiasm's offspring?" And he concludes, "Adieu! Down with Bigotry! Down with Intolerance! In this endeavour your most sincere friend will join his every power, his every feeble resource. Adieu!"

But there was another and, for the moment, deeper sorrow that saddened Shelley and made him exclaim to Hogg, "Oh, here we are in the midst of all the uncongenial jollities of Christmas, when you are compelled to contribute to the merriment of others—when you are compelled to live under the severest of all restraints, concealment of feelings pregnant enough in themselves, how terrible is your lot! I am learning abstraction, but I fear that my proficiency will be but trifling. I cannot, dare not, speak of myself. Why do you still continue to say, ' Do not despond, that you must not despair.' "

The cause of this despair was Miss Harriet Grove, Bysshe's pretty cousin, whose love for him had apparently for some time been lukewarm, and had now, he realised, expired. The last poem in the *Posthumous Fragments of Margaret Nicholson,* published during

the middle of the preceding November, is a serious
piece entitled, " Melody to a scene of Former Times,"
beginning :

> "Art thou, indeed, for ever gone,
>   For ever, ever lost to me?"

which seems to strike a personal note, and perhaps
alludes to a coolness on the part of Miss Grove.   When
he says :

> "Two years' speechless bliss are gone,
>   I thank thee, dearest, for the dream,"

as I have before pointed out, he appears to be speaking
of the two years that had elapsed since that occasion
when he and his cousin met for the first time after
childhood.   Bysshe was an assiduous letter writer, and
we know that Miss Grove was one of his correspondents.
Religious discussion was at this time as the breath of
his life, and he found it impossible to restrain himself
from entering upon his favourite topic even in his love-
letters.   To quote the words of her brother, the Rev.
Charles Grove, " She became uneasy at the tone of his
letters on the subject of religion, at first consulting my
mother, and subsequently my father also on the subject.   This led at last, though I cannot exactly tell
how, to the dissolution of an engagement between
Bysshe and my sister H., which had previously been

permitted, both by his father and mine." [1] Grove spent the Christmas vacation at Field Place, and perhaps he conveyed to Bysshe these unwelcome tidings. In his letters to Hogg, Bysshe had much to say on the subject, of her want of enthusiasm ; he speaks of " the never-dying remorse, which my egotising folly has occasioned," and attributes the cause of her disloyalty to worldly prejudice and bigotry. His sister Elizabeth attempted sometimes to plead his cause, but in vain. Miss Grove said :

" Even supposing I take your representation of your brother's qualities and sentiments, which as you coincide in and admire, I may fairly imagine to be exaggerated, although *you* may not be aware of the exaggeration, what right have *I*, admitting that he is so superior, to enter into an intimacy, which must end in delusive disappointment, when he finds how really

[1] An interesting sidelight is thrown on this episode by Dr. John William Polidori, who accompanied Byron in 1816 as his physician to Switzerland, where he made Shelley's acquaintance for the first time. He notes, somewhat crudely, in his Diary (edited by Mr. W. M. Rossetti, 1911) some facts on the life of Shelley, who undoubtedly confided them to him :

" Shelley is another instance of wealth inducing relations to confine for madness, and was only saved by his physician [Dr. Lind] being honest. He was betrothed from a boy to his cousin, for age ; another came who had as much as he *would* have, and she left him ' because he was an atheist.' When starving, a friend [? Godwin] to whom he had given £2000, though he knew it, would not come near him." The last statement seems to relate to William Godwin, who held himself aloof from Shelley when he was in dire need during the winter of 1814, after his elopement with Mary Godwin.

inferior I am to the being which his heated imagination has pictured." " This was unanswerable," adds Shelley in quoting Miss Grove's decision in a letter to Hogg.[1] Later he writes :. " Is she not gone and yet I breathe, I live ! But adieu to egotism ; I am sick to death of the name of *self*." [2] And again : " Believe me, my dear friend, that my only ultimate wishes *now* are for your happiness, and that of my sisters." [3]

When at last he realised that it was vain to hope for a reconciliation, and that it was now all over between himself and Miss Grove, he wrote : " She is no longer mine ! She abhors me as a sceptic, as what *she* was before ! Oh, bigotry ! When I pardon this last, this severest of thy persecutions, may Heaven (if there be wrath in Heaven) blast me ! Has vengeance, in his armoury of wrath, a punishment more dreadful ? [4] . . . Is suicide wrong ? I slept with a loaded pistol, and some poison, last night, but did not die. I could not come on Monday, my sister would not part with me ; but I must—I will see you soon. My sister is now comparatively happy ; she has felt deeply for me. Had it not been for her—had it not been for a sense of what I owe her, to *you*, I should have bidden you a

[1] Shelley to Hogg, December 23, 1810.
[2] Shelley to Hogg, January 2, 1811.
[3] Shelley to Hogg, December 28, 1810.
[4] Mr. W. M. Rossetti points out that this sentence is repeated almost verbatim from Schubart's " Ahasuerus."

final farewell some time ago. But can the dead feel ;
dawns any day-beam on the night of dissolution ? " [1]

Elizabeth " saw me when I received your letter of
yesterday," he wrote to Hogg. " She saw the con-
flict of my soul. At first she said nothing ; and then
she exclaimed, ' Re-direct it, and send it instantly to
the post ! ' Believe me, I feel far more than I will
allow myself to express, for the cruel disappointments
which I have undergone." Shelley seemed to have
believed that the letter was about Miss Grove, as he
added : " Write to me whatever you wish to say ;
you may say what you will on *other* subjects ; but on
that I dare not even read what you would write. *Forget* her ? What would I not have given up to have
been thus happy." [2]

" Forsake her ! Forsake one whom I loved ! Can
I ? Never ! But she is gone—she is lost to me for
ever ; for ever ! " he writes in a fit of agony. " I am
cold this morning, so you must excuse bad writing, as
I have been most of the night pacing a churchyard. I
must now engage in scenes of strong interest." Then
on January 11, 1811, comes one of Bysshe's last references to Harriet Grove in his letters to Hogg : " She
is gone ! She is lost to me for ever ! She married ! [3]

---

[1] Shelley to Hogg, January 3, 1811.

[2] Shelley to Hogg, January 6.

[3] Hogg prints "She is married," but Peacock's suggested emendation
as given above would seem to be correct, as Miss Grove does not appear

Oxford

Married to a clod of earth ; she will become as insensible herself ; all those fine capabilities will moulder ! Let us speak no more on the subject. Do not deprive me of the little remains of peace, which yet linger : that which arises from endeavours to make others happy."

His solicitude for the happiness of others included a plan which involved Hogg and his sister Elizabeth, " with whom except an occasional tiff, when she preferred less dry and abstruse matters to his ethical and metaphysical speculations, he agreed most affectionately, cordially, and perfectly." [1] To Elizabeth (of whom he generally spoke to Hogg as " my sister," as if he only had one), he had turned for sympathy, and found it, while he was suffering the tortures of unrequited love. Bysshe had arranged that Hogg should go to Field Place, having undertaken to fall in love with Elizabeth, who had not yet turned seventeen. " If I did not," he adds humorously, in writing years after this incident, " I had no business to go to Field Place, and he would never forgive me. I promised to do my best." Bysshe read Hogg's letters to her, and he was happy when he was able to write

to have married Mr. Heylar until the autumn of 1811. On October 28 of that year, in a letter which Professor Dowden quotes, from Shelley to Charles Grove from York, he says, " How do you like Mr. Heylar? a new brother as well as a new cousin [the new cousin was Shelley's bride] must be an invaluable acquisition."

[1] Hogg, vol. i. p. 201.

143

to him, "She frequently inquires after you, and we talk of you often. I do not wish to awaken her intellect too powerfully ; this must be my apology for not communicating all my speculations to her. . . . I wish you knew Elizabeth, she is a great consolation to me ; but, if all be well, my wishes on that score will soon be accomplished." Bysshe encouraged Hogg to publish a tale, so that he might give Elizabeth a copy, but his great hope of bringing her and his friend together was for the present out of the question. Hogg was in Mr. Timothy Shelley's bad books, thanks to Stockdale, who had already used him as a scapegoat for Bysshe's sins, and was preparing for him an additional burden.

During these days of trouble at home, Shelley did not entirely abandon certain literary projects which he had set on foot at Oxford. It was there that he became acquainted with a literary character named Browne, better known as Bird, who had written a voluminous historical and political work on Sweden. He applied for assistance to Shelley, who with his characteristic generosity agreed to purchase the copyright of the work. To Munday and Slatter, the Oxford printers, Shelley applied for aid in raising the necessary amount, and they, knowing his family and wishing to save him from money-lenders, advanced a sum of £200, and went security for the remaining £400. Type and paper were purchased, but the work had not progressed very far when Shelley left the University, and the printers' hopes of recovering their liabilities vanished. Mr. Slatter, who related these facts, did not doubt the intention of Shelley in entering into the engagement, but his prospects suddenly changed, and he was never afterwards in a position to fulfil it.

Hogg, who was staying in London during the Christmas holidays, had literary ambitions, which were fostered by Shelley, and among other attempts he composed some verses on " The Dying Gladiator," the subject of the Oxford English prize poem for 1810. Hogg was not awarded the prize, and Shelley, usually an admirer of his friend's poems, was unenthusiastic over " The Dying Gladiator." But he had faith in Hogg's talents, and it is said, that he wrote with him a novel entitled *Leonora*. This story, like other flotsam and jetsam from Shelley's pen, has not survived, although it went very near to being printed. What little we know of this work is told by Slatter, but there are several references in Shelley's correspondence to a novel which appears to be *Leonora*. Shelley confided to Stockdale, in a letter on December 18, 1810, that he had a novel in preparation. " It is principally constructed," he said, " to convey metaphysical and political opinions by way of conversation,[1] it shall be

---

[1] A plan subsequently adopted by T. L. Peacock with great success in his novels *Nightmare Abbey*, *Crotchet Castle*, &c.

sent to you as soon as completed : but it shall receive
more correction than I trouble myself to give to wild
romance and poetry." The reception of *St. Irvyne*
probably did not inspire Stockdale with any desire to
become the publisher of another of Shelley's works
of fiction. And two days later when writing to Hogg,
after he had learnt that Stockdale had been talking
him over with his father, he declares that "Stockdale
will no longer do for me. I am at a loss whom to
select. S.'s skull is very thick, but I am afraid he will
not believe my assertion ; indeed, should it gain credit
with him, should he accept the offer of publication,
there exist numbers who will find out, or imagine, a
real tendency ; and booksellers possess more power
than we are aware of in impeding the sale of any book
containing opinions displeasing to them. I am disposed to offer it to Wilkie & Robinson,[1] Paternoster
Row, and to take it there myself ; they published
Godwin's works, and it is scarcely possible to suppose
anyone, layman or clergyman, will assert that these
support Gospel doctrines. If that will not do, I must
print it myself. Oxford, of course, would be most con-
venient for the correction of the press. Mr. Munday's
principles are not *very* severe ; he is more a votary to
Mammon than God. . . . Inconveniences would now
result from my *owning* the novel, which I have in pre-

---

[1] The publishers of *Zastrossi*.

paration for the press. I give out therefore, that I will publish no more ; everyone here, but the select few who enter into my schemes, believe my assertion." [1]

Shelley's recent " publishing freaks " had evidently met with scant sympathy from the household at Field Place, and he was therefore determined to keep his counsel, to which, besides Hogg, his sister Elizabeth was perhaps admitted. *Leonora*, if this was the novel referred to in the above letter, was put into the hands of the printer at Oxford who was at work on Mr. Bird's *History of Sweden*, but, as Slatter tells us, " the printers refused to proceed with it, in consequence of discovering that he had interwoven his free notions throughout the work, and at the same time they strongly endeavoured to dissuade him from its publication altogether." This advice was, however, disregarded, and Shelley took the " copy " to Mr. King, a printer at Abingdon, who had nearly completed it when Shelley's expulsion from the University stopped further progress of the work. After that event, in writing to Hogg on May 15, 1811, he says, " How goes on your tale ? I have heard nothing of it. As for mine, I cannot get an answer from Munday's.[2] Do they tremble ? I thought the A[bingdon ?] printer too stupid ; and I defy a zealot to

---

[1] Shelley to Hogg, December 20, 1810.
[2] The name is printed by Hogg as " L . . ." In the copy of this letter corrected by Lady Shelley, presumably from the original, the name is given as " Munday's," which is evidently what was written by Shelley.

say it does not support orthodoxy. If an author's own assertion in his own book may be taken as an avowal of his intentions, it does support orthodoxy. I could not do more, and yet they say *Mine* is not printable; it is as bad as Rousseau, and would certainly be prosecuted." A novel by Shelley in the manner of Jean Jacques would certainly be an interesting recovery, if recovery were possible, but printers' proofs (for the book seems to have gone no further than that stage) have usually a very transitory existence, and the chances of its survival are remote.

"I am composing a satirical poem; I shall print it at Oxford, unless I find on visiting him, that R[obinson] is ripe for printing whatever will sell. In that case he is my man," thus wrote Shelley to Hogg in his letter of December 20, 1811. It is possible, though by no means certain, that he here referred to a poem mentioned by C. K. Sharpe in a letter, already quoted from, in which he says: "Shelley's last exhibition is a poem on the State of Public Affairs." Such a poem seems to have been published, as the late Mr. D. F. MacCarthy discovered in the *Oxford Herald* for March 9, 1811, the following advertisement:

"LITERATURE. *Just Published, Price Two Shillings,* A Poetical Essay on the Existing State of Things [Quotation from Southey's "Curse of Kehama"]. By a gentleman of the University of Oxford. For assisting to maintain in Prison Mr. Peter Finnerty, imprisoned for a libel. London, sold by B. Crosby and Co., and all other booksellers, 1811."

The title also figures in a list of books published during 1810–11 in *The Poetical Register*.

No copy of the *Poetical Essay* has as yet come to light, and it is not mentioned by this title in Shelley's published correspondence. But in assigning the book to Shelley there is the evidence of C. K. Sharpe, and, as in the case of *St. Irvyne*, it is described on the title-page as " by a gentleman of the University of Oxford." The quotation from the " Curse of Kehama " also suggests Shelley, who inquired of Stockdale, in his letter of December 2, if he knew when Southey's poem would come out, as he was curious to see it. We know that he procured " Kehama " as soon as it was published, and it long remained a favourite with him.

Peter Finnerty was an Irish journalist, born in 1766, who got into trouble during the Rebellion of 1798, as printer of the *Dublin Press*. For a political libel he suffered imprisonment, and his types and press were destroyed. On his release he went to England and became a reporter on the *Morning Chronicle*. To this paper, on January 23, 1810, he contributed a letter on Lord Castlereagh, whom Leigh Hunt said " he accused of an intention to harass and destroy him, and reminded the Viscount of the tyrannous and horrible cruelties practised upon the people of Ireland during his administration of that country." A year later Finnerty was tried for libel and sentenced to eighteen months' imprisonment. His case was reported in the *Oxford Herald*, in which journal a subscription to maintain him during his imprisonment was opened. Shelley's name as a subscriber of one guinea appears in the *Herald* for March 2, 1811, and a like amount is acknowledged to Mr. Hobbs, of whom more presently, and to Mr. Bird, evidently the Historian of Sweden. Shelley's interest in Finnerty did not cease with the publication of the " Poetical Essay." He mentioned him in his "Address to the Irish People "; and in a speech which he made during his Irish campaign in the spring of 1812, at the Fishamble Theatre, Dublin, he was reported to have commiserated with the sufferings of Finnerty, and to have written " a very beautiful poem, the profits of which we understand, from *undoubted* authority, Mr. Shelly [*sic*] remitted to Mr. Finnerty ; we have heard that they amounted to nearly a hundred pounds." [1] This statement cannot be reconciled with the fact that the book has entirely disappeared, as, in order to yield such a sum, it would have been necessary to sell a considerable number

[1] *The Dublin Weekly Messenger*, March 7, 1812. A copy of this paper with a mark against the article on " Pierce Byshe Shelly, Esq.," is among the Shelley-Whitton papers.

of copies at the price of two shillings. Professor Dowden suggested that the " Poetical Essay " may possibly have comprised an earlier form of the portion of " Queen Mab " [printed in 1813] that relates to the present time, and that this part constituted the germ of the poem : the other sections dealing with the past and the future being afterwards added. Some reason for this theory may be found in an information laid before the Lord Chancellor in 1817, who was in possession of Eliza Westbrook's copy of " Queen Mab," that that poem was actually written and published when the author was of the age of nineteen.

CHAPTER VIII

PHILOSOPHIC DOUBTS

Metaphysical studies—Religious doubts—Shelley's passion for dispute—His miscellaneous correspondents—On the existence of the Deity—His tirade against intolerance—A first cause—" Armageddon heroes "—The fears of his father and mother—Hogg's tale—Stockdale makes trouble—Timothy Shelley reconciled—Exit Stockdale—Shelley's return to Oxford—On the evidences of Christianity—" Parthenon "—Shelley's belief in pre-existence—The adventures of a coat.

SHELLEY went up to Oxford, as we have seen, a devoted student of natural philosophy, but he failed to imbue his friend Hogg with his love of chemistry and electricity. Lacking the sympathy of his companion in this direction, he discovered it in another, namely, in the study of metaphysics, into which science he plunged with his characteristic energy. The course of his incessant reading included theology, and his confession to a correspondent [1] in the spring of 1811, " I was once an enthusiastic Deist, but never a Christian," is evidently in allusion to his state of mind during the winter of 1810-11.

There seems to be no reason to suppose that Shelley had troubled himself very much with questions of

[1] Janetta Philipps.

152

Philosophic Doubts

religion during his Eton days, and his interest in the subject at Oxford may be said to have been mainly polemical. He was concerned at this time with such discussions as those referring to the evidences of Christianity and the existence of the Deity, but he had not then been moved by the deeper spiritual issues which afterwards attracted him when he was writing his Essay on Christianity. We can see in his letters to Hogg, during the Christmas of 1810, how his mind alternates between the acceptance of a belief in a Supreme Being and total disbelief.

But before Christmas he had grown tired of the works of controversial divines, and he announced, in a letter to Hogg on December 23, that he had done with such studies. " I shall not read Bishop Prettyman,[1] or any more of them," he said, " unless I have some particular reason. Bigots will not argue ; it destroys the very nature of things to argue ; it is contrary to faith. How therefore could you suppose that one of these liberal gentleman would listen to scepticism on the subject even of St. Athanasius's sweeping anathema ? "

[1] Sir George Pretyman Tomline, Bishop of Winchester, was until 1803 known by the name of Pretyman. In 1799 he published his popular, though not very deep, *Elements of Christian Theology*, dedicated to Pitt (whose tutor he had been), and used by candidates for ordination. Tomline was described in the *Dict. Nat. Biog.* as "a supporter of the prerogative and an uncompromising friend to the existing state of things." He objected, however, so strongly to Catholic Emancipation, that he declared (and evidently did so to give a proof of his courage) that he was prepared to oppose it, even if supported by his patron.

Shelley in England

Argument was the breath of Shelley's life; he loved it passionately as he did letter-writing. Logic and Letters were to him toys and mascots. He would relinquish neither. His investigations in pursuit of Truth included a vigorous correspondence upon controversial religion, and among those personally unknown to him, to whom he had written while in London, " by way of a gentle alterative," apparently on the subject of the Athanasian Creed, was a certain Mr. W. It is not known whether Shelley had posed as a clergyman in order to " draw " his correspondent, or whether W. was merely puzzled at the recondite character of his letter. "He promised to write to me when he had time," exclaimed Shelley, "seemed surprised at what I had said, yet directed me as the Reverend : his amazement must be extreme." When at length the letter from W. arrived at Field Place, Shelley wrote to Hogg that it was too long to answer ; but three days later he promised to send it to his friend, who had then returned to Oxford, and added, " If it amuses you, you can answer him, if not I will." Hogg returned W.'s letter with his reply to Shelley, who pronounced the rejoinder " excellent," and wrote : " I think it will fully (in his own mind) convince Mr. W. I enclosed five sheets of paper full this morning, and sent them to the coach with yours. I sate up all night to finish them ; they attack his hypothesis at

Philosophic Doubts

its very basis which, at some future time, I will explain to you : and I have attempted to prove, from the existence of a Deity and a Revelation, the futility of the superstition upon which he forms his whole scheme."

But to go back. On December 23, Shelley adduces the popular objection to the free discussion of religious topics to prejudice and superstition. " You have said that the philosophy, which I pursued, is not uncongenial with the strictest morality ; you must see that it militates with the received opinions of the world ; that, therefore, does it offend but [offends only] prejudice and superstition, that superstitious bigotry, inspired by the system upon which at present the world acts, of believing all that we are told of as incontrovertible facts."

In his letter to Hogg of January 3, in which he communicates the news that he had been thrown over by Harriet Grove, before coming to the subject, as if he desired to defer it as long as possible, he pauses to discuss the subject of the existence of God, and says :

" Before we deny or believe the existence of anything, it is necessary that we should have a tolerably clear idea of what it is. The word ' God,' a vague word, has been, and will continue to be, the source of numberless errors, until it is erased from the nomenclature of philosophy. Does it not imply " the soul of the Universe, the intelligent and *necessarily* beneficent actuating principle ? ' This it is impossible not

155

to believe in; I may not be able to adduce proofs;
but I think that the leaf of a tree, the meanest insect
on which we trample, are, in themselves, arguments
more conclusive than any which can be advanced,
that some vast intellect animates infinity. If we
disbelieve *this*, the strongest argument in support of
the existence of a future state instantly becomes
annihilated. I confess that I think Pope's

"All are but parts of one stupendous whole"

something more than poetry. It has ever been my
favourite theory. For the immortal soul ' never to be
able to die, never to escape from some shrine as chilling
as *the clay-formed dungeon*,[1] which now it inhabits '—
it is the future punishment which I can most easily
believe in.

" Love, love, *infinite in extent*, eternal in duration,
yet (allowing your theory in that point) perfectible,
should be the reward; but can we suppose that this
reward will arise, spontaneously, as a necessary appendage to our nature, or that our nature itself could be
without cause—a first cause—a God? When do we
see effects arise without causes? What causes are
there without corresponding effects? Yet here I
swear—and as I break my oath may Infinity Eternity
blast me—here I swear, that never will I forgive intolerance! It is the only point on which I allow myself
to encourage revenge; every moment shall be devoted
to my object, which I can spare; and let me hope that
it will not be a blow which spends itself, and leaves the
wretch at rest—but lasting, long revenge! I am
convinced too that it is of great dis-service to Society,

[1] So in Schubart.

that it encourages prejudices, which strike at the root of the dearest, the tenderest of ties. Oh ! how I wish I were the avenger !—that it were mine to crush the demon ; to hurl him to his native hell, never to rise again, and thus to establish for ever perfect and universal toleration. I expect to gratify some of this insatiable feeling in poetry. You shall see—you shall hear—how it has injured me."

Shelley then goes on to break the tidings that Harriet Grove was lost to him, and her reason for proving faithless was that she " abhorred " him for being " a sceptic " and holding opinions which she herself had once held.

Hitherto he had been a questioner, but what he considered as an act of bigotry on the part of Harriet Grove and her parents, in cancelling his engagement, had prompted him to exclaim on January 6, " I will crush Intolerance. I will, at least, attempt it. To fail even in so useful an attempt were glorious ! " To this and similar expressions Shelley gave vent in his letters to Hogg while suffering under the loss of Harriet Grove. It was his first challenge to the world, a defiance which in later years rang forth in "Queen Mab," " The Revolt of Islam," and " The Masque of Anarchy."

In this same letter he proceeds to consider an argument which he had received from Hogg " against the Non-existence of a Deity. Do you allow," he says, "that some *supernatural* power actuates the organization of physical causes ? . . . If this Deity thus influences the action of the Spirits (if I may be allowed the expression) which take care of minor events (supposing your theory be true), why is it *not* the soul of the Universe ; in what is it not analogous to the soul of man ? Why *too* is *not* gravitation the soul of a clock ? . . . I think we may not inaptly define *Soul* as the most supreme, superior, and distinguished abstract appendage to the nature of anything."

These extracts from Shelley's letters, with the following, show the incertitude of his mind :

" What necessity is there for continuing in existence ? But Heaven ! Eternity ! Love ! My dear friend, I am yet a sceptic on these subjects ; would that I could believe them to be, as they are represented ; would that I could totally disbelieve them ! But no ! That would be selfish. I still have firmness enough to resist to the last, this most horrible of errors. . . . I wish, ardently wish, to be profoundly convinced of the existence of a Deity, that so superior a spirit might derive some degree of happiness from my feeble exertions :

" For love is heaven and heaven is love." [1]

You think so, too, and you disbelieve not the existence

[1] From Walter Scott's *Lay of the Last Minstrel*, quoted also by Shelley as a motto for a chapter in *St. Irvyne*.

Philosophic Doubts

of an eternal, omnipresent Spirit. . . . Stay! I have an idea. I think I can prove the existence of a Deity —a First Cause. I will ask a materialist, how came this universe at first? He will answer by chance. What chance?"[1] Then he proceeds to argue his case in support of "A First Cause," and he adds: "Oh, that this Deity were the soul of the universe, the spirit of universal, imperishable love! Indeed I believe it is: but now to your argument of the necessity of Christianity. I am not sure that your argument does not tend to prove its unreality." Here we see Shelley pleading the cause of Deism, but he cannot resist a sally at Orthodoxy: "Hideous, hated traits of Superstition. Oh! Bigots, how I abhor your influence; they are all bad enough—but do we not see Fanaticism decaying? is not its influence weakened, except where Faber, Rowland Hill, and several others of the Armageddon heroes maintain their posts with all the obstinacy of long-established dogmatism?"

Apart from this grief at the loss of Harriet Grove, Bysshe cannot have found the atmosphere of Field Place congenial, and but for the prospect of having to leave his sister Elizabeth, he must have looked forward with pleasure to his return to Oxford. If he were not actually in disgrace with his father, there was probably a coolness between them arising out of the reasons that

---

[1] Shelley to Hogg, Jan. 12, 1811.

the Groves had given for breaking off Harriet's engagement. Mr. Timothy Shelley was conventional, and to avow, as Bysshe had done to Stockdale, opinions such as were held by Tom Paine and other Deists was against the canons of respectability. To be respectable was the whole duty of a gentleman. Although Timothy Shelley was prepared to do anything within reason for Bysshe, and to provide handsomely for him, his feelings had been trampled on and his sense of dignity injured. Mrs. Shelley likewise had her fears : " My Mother imagines me to be in the high road to Pandemonium, she fancies I want to make a deistical. coterie of all my little sisters : how laughable ! " And it was, perhaps, for Bysshe had told Hogg that he did not communicate to Elizabeth all his speculations, and on another occasion he withheld a letter which his friend had sent apparently to guide her on some speculative matter.

One should not so much blame Mr. Timothy Shelley and his wife for their attitude, as deplore the irony of fate that enabled an old-fashioned, middle-aged squire to beget in the reign of George the Third a son of Bysshe's temperament and genius.

Before Bysshe returned to Oxford other troubles arose for him. Stockdale, the publisher of *St. Irvyne*, had received the confidences of Shelley as well as Hogg, both of whom had placed manuscripts in his hands. It seems clear that Shelley's manuscript was the *Necessity of Atheism;* Hogg's may have been a tale [1] that he had written, which Shelley, who evinced great interest, had urged him to get published. In his account of the matter, Stockdale tells us, Shelley had informed him of a metaphysical essay, in support of Atheism, that he had completed: this he intended to promulgate through the University. Stockdale warned him " that his expulsion would be the inevitable consequence of so flagrant an insult to such a body. He, however, was unmoved," and Stockdale added, " I instantly wrote to his father."

Hogg had called occasionally at Stockdale's shop as Shelley's friend, but he failed to make a favourable impression on the publisher, who did not consider that he could have led Shelley " astray " ; he regarded his mind " so infinitely beneath that of his friend." Hogg was evidently viewed with suspicion by Stockdale who, however, had what he may have considered a lucky inspiration. He had noticed by Hogg's address that he was connected in some way with " the worthy " Rev. John Dayrell, of Lynnington Dayrell, not far from Mrs. Stockdale's native place ; he also believed that "Shelley was unquestionably in a most devious

---

[1] " Pray publish your tale ; demand one hundred pounds for it from any publisher ;—he will give it in the event. It is delightful, it is divine—not that I like your heroine—but the poor Mary is a character of heaven I adore her ! " (Shelley to Hogg, Jan. 3, 1811).

path." Stockdale therefore promptly asked his wife
if she knew anything of the young man. Whereupon
good Mrs. Stockdale busied herself in the matter, with
the result that her " recollection and enquiry " confirmed the worst suspicions of her husband, who declared, in a manner worthy of the publisher of *St.
Irvyne*, " that if I did not rush forward, and, however
rudely, pull my candidate for the bays from the preci-
pice, over which he was suspended by a hair, his fate
must be inevitable."

Mr. Timothy Shelley, with Stockdale's letter in his
hand, must have questioned Bysshe about his friend
and his latest " printing freaks," as they were both calculated to become a source of trouble. I do not think
it unlikely that he may have tried to help the boy in
a fatherly way, to allay his religious doubts. Bysshe,
however, wrote in anger to Hogg on January 14:
" Stockdale has behaved infamously to me : he has
abused the confidence I reposed in him in sending him
my work ; and he has made very free with your
character, of which he knows nothing, with my father.
I shall call on Stockdale in my way, that he may
explain." And again, three days later : " Stockdale
certainly behaved in a vile manner to me ; no other
bookseller would have violated the confidence reposed
in him. I will talk to him in London, where I shall be
on Tuesday [January 22]."

Philosophic Doubts

Bysshe did not take his father's ministrations kindly, and gave vent in the same letter to the following unfilial remarks : " Your systematic cudgel for blockheads is excellent. I tried it on with my father, who told me that thirty years ago he had read Locke, but this made no impression. The ' *equus et res* ' are all that I can boast of ; the ' *pater* ' is swallowed up in the first article of the catalogue. You tell me nothing. of the tale ; I am all anxiety about it."

These communications naturally roused Hogg's ire ; he had been accused of some unspecified infamy ; he was determined to bring the meddling bookseller to account, and addressed to him the following letter :

T. J. Hogg to J. J. Stockdale

OXFORD, *Jan.* 21, 1811.

SIR,—I have just heard from a friend to my great surprise that you have made very free with my character to Mr. Shelley. I feel it my duty as a gentleman closely to investigate this extraordinary conduct. I ask what there was in my behaviour to you contrary to the strictest politeness, what there was to justify such an infamous proceeding ?

I insist, Sir, upon knowing the precise nature, the very words of your conversation with Mr. S. . . .

I insist upon being informed upon what authority you spoke thus of me. I demand a full, a perfect apology from yourself. I desire that you should

Shelley in England

immediately write in order to contradict whatever you may have told Mr. Shelley or anyone else.

When I am informed of the exact nature of the offence I can judge of the necessary apology.

The bare mention, of the MS. with which I entrusted you to any one was an unparalleled breach of confidence.—There may have been instances of booksellers who have honourably refused to betray the authors whose works they have published altho' actions were brought against them. I believe that one gentleman had honour enough to submit to the pillory rather than disgrace himself by giving up the name of one who had confided in him, however unworthy · he might be of such generous treatment. Altho' I might be disposed to pardon this offence against myself, I feel it my duty to caution the world against such flagrant violation of principle.

I shall consequently insert in the public newspapers an anonymous advertisement containing a plain statement of the manner in which you have acted. An immediate answer to this letter is desired by, Sir, yours &c. &c.,

T. Jefferson Hogg.

Univ. Coll.

The gentleman who submitted to the pillory was no doubt the long-suffering Peter Finnerty.

Mr. Timothy Shelley went to London to see Stockdale and find out what was amiss, for, as he wrote in his reply to that worthy man, " I cannot comprehend the meaning of the language you use." He was, however, by no means pleased with the bookseller,

SIR TIMOTHY SHELLEY, BART.

*After the picture by George Romney, R.A.,
in the possession of Sir John Shelley, Bart.*

and turning his back on him he proceeded in the direction of Westminster to make inquiries about Hogg.

The result was most satisfactory, and he returned home evidently in a good humour, for Bysshe wrote cheerfully to his friend : " My father's prophetic pre-possession in your favour is become as high as before it was to your prejudice. Whence it arises, or from what cause, I am inadequate to say ; I can merely state the fact. He came from London full of your praises ; your family, that of Mr. Hogg of Norton House, near Stockton-upon-Tees. Your principles are *now* as divine as before they were diabolical. I tell you this with extreme satisfaction, and to sum up the whole, he has desired me to make his compliments to you, and to invite you to make Field Place your headquarters for the Easter Vacation. I hope you will accept of it. I fancy he has been talking in town to some of the northern Members of Parliament who are acquainted with your family. However that may be, I hope you have no other arrangement for Easter which can interfere with granting me the pleasure of introducing you personally here."

On his return to Oxford, Bysshe learnt some further particulars about Stockdale, whose reply to Hogg's letter had been so unsatisfactory that he had written again, only to receive an equally evasive answer.

Shelley in England

Shelley therefore took up the matter himself and wrote :

P. B. Shelley to J. J. Stockdale

OXFORD, *Jan.* 28, 1811.

SIR,—On my arrival at Oxford, my friend Mr. Hogg communicated to me the letters which passed in consequence of your misrepresentations of his character, the abuse of that confidence which he invariably reposed in you. I now, sir, desire to know whether you mean the evasions in your first letter to Mr. Hogg, your insulting *attempt* at coolness in your second, as a means of escaping *safely* from the opprobrium naturally attached to so ungentlemanlike an abuse of confidence (to say nothing of misrepresentation) as that which my father communicated to me, or as a *denial* of the fact of having acted in this unprecedented, this *scandalous* manner. If the former be your intention, I will compassionate your cowardice, and my friend, pitying your *weakness*, will take no further notice of your contemptible *attempts* at calumny. If the latter is your intention, I feel it my duty to declare, as my veracity and that of my father is thereby called in question, that I will never be satisfied, despicable as I may consider the author of that affront, until my friend has ample apology for the injury you have attempted to do him. I expect an immediate, and demand a satisfactory letter.—Sir, I am your obedient humble servant,   PERCY B. SHELLEY.

After Shelley's expulsion from Oxford he wrote to ask Stockdale how many copies had been sold of *St.*

Philosophic Doubts

Irvyne, and requested him to make out his accounts. The bookseller's reply took some time to reach Shelley, who was then at Rhayader : he replied on August 1, 1811 : "I am sorry to say, in answer to your requisition, that the state of my finances renders immediate payment perfectly impossible. It is my intention, at the earliest period of my power to do so, to discharge your account. I am aware of the imprudence of publishing a book so ill-digested as *St. Irvyne ;* but are there no exceptions on the profits of its sale ? My studies have, since writing it, been of a more serious nature. I am at present engaged in completing a series of moral and metaphysical essays—perhaps their copyright would be accepted in lieu of part of the debt."

Stockdale very wisely declined this offer, but he stated in 1827, in his recollections of Shelley, that he did not question his intention of paying the account for the publication of *St. Irvyne*, and that it was his conviction that Shelley " would vegetate rather than live, to effect the discharge of every honest claim upon him." Recognising that there was little to be hoped from Shelley, he applied to his father, who said that his son was not of age, and that he would never pay a farthing of the account. So it was never settled.

Pondering alone at Field Place over his conversations on religion with Bysshe after he had left Oxford, Timothy Shelley was resolved to try to win his son back to the fold. In the letter which he addressed to Bysshe he probably wrote on the evidences of Christianity, having fortified himself during his task with deep draughts from the works of his favourite divine, Paley. In order to show that some men of great mental powers have been Christians, he cited the instances, among others, of Locke and Newton. Bysshe's reply is the first of a series of unpublished letters which I shall print in the following pages :

P. B. Shelley to Timothy Shelley

UNIV. COLL. OX., *Feb.* 6, 1810
[misdated for 1811].

MY DEAR FATHER,—Your very excellent exposition on the subject of Religion pleases me very much. I have seldom seen ideas of Orthodoxy so clearly defined. You have proved to my complete satisfaction that those who do not think at all, a species which contains by far the major part of even uncivilised society, ought to be restrained by the bonds of *prejudicative* religion, by which I mean that it is best that they should follow the religion of their fathers whatever it may be, not having sufficient principle to discharge their duties without leaning on some support, a slight support being better than none at all. So much for the beings who ought to take things upon trust ; But after a rational being, or rather a being

168

Philosophic Doubts

possessing *capabilities* for superadded *rationability*, has proceeding to perfectibility passed that point, before which he could not or used not to reason, after which he both *did* reason, and took interest in the inferences which he drew *from* that reason. Do you then deny him to *use* that reason in the very point which is most momentous to his present, to his future happiness, in the very point which, as being of greater importance, demands a superior energization of that most distinguishing faculty of man. You cannot deny him *that* which is, or ought to be the essence of his being, you cannot deny it him without taking away that essentia and leaving him not an " animal rationale " but " irrationale," retaining no distinguishing characteristic of " *Man* " but " animal bipeds implume risibile."—I then have passed that point, because I *do* reason on the subject, I *do* take interest in that reasoning and from that reasoning I have adduced to my own, I think I could to your *private* satisfaction, that the testimony of the twelve Apostles is insufficient to establish the truth of their doctrine, not to mention how much *weaker* the evidence must become, when filtered thro' so many gradations of history, so many ages.

Supposing twelve men were to make an affidavit before you that they had seen in Africa a vast snake three miles long, suppose they swore that this snake eat nothing but Elephants, and that you knew from all the laws of nature, that enough Elephants could not exist to sustain the snake, would you believe them ? The case is the same, . . . it is clearly therefore proved that we cannot, if we *consider* it, believe facts inconsistent with the general laws of Nature, that there is no evidence sufficient, or rather that evidence is insufficient to prove such facts. I could give you a methodical proof if you desire it, or think this to be inconclusive.

As to Locke, Newton, etc., being Christians, I will relate an anecdote of the latter. At Cambridge he kept chickens, and making a Box for them he provided a large hole for the Hen to go out of, smaller ones for the chickens. What an inconsistency for a Genius who was searching into the mechanism of the Universe. Locke's Christianity cannot *now* appear so surprising, particularly if we mention Voltaire, Lord Kames, Mr. Hume, Rousseau, Dr. Adam Smith, Dr. Franklin et *mille alios*, all of whom were Deists, the life of all of whom was characterised by the strictest morality : all of whom whilst they lived were the subjects of panygeric [*sic*], were the directors of literature and morality. *Truth*, whatever it may be, has never been known to be prejudical to the best interests of mankind, nor was there ever a period of greater tranquillity in which the name of Religion was not even mentioned. Gibbon's History of the decline and fall of the Roman empire proves this truth satisfactorily.

Thus far, my dear Father, have I thought it necessary to explain to you my sentiments, to explain to you upon what they are founded, as far as the imperfect medium of a letter will allow. At some leisure moment may I request to hear your objections (if any yet remain) to my private sentiments—"Religion fetters a reasoning mind with the very bonds which restrain the unthinking one from mischief." This is my great objection to it. The coming of Christ was called εὐαγγελλιον [*sic*] or good tidings ; it is hard to believe

Philosophic Doubts

how those tidings *could* be *good* which are to condemn
more than half of the world to the Devil, for, as St.
Athanasius says, " He who does not believe should go
into eternal fire "—As if belief were voluntary, or an
action, not a passion (as it is) of the mind. I will
now conclude this letter, as, knowing your dislike to
long scrawls, I fear I must have tired you. Believe
me, whatever may be my sentiments, Yrs. most
dutiful affect. P. B. SHELLEY.

[Addressed]
    T. SHELLEY, ESQ., M.P.,   *Postmark*, OXFORD.
    Miller's Hotel,   8 *Feb*. 1811.
            Westr. Bridge,
            London.

[Readdressed] Horsham, Sussex.

Mr. Timothy Shelley apparently wrote to inform
Bysshe of the death of his aunt, Mrs. Sidney, who
was the wife of Timothy's half-brother, afterwards Sir
John Shelley-Sidney of Penshurst. He also seems to
have given some paternal counsel on the subject of
attending College lectures. In the following letter,
perhaps the last addressed to his father on an entirely
friendly footing, Bysshe reassured him that he was
on the right road, and that, whatever doubts he
might himself entertain, there was no fear of him trying
to convert the University. Mr. Shelley had suggested
that Bysshe should enter into competition for the
Prize Poem, the subject being " Parthenon." In

order to help him, "he had induced a distinguished scholar, a considerable antiquary and an eminent man, the Rev. Edward Dallaway, vicar of Leatherhead, secretary to the Earl Marshal, and the historian of the county of Sussex, to furnish a long letter, accompanied with sketches and much valuable information relative to the subject." Bysshe actually began to compose the poem, but he was sent away from Oxford before the time arrived for submitting his attempt to the judges.[1] And in this reply Bysshe promised to meet his father's wishes, that he should submit his verses to Mr. Dallaway. The prize was awarded to Richard Burdon of Oriel College. In his letter to Hogg of July 28, 1811, Shelley offers some criticism on Burdon's poem, and says, "It is certainly admirable as an architectural poem ; but do not let *me* be considered *envious* when I say, that it appears to me to want energy, since the very idea of my being able to write like it is eminently ludicrous. I wonder whether B . . . is a fool or a hypocrite ; he must be the latter."

The whole of the letter is satisfactory, even to the sanguine news about the sale of *St. Irvyne*, and it shows that Shelley was anxious to please his father and resume the old footing of confidence.

---

[1] Hogg, vol. i. p. 317.

Philosophic Doubts

P. B. Shelley to Timothy Shelley

OXFORD, 17th Feb. 1811.

MY DEAR FATHER,—I suppose that by this time you are at Horsham. I dress in black for the late Mrs. Sidney, her death was certainly a necessary consequence of her complaint.

Mr. Rolleston's logic lectures yet continue, as to divinity it is a study which I have very minutely investigated, in order to detect to my own satisfaction the impudent and inconsistent falsehoods of priestcraft, I am in consequence perfectly prepared to meet any examination on the subject : It is needless to observe that in the Schools, Colleges, etc., which are all on the principle of Inquisitorial Orthodoxy, with respect to matters of belief I shall perfectly coincide with the opinions of the learned Doctors, although by the very rules of reasoning which their own *systems* of logic teach me I *could* refute their errors. I shall not therefore publickly come under the act " De heretico comburendo."

I have not yet finished " Parthenon." I hope I shall make it à Poem, such as you would advise me to subject to Mr. Dallaway's criticism. *St. Irvyne* sells fast at Oxford.—I am, My dear Father, your very dutiful affect. PERCY B. SHELLEY.

[Addressed outside]
  T. SHELLEY, Esq.
     Field Place,
M.P.   Horsham, Sussex.

On his return to Oxford, Shelley resumed his studies, and, although his mind was occupied, as we have seen,

with religious topics, he found time to take his walks
with Hogg which had been interrupted by the vacation.
In these excursions he would often stop to gaze at
the children of the country people, and speculate on
their future sorrows and sufferings. Hogg tells us
that one day while he was strolling in the neighbourhood of Oxford he stopped to observe a pretty little
gipsy girl of about six years, who, bare-legged and with
tattered clothes, was busily employed in collecting
empty snail shells. He "was forcibly struck by the
vivid intelligence of her wild and swarthy countenance, and especially by the sharp glance of her fierce
black eyes. ' How much intellect is here ! ' he exclaimed, ' in how humble a vessel, and what an unworthy occupation for a person who once knew perfectly
the whole circle of the sciences ; who has forgotten
them all, it is true, but who could certainly recollect
them, although most probably she will never do
so ; will never recall a single principle of any of
them.' " A boy, a little older than the girl, who
was in charge of her, then appeared and, signalling
to his sister, disappeared with her. The intelligence
of the children appealed to Shelley, who "compared them to birds, and to the two wild leverets,
which that wild mother, the hare, produces." He
encountered them again later, in their gipsy encamp-
ment, and on being recognised by the children followed

them into the tent, with the agility and ease of one who had been accustomed to dwell in such narrow tenements.

A devoted student of Plato, he used to say that every true Platonist must be a lover of children as he truly was. His belief in pre-existence is shown by the following story. One Sunday, after Shelley and Hogg had been reading Plato together, they encountered a woman carrying a child in her arms on Magdalen Bridge. Without ceremony Shelley seized hold of the child, and its mother, fearing that he intended throwing it into the water, held it fast by the clothes. " ' Will your baby tell us anything about pre-existence, Madam ? ' he asked, in a piercing voice and with a wistful look." As she did not reply, he repeated the question, when she said, " He cannot speak." Shelley exclaimed, " But surely he can if he will, for he is only a few weeks old. He may fancy perhaps that he cannot, but it is only a silly whim ; he cannot have forgotten entirely the use of speech in so short a time ; the thing is absolutely impossible." The woman replied meekly, " It is not for me to dispute with you, gentlemen, but I can safely declare that I never heard him speak, nor any child, indeed, of his age." After making some remark about the healthy appearance of the child, Shelley walked on, and with a deep sigh said, " How provokingly close are these new-born babes ! "

175

Shelley in England

Hogg, who observes that Shelley was commonly indifferent to matters of dress, has recorded an occasion on which he showed an exceptional interest in a coat. Calling at his friend's rooms one morning at the usual hour, he found him standing in the middle of the room in a new blue coat with gilt buttons, while his tailor (who had promised to send home a new coat the previous evening and had not done so, to Shelley's disappointment) was now extolling the beauty of the garment. The tailor having departed, Shelley took up his hat and went forth with Hogg, who questioned the prudence of walking in the fields in such splendid attire. Hogg's fears were well grounded, for, in picking their way through a muddy farmyard, a mastiff which had stolen upon them unheard, and without so much as a growl or bark, seized Shelley by the skirts of his coat. Both Hogg and Shelley kicked the unwelcome beast off, but not before the skirts had almost been severed from the waist. Shelley finished the work by rending them completely asunder, and he appeared to be more angry than Hogg had ever seen him either before or since that incident. He threatened to return with pistols to shoot the unfortunate dog, and proceeded home carrying the skirts of the coat on his arm. But at length he stopped short and, spreading out the skirts on a hedge, he looked at them for a few moments and "continued his march."

When Hogg suggested that they should take the skirts with them, Shelley replied despondently, " No, let them remain as a spectacle for men and gods ! " They returned to Oxford, and reached their College by the back streets. At Shelley's appearance his astonished scout inquired for the skirts so that he might carry the damaged garment at once to the tailor. But Shelley's pensive reply was that " they are upon the hedge." The scout seemed to be on the point of running forth instantly in quest of them, when Hogg, like a conjurer, drew the skirts from his pocket. In the evening, when they were sitting over their tea, the tailor brought back the coat, so skilfully repaired that it easily won Shelley's admiration.

Prior has printed in his *Life of Goldsmith* some of the bills of Mr. Filby who fashioned the immortal plum-coloured coat for the little Doctor. There is a precedent therefore for printing the following old tailor's bill for clothes supplied to Shelley, which has survived the usual fate of such documents, and especially as one of the garments mentioned in it appears to be that which figures in the above story :

Shelley in England

P. B. Shelley, Esqr., Univy. Coll.

To Willm. & Richd. Dry.

1810.

Nov. 1.	A Superfine Olive Coat Gilt Buttns.	4	8	0
	A Pair Rich Silk Knitt Pantaloons	3	8	0
	A Pair Rich Silk Knitt Breeches .	2	12	0
	Two Stripd. Marcela Waistcoats Double Breastd. . . .	2	0	0
9.	Mending a pair of Breeches .			4
Dec. 10.	Mending two pair do. . .	0	1	0

1811.

Feb. 28.	1 Pair Patent Silk Braces . .	0	8	0
March 2.	A Pair mixt Double milld. Worsted Pantaloons . .	1	15	0
	A Pair fine Blue Ribbd. Worsted do.	1	16	0
14.	A Pair gloves		4	0
21.	A Pair do.		3	0
23.	A Superfine Blue Coat Velvett Collr. & Gilt Buttns. . .	4	12	0
	A Pair Fine Worsted Pantaloons	1	15	
	A Pair Stout Cord Breeches .	1	7	
	A Figd. Marcela Waistcoat .	1	0	0
25.	Mending a pair Pantaloons .			8

£25	10	0

Philosophic Doubts

The following receipt is annexed to the above :

January 11, 1813 [error for 1814]. Recd. of Wm. Whitton, Esq. for P. B. Shelley, Esqr. Twenty-five pound ten shilling for the acct. of Mess. Dry, Taylors, Oxford.   JOSEPH KENNERLEY.

£25 : 10 : 0.

The last item in this account bears the actual date of Shelley's expulsion.

CHAPTER IX

EXPELLED FROM OXFORD

Political Justice, its message to and influence on Shelley—His letter to Leigh Hunt—Shelley's prospects of entering Parliament—Mr. Hobbes and his poem *The Widower* — *The Necessity of Atheism* — Shelley learns printing — The object of the syllabus — "Jeremiah Stukeley" — The publication of *The Necessity* — Munday & Slatter—Rev. John Walker's advice—Shelley and Hogg expelled—Accounts of the transaction—They leave Oxford.

WHILE at Eton, Shelley had borrowed from Dr. Lind his copy of *Political Justice ;* and the book no doubt formed the subject of many conversations and warm discussions between the old doctor and his young friend. Shelley was of an impressionable age ; the influence of this work on his mind and character was powerful and lasting, and he acknowledged the debt in his second letter to Godwin.[1]

"It is now a period of more than two years," he wrote, "since first I saw your inestimable book on *Political Justice ;* it opened to my mind fresh and more extensive views ; it materially influenced my character, and I rose from its perusal a wiser and a better man. I was no longer the Votary of romance ;

[1] Shelley to Godwin, Jan. 10, 1812.

Expelled from Oxford

till then I had existed in an ideal world—now I found that in this universe of ours was enough to excite the interest of the heart, enough to employ the discussions of reason ; I beheld, in short, that I had duties to perform. Conceive the effect which the *Political Justice* would have upon a mind before jealous of its independence and participating somewhat singularly in a peculiar susceptibility."

On taking up the study of metaphysics with Hogg at Oxford, Shelley's interest in *Political Justice* was revived, as we find that he wrote, on November 19, 1810, to request Stockdale to send him a copy of the book. It is likely that he gave it closer attention at the University than he did during his Eton days, and that his reference to its influence in his letter to Godwin applies specially to the later period.

The primary effect of *Political Justice* on Shelley was to cause him to think, and he did not overestimate its importance as an influence on his character. It is not possible to understand Shelley's state of mind at this time without taking *Political Justice* into account. Among other things he was made to realise something about the wretched social condition of the poorer classes.

Offences against property have always been dealt with severely in England, but in the eighteenth century delinquents were punished with inhuman cruelty.

Shelley in England

Thieves and suspected thieves were commonly hanged, irrespective of age or sex. The press-gang was in operation, and flogging in the Navy and Army of frequent occurrence. The cost of food was high ; wages were low and the hours of work long. Women, especially of the poorer classes, had practically no means of redressing wrongs, and children were permitted to toil without restriction as to time at dangerous occupations. Little boys, the younger the better, were sent up chimneys to clean them.

That such a state of affairs should prevail in Christian England had caused Shelley to blame Christianity. He also learnt something from Godwin's habit of stating the most unpalatable facts unflinchingly and in all their ugly nakedness. An uncompromising advocate of the liberties and rights of the classes that were unrepresented by Parliament and neglected by the Church, Godwin was one of the first to reawaken in this country, by his book, sympathy for the cause of the common people. *Political Justice* had appeared in 1793, the year of the Terror, while the sensibility of the public was easily moved. When this book fell into Shelley's hands in 1810, England had not only neglected to follow its lessons but had put it on the shelf, and Godwin was more widely known as the author of his novel *Caleb Williams*.

Expelled from Oxford

But England was not entirely apathetic in 1811: the claims of a large section of the poorer classes were becoming more and more urgent, and these claims had their supporters, though some of them were little better than demagogues. Leigh Hunt, however, was a sincere, though perhaps not always a very tactful, champion of the people's cause, who week by week pursued, in his newspaper *The Examiner*, a course of warfare in favour of free speech and against the privileged classes. The campaign was not conducted without danger. Hunt disdained to mince his words, and on two occasions the Government had instituted prosecutions against him, both of which had failed. An article on Military flogging, which was reprinted in *The Examiner* for February 24, 1811, from a provincial newspaper, with the title " One thousand Lashes," had resulted in another Government prosecution against Leigh Hunt as editor, and his brother John Hunt as printer of the paper. But Brougham, who stoutly defended the Hunts, obtained for them a verdict of " Not Guilty."

We have seen that Shelley had begun to show an active interest in the cause of free speech by contributing to the fund in aid of Peter Finnerty, and he seems to have been hardly less interested in the prosecution of the Hunts. Full of enthusiasm, he wrote

Shelley in England

to Leigh Hunt as editor of *The Examiner*, from Oxford, on March 2 :

"Permit me, although a stranger, to offer my sincerest congratulations on the occasion of the triumph, so highly to be prized by men of liberality ; permit me also to submit to your consideration, as one of the most fearless enlighteners of the public mind at the present time, a scheme of mutual safety, and mutual indemnification for men of public spirit and principle, which, if carried into effect, would evidently be productive of incalculable advantages : of the scheme the following is an address to the public, the proposal for a meeting, and shall be modified according to your judgment, if you will do me the honour to consider the point.

"The ultimate intention of my aim is to induce a meeting of such enlightened and unprejudiced members of the community, whose independent principles expose them to evils which might thus be alleviated ; and to form a methodical society, which should be organized so as to resist the coalition of the enemies of liberty, which at present render any expression of opinion on matters of policy dangerous to individuals. It has been for want of societies of this nature, that corruption has attained the height at which we now behold it ; nor can any of us bear in mind the very great influence, which some years since was gained by *Illuminism*, without considering that a society of equal extent might establish national liberty on as firm a basis as that which would have supported the visionary schemes of a completely equalized community.

Expelled from Oxford

"Although perfectly unacquainted with you privately, I address you as a common friend to *liberty*, thinking that, in the case of this urgency and importance, etiquette ought not to stand in the way of usefulness.

"My father is in parliament, and on attaining twenty-one I shall in all probability fill his vacant seat. On account of the responsibility to which my residence in the University subjects me, I, of course, dare not publicly avow all I think, but the time will come when I hope that my every endeavour, insufficient as this may be, will be directed to the advancement of liberty."

Professor Dowden explained Shelley's reference to Illuminism as probably the result of his having read in the Abbé Barruel's *Mémoires pour servir à l'Histoire du Jacobinisme*, "how Spartacus Weishaupt founded the Society of Illuminists, not so many years ago, for the defence and propagation of free-thought and revolutionary principles; [and] he remembers how formidable that society had grown."[1]

Not the least interesting portion of this letter is the passage dealing with Shelley's prospect of becoming a Member of Parliament, and with the danger which he desired to avoid of avowing opinions that would not be acceptable to the authorities at Oxford. The circumstances, therefore, that subsequently caused his

---

[1] Dowden's *Life of Shelley*, vol. i. p. 112.

expulsion from Oxford were not the result of a deliberate plan on his part to bring about that misfortune. After he left Oxford he might still have entered Parliament had he chosen to become a party man, but the prospect had ceased to attract him ; he probably recognised that he could not give his allegiance to any party represented in the House, where there was no place then for independent members.

Shelley frequently went into the shop of Munday & Slatter, the Oxford printers, in regard to his literary projects, and they, like Stockdale, becoming alarmed at the tone of his conversation, in the words of Mr. Henry Slatter [1] " used more than ordinary endeavours to reclaim the waywardness of his imagination," and they applied to Mr. Hobbes, a literary friend, to talk to him. This Mr. Hobbes " undertook to analyze " Shelley's arguments, and " endeavoured to refute them philosophically." Slatter tells us that, although Mr. Hobbes " appeared to make a strong impression at the time," Shelley at length declared " that he would rather meet any or all the dignitaries of the Church than one philosopher," and declined to reply in writing to the philosophical arguments of Slatter's literary friend. On turning to a poetical production

[1] " *Oxford*, a poem by Robert Montgomery. Fourth Edition. Oxford, 1835. With biographical recollections," to which Henry Slatter contributed a letter to the author containing some interesting reminiscences of Shelley.

Expelled from Oxford

of Mr. Hobbes entitled *The Widower*, published anonymously in 1812 by Munday & Slatter, it is not difficult to see why Shelley refused to pursue the argument. One extract from this work will suffice, namely, that which he describes in his synopsis as " Vicious infidels addressed " :

> " Deem ye my verse too serious—still too grave?
> Fain would my muse employ her calmer pow'rs,
> Persuasive reason's force, if haply she
> Might urge your heedless feet from erring ways,
> To tread reclaim'd in virtue's sacred path.
>
> Say then, ye scoffers of religion, whose
> Dread laugh proceeds from deep depravity,
> And wicked hate of all that's good, rather
> Than from settled disbelief, resulting
> From evestigating, [sic] studious research ;
> 'Tis infidelity of heart, sensual
> Its character ; not infidelity
> Of intellect, a principle of mind.—
> Say then, ye giddy votaries of vice,
> Who scorn alike the robe of sanctity
> And virtue's diadem, are nature's laws
> Unfixed and mutable? Can man, with all
> His boasted powers, arrest or change their course,
> In order t'effect some diff'rent design? "

The rest of the poem is no better, and it is therefore unlikely that Mr. Hobbes' philosophy was superior to his verse.

During Shelley's first term at Oxford he read, together with Hogg, several metaphysical works, such as Locke *On the Human Understanding*, and Hume's *Essays*.

Shelley in England

Of these works they prepared careful analyses which, said Hogg, although their joint production, were in Shelley's handwriting, and remained in his custody. From these papers he drew up, perhaps at Field Place during the Christmas vacation, the small "metaphysical essay in support of Atheism," in regard to which, as we have already seen, he had approached Stockdale. This publisher, so far from agreeing to issue the pamphlet, had promptly written in alarm to Shelley's father.

Stockdale having failed him as a publisher, Shelley either sent or took the manuscript to C. & W. Phillips, the Worthing printers, from whose press had issued his first volume of verse, the *Original Poetry of Victor and Cazire*. An interesting sidelight is thrown on the printing of this book and the *Necessity* by the extract from a letter of Mr. Barclay Phillips to Dr. Clair J. Grece, which is given by Messrs. Thomas J. Wise and Percy Vaughan in their introduction to a reprint of Shelley's pamphlet.[1] " The active member of the firm," they say, " was an intelligent brisk young woman, with whom Shelley was on very good terms." Mr. Barclay Phillips writes of her : " She was amiable and clever. She thoroughly learned ' the art and mystery of printing,' and did much of the printing herself. . . .

---

[1] *The Necessity of Atheism.* A reprint of the original edition. Issued by the Rationalist Press Association by arrangement with the Shelley Society. Watts & Co., London, 1906.

Expelled from Oxford

At one time (eighty years ago) my Aunt Philadelphia Phillips lived with us at Brighton. I there frequently heard her talk of Shelley. She said he took great interest in the art of printing, and would often come in and spend hours in the printing office learning to set up the types, and help my cousin (the daughter)."

Shelley as a compositor, sitting on a high stool over the type-cases, is a character in which the poet has not hitherto been described. It does not seem, however, to be at all out of keeping with the trend of his mind that he should wish to master the details of typography. He was not satisfied with a theoretical knowledge of chemistry and electricity, but always took pleasure in practical experiments; he probably soon acquired an elementary knowledge of printing. It is not known whether he actually set up the type for the *Necessity of Atheism*, a very rough piece of work which might well have been the production of some 'prentice hand.

In getting his essay printed Shelley had a specific purpose. He had continued, Hogg tells us, his practice of writing to public men on religious matters, and his correspondence had increased, so that "the arrival of the postman was always an anxious moment with him." At Eton he began to address inquiries on subjects of chemistry anonymously, or rather that he might receive an answer, as Philalethes and the like; but as postmen do not ordinarily understand

189

Greek, " to prevent miscarriages, it was necessary to adopt a more familiar name, as John Short or Thomas Long." He kept up the practice at Oxford, and he intended to utilise his little printed extract of some of the doctrines of Hume to assist him in his correspondence. " It was a small pill, but it worked powerfully " : his mode of operation was to enclose a copy of the pamphlet with a letter bearing a London address, in which he stated " with modesty and simplicity, that he had met accidentally with the little tract, which appeared unhappily to be quite unanswerable." If this appeal secured a refutation, by way of answer, Shelley " in a vigorous reply would fall upon the unwary disputant and break his bones." Sometimes the attack " provoked a rejoinder more carefully prepared, when an animated and protracted debate ensued." He seemed to attach a potency to the three letters Q.E.D. with which the pamphlet concludes, and had often remarked to Hogg, " if you ask a friend to dinner, and only put Q.E.D. at the end of the invitation, he cannot refuse to come."

Although we are told that " he loved dearly victory in debate, and warm debate for its own sake," [1] the

---

[1] Hogg (i. 275), who adds: "Never was there a more unexceptional disputant, he was eager beyond the most ardent, but never angry and never personal: he was the only arguer I ever knew who drew every argument from the nature of the thing, and who could never be provoked to descend to personal contentions."

object of his inquiries was to endeavour to obtain an indisputable proof of the truth of his theories. His belief in Deism had failed, and he had become, as he told Godwin,[1] "in the popular sense of the word 'God' an atheist."

Shelley did not neglect to test the powers of his pamphlet, and he informed Henry Slatter,[2] a statement which is supported by Medwin, that he had sent a copy to every bishop in the Kingdom, to the Vice-Chancellor, and to other dignitaries, besides the heads of houses in Oxford, addressing them under the fictitious signature of "Jeremiah Stukeley."

Apparently the earliest public announcement of *The Necessity of Atheism* is that which appeared on February 9 in the *Oxford University and City Herald*, where the tract was advertised by its title and, it was stated, "Speedily will be published, to be had of all booksellers of London and Oxford." On the 13th of the same month Shelley wrote to Graham, evidently with reference to *The Necessity*, and said, "I send you a book, you must be particularly intent about it. Cut out the title-page, and advertise it in eight famous papers, and in the *Globe*, advertise the *advertisement* in the third page. I wish you to be particularly quick about it. I will write more to-morrow. Now can

---

[1] In his letter dated Jan. 10, 1812.
[2] *Cf.* Montgomery's *Oxford* (4th ed., 1835), p. 168.

only say silence and dispatch." There is another letter to Graham, with no more definite date than 1811, but it was apparently written after February 13, for Shelley says, as if he were cancelling his former request : " You need not advertise the Atheism, as it is not yet published, we are afraid of the Legislature's power with respect to Heretics."

Shelley's connection with the tract was soon known at Oxford, though to what extent it is not possible to say. However, Charles Kirkpatrick Sharpe knew about it on March 15, for on that date he wrote from Christ Church, " Our Apollo next came out with a prose pamphlet in praise of Atheism, which I have not yet seen."

That Sharpe knew Shelley personally is probable, but they had little in common, and there is no reason for supposing that they were more than acquaintances. The Rev. W. K. R. Bedford, the biographer of this minor " Horace Walpole," with rather more vehemence than was necessary, said that Sharpe while admitting the genius of Shelley's writings had for him " an intrinsic loathing." In a copy of Lady Charlotte Bury's *Memoirs*, Sharpe scribbled on the margin of a page containing an anecdote of the poet—" Mr. S. was a strange tatterdemalion looking figure, dressed like a scarecrow ; he had no credit for talents at Oxford, where he was thought to be insane."

Expelled from Oxford

And in an undated letter, after 1819, he wrote:
"I send you the *Cenci*, written by that wicked wretch,
Shelley, and well written. I remember him at Oxford,
mad and bad—and trying to persuade people that he
lived on arsenic and aqua fortis." [1]

Slatter tells us that Shelley himself strewed the
windows and counters of Munday's shop, without their
knowledge, with copies of *The Necessity*, and gave
instructions to their shopman to sell the pamphlet as
fast as he could at a charge of sixpence a copy.
Apparently little time was given for these operations,
for a " judicious " friend of the booksellers, the Rev.
John Walker, Fellow of New College, happened to
drop in to the shop. The title of the pamphlet
attracted his notice ; after examining it he asked to
see Messrs. Munday & Slatter ; and at once drew their
attention to its dangerous tendency. He counselled
them to destroy the copies forthwith, which advice
they agreed to adopt, and promptly proceeded with
Mr. Walker to the back-kitchen, where the offending
pamphlets were burnt. They also sent a friendly hint
to the printers, C. & W. Phillips of Worthing, warning them of the danger of circulating the pamphlet
and of the liability they ran of a prosecution by
the Attorney-General, and advising them to destroy

---

[1] *Letters of Charles Kirkpatrick Sharpe*, 2 vols., 1888.

every remaining copy together with the MS. and types.[1]

In the meantime the booksellers had sent to ask Shelley to come to their house. He came instantly, and found that Councillor Clifford " of O.P. notoriety " was with them. The subject was broached by the booksellers and councillor, who all proceeded, " first by entreaties, and next by threats, to dissuade Shelley from the error of his ways, for the sake of himself, his

---

[1] The following letter, found among the Shelley-Whitton papers, was never sent. It is curious as showing that a prosecution was contemplated, and that Mr. Shelley was evidently alarmed lest other publications, similar to *The Necessity of Atheism*, should appear from Messrs. Phillips's press.

William Whitton to C. & W. Phillips

10 GREAT JAMES STREET, BEDFORD ROW,
April 13, 1811.

GENT,—I have a publication before me intituled " The Necessity of Atheism," which was printed by you, and by which you have been instrumental to two young students of Oxford being expelled their college, and you must therefore know that you have done to them and to their families an injury for which no sacrifice within your power can compensate. I have been informed that a prosecution is intended against you, and my motive for writing this to you is to caution you against incurring further censure and responsibility, and heaping difficulties upon the two young men by any attempt to put to the press any other work from the same authors or at their instance. How you could venture to give publicity to such blasphemous work at the instance of a stripling only nineteen years of age, whose father and mother you must have known, without the least communication with them, must be a matter of astonishment and surprise to every one.

If you have in your possession any manuscripts for publication from the same author, it is my strong recommendation to you to retain them, and not to proceed in the printing thereof.—I am, your obedient servant,

WM. WHITTON.

friends and connections ; all seemed of no avail—he appeared to glory in the course he had adopted."[1] Slatter adds that Shelley's conduct became so unguarded that he was suspected as the author of the pamphlet, and also of having sent a copy to the head of his own college. The distribution of the tract, as we shall see, was attended with serious consequences.

In the following passage from Shelley's letter to Godwin, in which he sketched his early life, he also summed up his short University career, and related the cause which brought it to an abrupt conclusion.

"I went to Oxford," he wrote, "Oxonian society was insipid to me, uncongenial with my habits of thinking. I could not descend to common life ; the sublime interest of poetry, lofty and exalted achievements, the proselytism of the world, the equalisation of its inhabitants, were to me the soul of my soul. You can probably form some idea of the contrast exhibited to my character by those with whom I was surrounded. Classical reading and poetical writing employed me during my residence at Oxford.

"In the meantime I became in the popular sense of the word ' God ' an Atheist. I printed a pamphlet avowing my opinions, and its occasion. I distributed this anonymously to men of thought and learning,

---

[1] Montgomery's *Oxford* (4th ed., 1835), p. 168.

wishing that Reason should decide on the case at issue : it never was my intention to deny it. Mr. Copleston at Oxford, among others, had the pamphlet ; he showed it to the Master and Fellows of University College, and *I* was sent for. I was informed, that in case I denied the publication, no more would be said. I refused and was expelled." [1]

The Reverend Edward Copleston, who subsequently became Bishop of Llandaff, was a Fellow of Oriel and Professor of Poetry in 1811. From Shelley he probably received a copy of *The Necessity of Atheism* with a letter, and more vigilant than other recipients of the pamphlet he tracked its author to University College. Charles Kirkpatrick Sharpe [2] of Christ Church knew that Shelley was author of the pamphlet, and probably others at Oxford were equally well-informed. If any doubt existed in the minds of the Master and Fellows of University College, a comparison of the letter which accompanied the tract

---

[1] Shelley to Godwin, Jan. 10, 1812.

[2] Another reference to *The Necessity of Atheism* is to be found in a letter written by C. Kirkpatrick Sharpe from Oxford, and printed in Lady Charlotte Bury's anonymous *Diary Illustrative of the Reign of George the Fourth*, 1838, vol. i. p. 88 : " Meanwhile, be it known unto you that the ingenious Mr. Shelley hath been expelled from the University on account of his Atheistical pamphlet. Was ever such bad taste and barbarity known ? He behaved like a hero, ' he showed to Fortune's frowns a brow serene,' and declared his intention of emigrating to America."—October 1811.

with Shelley's handwriting supplied them with the necessary proof of identity.

Hogg's description of Shelley's expulsion is vivid, and must be given in his own words ; though written more than twenty years after the actual event, it seems to be fairly accurate, except that Shelley states that he refused to deny the authorship of *The Necessity*, a statement which Mr. Ridley's account also supports.

Lent term of 1811 was drawing to a close. Shelley and Hogg had planned a course of reading, and had agreed to meet at an earlier hour than usual in order to get through their studies before the vacation. On March 25, Lady Day, a fine spring morning, Hogg called at Shelley's rooms : he was absent, but soon returned, and in a state of agitation. Hogg inquired anxiously what was amiss, and Shelley exclaimed, after he had recovered himself a little, " ' I am expelled ! I was sent for suddenly a few minutes ago : I went to the Common-room, where I found our Master [Dr. Griffith] and two or three of the Fellows. The Master produced a copy of the little syllabus, and asked me if I were the author of it. He spoke in a rude, abrupt and insolent tone. I begged to be informed for what purpose he put the question. No answer was given ; but the Master loudly and angrily repeated ' :

" ' Are you the author of this book ? '

Shelley in England

" ' If I can judge from your manner,' I said, ' you are resolved to punish me, if I should acknowledge that it is my work. If you can prove that it is, produce your evidence ; it is neither just nor lawful to interrogate me in such a case and for such a purpose. Such proceedings would become a court of inquisitors, but not free men in a free country.'

" ' Do you choose to deny that this is your composition ? ' the Master reiterated in the same rude and angry voice.

" Shelley complained much of his violent and ungentlemanly deportment, saying :

" ' I have experienced tyranny and injustice before, and I well know what vulgar violence is ; but I have never met with such unworthy treatment. I told him calmly, but firmly, that I was determined not to answer any questions respecting the publication on the table. He immediately repeated his demand ; I persisted in my refusal ; and he said furiously :

" ' Then you are expelled ; and I desire you will quit the College early to-morrow morning at the latest.'

" ' One of the Fellows took up two papers, and handed one of them to me ; here it is.' He produced a regular sentence of expulsion, drawn up in due form, under the seal of the College."

Shelley " sat on the sofa, repeating, with convulsive

· vehemence, the words, ' Expelled, expelled ! ' his head shaking with emotion, and his whole frame quivering."

Hogg, justly indignant, " so monstrous and so illegal did the outrage seem," was resolved to stand by his friend, and at once wrote a short note to the Master and Fellows asking them to reconsider their sentence. The " conclave " was still sitting when the note reached them ; Hogg was instantly sent for, and on his arrival he was asked by the Master, as Shelley had been, if he had written the tract. Hogg said that he pointed out the unfairness of the question, and the injustice in punishing Shelley for refusing to answer it. No one spoke except the Master, who told Hogg to retire and consider whether he was resolved to persist in refusing to answer the question : but he had scarcely passed the door when he was recalled. The Master again showed him the book, and again asked if he was the author of it. Hogg once more declined to admit or deny his responsibility for its publication, at which the Master exclaimed " angrily, in a loud great voice, ' Then you are expelled.' " As in Shelley's case, a formal sentence signed and sealed was handed to him, and he was told to quit the College at an early hour on the following day.

Peacock, in writing of the expulsion, stated that Hogg's account differed materially from that which Shelley gave of the transaction. " Making all allow-

Shelley in England

ance," he says, " for the degree in which his imagination coloured the past, there is one matter of fact which remains inexplicable. According to him, his expulsion was a great matter of form and solemnity ; there was a sort of public assembly, before which he pleaded his own cause, in a long oration, in the course of which he called on the illustrious spirits who had shed glory on those walls to look down on their degenerate successors. Now, the inexplicable matter to which I have alluded is this : he showed me an Oxford newspaper, containing a full report of the proceedings, with his own oration at great length. I suppose the pages of that diurnal were not deathless, and that it would now be vain to search for it, but that he had it, and showed it to me, is absolutely certain. His oration may have been, as some of Cicero's published orations were, a speech in the potential mood ; one which might, could, should, or would, have been spoken : but how in that case it got into the Oxford newspaper passes conjecture."

Peacock's statements are generally reliable, but the search which has been made for the report has proved fruitless.

These proceedings, as narrated by Hogg, can be compared with an independent account written by Mr. C. J. Ridley, junior Fellow of University College, who became Fellow in 1813. Ridley's letter, which is undated, describes the affair from his recollection some time after the event ; and is now pasted into the College Register. He said that " It was announced one morning at a breakfast party, towards the end of Lent Term, 1810 [an error, it was 1811] that P. B. Shelley, who had recently become a member of University College, was to be called before a meeting of the Common-room for being the supposed author of a pamphlet entitled *The Necessity of Atheism*. This anonymous work, consisting of not many pages had been studiously sent to most of the dignitaries of the University, and to others more or less ' connected with Oxford.' The meeting took place the same day, and it was understood that the pamphlet, together with some notes sent with it, in which the supposed author's handwriting appeared identified with that of P. B. Shelley, was placed before him. He was asked if he could or would deny the obnoxious production as his. No direct reply was given either in the affirmative or negative. Shelley having quitted the room, T. J. Hogg immediately appeared, voluntarily on his part to state that, *if* Shelley had anything to do with it, he (Hogg) was equally implicated, and desired his share of the penalty, whatever was inflicted. It has always been supposed that T. J. Hogg wrote the preface. Towards the afternoon, a large paper bearing the College seal and signed by the Master

and Dean was affixed to the hall door, declaring that
the two offenders were publicly expelled from the
College, for *contumacy in refusing to answer certain
questions put to them.* The aforesaid two had made
themselves as conspicuous as possible by great singularity of dress, and by walking up and down the centre
of the quadrangle, as if proud of their anticipated
fate. 1 believe no one regretted their departure ;
for there were but few, if any, who were not afraid of
Shelley's strange and fantastic pranks, and the still
stranger opinions he was known to entertain, but all
acknowledged him to [have] been very good-humoured
and of kind disposition. T. J. Hogg had intellectual
powers to a great extent, but unfortunately misdirected. He was most unpopular." [1]

The Register bears the following entry : " *Martii*
25°, 1811. At a meeting of the Master and Fellows
held this day it was determined that Thomas Jefferson
Hogg and Percy Bisshe Shelley, be publicly expelled
for contumaciously refusing to answer questions proposed to them, and for also repeatedly declining to
disavow a publication entitled 'The Necessity of
Atheism.'"

In this peremptory manner was Shelley driven

---

[1] First given by Professor Dowden in his *Life of Shelley*, and afterwards printed in the *Notebook of the Shelley Society*, Part i., 1888, pp.
99–100.

from the University where his presence and that of his friend Hogg had become a source of discomfort to the dignified, wine-bibbing dons. Secure in their positions of ease, they were too indolent to rouse themselves to the effort of obtaining the confidence of the students, or of exercising their personal influence. Having been forced to take notice of the pamphlet, to which Copleston had drawn their attention, they chose the simplest course of dealing with the case, namely, of getting rid of the young men as quickly as possible. They devoted half an hour to their dismissal, after which they returned to their port and scandal, with the smug satisfaction of an unpleasant duty cleverly performed.

Hogg was told that, should it be inconvenient for them to quit Oxford immediately, they might remain for a time if Shelley would ask permission of the Master to be allowed to delay their departure. But he was too indignant at the insult that he had received to ask for any such favour.[1] Hogg says Shelley had never received any admonition or the slightest hint that his speculations were inproper or unpleasing to anyone. He was probably unaware of the ministrations of the Rev. Mr. Walker, which were of a semi-official character. Shelley might have been amenable

---

[1] Hogg, vol. i. p. 287.

to a reproof from the head of his college, and have submitted to the punishment of rustication ; at least Hogg seemed to think so.

So with heavy hearts Shelley and his friend bade a long farewell to Oxford, and to those hopes which some nine months earlier had seemed so bright. There was much at the University that Shelley appreciated. He enjoyed the comparative liberty of an under-graduate after the restrictions of Eton and Field Place, and the security from interruptions which " the bless-ings of the oak " ensured. " The oak," he said to Hogg, " alone goes to make this place a paradise." To Oxford he owed the pleasure of knowing T. J. Hogg, the companion of his long rambles and even longer con-versations. To him he had remarked, " I can imagine few things that would annoy me more severely than to be disturbed in our tranquil course ; it would be a cruel calamity to be interrupted by some untoward accident, to be compelled to quit our calm and agree-able retreat. Not only would it be a sad mortifica-tion, but a real misfortune, for if I remain here I shall study more closely and with greater advantage than I could in any other situation that I can conceive. I regret only that the period of our residence is limited to four years ; I wish they would revive, for our sake, the old term of six and seven years."

The election of Lord Grenville to the Chancellor-

Expelled from Oxford

ship of the University, some months before Shelley went up to Oxford, had given rise to bitter feuds. This feeling had died down, but some of it probably still lingered during Shelley's time. Shelley, like his father, was a Grenvillite, and the winning competitor had also received the support of the undergraduates. Lord Grenville's liberalism was odious to the dons, who equally disliked him for his disposition to favour Catholic emancipation. The defeated candidate, Lord Eldon, was a member of University College, and Hogg implies that Shelley was "regarded from the beginning with jealous care" because he delighted in Lord Grenville's policy. The opinions of an undergraduate on such matters are unlikely to have interested the authorities, although Shelley's liberal views on politics and religion, as well as his eccentric habits, undoubtedly excited attention.

CHAPTER X

POLAND STREET

Shelley leaves Oxford with Hogg and arrives in London—Takes lodgings in Poland Street—Visits the Groves—Acquaints Medwin of his expulsion—Kensington Gardens—Dr. Abernethy's anatomy lectures—Mr. Shelley's letter to Hogg—Bysshe writes to his father —Mr. Shelley in London—His conditions—which Bysshe rejects— Mr. Shelley and Mr. Hogg—R. Clarke—Bysshe and Hogg dine with Mr. Shelley—Mr. William Whitton—Mr. Hurst's fruitless intervention—Robert Parker and John Grove talk to Bysshe—Hogg and Bysshe offer proposals—Sir Bysshe Shelley's opinion—Bysshe's place filled at Oxford—Hogg leaves London—Bysshe offers to renounce his interest in the entail—Angry correspondence with Whitton.

SHELLEY and Hogg decided to leave Oxford without delay, and after breakfasting on the following morning, March 26, they took their places on the outside of the coach for London. It is stated that Shelley had no money wherewith to defray the expenses of his journey and that he obtained a loan of £20 for that purpose from Slatter, a brother of the Oxford bookseller.[1] A lodging for the night was found at a

[1] Henry Slatter stated in his contribution to Montgomery's *Oxford*, 4th ed., that Shelley gave a written memorandum that he had borrowed this sum from Slatter, who subsequently was unable to obtain its repayment. Among the Shelley-Whitton papers there are two receipts signed by Shelley, for ten pounds each from Slatter, and dated respectively March 12 and 23, 1811. As both of these dates are anterior to the expulsion which occurred on March 25, they probably relate to another transaction.

coffee-house near Piccadilly; and having dined, they proceeded for tea to the house of Shelley's cousins, the Groves, at Lincoln's Inn Fields. The cousins appeared to Hogg taciturn people, and Shelley's attempts at conversation were not successful in dispelling their reserve. This is hardly surprising considering that Bysshe was Harriet Grove's rejected suitor, and, if he gave the reasons for the sudden appearance of himself and his friend in London, it would have more than accounted for his cousins' silence.

The next day Hogg and Shelley went in search of lodgings, and it proved no easy quest, for Bysshe was difficult to please. He objected to the street cries at one house, and the landlady or the maid at others, but at last they came to Poland Street, off Oxford Street, which captivated the poet, as it reminded him of Jane Porter's novel, *Thaddeus of Warsaw*, "and of freedom." They halted at a house where lodgings were announced in the window, and there they engaged apartments.

The sitting-room on the first floor especially attracted Shelley's fancy. It was somewhat dark and quiet, but the walls were covered with a gay paper of "trellises, vine-leaves with their tendrils, and huge clusters of grapes, green and purple, all represented in lively colours." Shelley found this delightful, and touching

the walls said, "We must stay here; stay for ever!"
His bedroom, which opened out of the sitting-room,
was papered with the same trellis of vines, and, while
touching and admiring it, he asked if grapes really
grew in that manner anywhere. Hogg, with his practical mind for creature comforts, ordered a fire, and
they then fetched their luggage in a hackney coach.

Probably one of Shelley's first thoughts when he
arrived in London was to carry the tidings of his misfortune to Medwin, who says: "I remember, as if it
occurred yesterday, his knocking at my door in
Garden Court, in the Temple, at four o'clock in the
morning, the second day after his expulsion. I
think I hear his cracked voice, with his well-known
pipe—'Medwin, let me in, I am expelled'; here
followed a sort of loud, half-hysteric laugh, and a
repetition of the words—'I am expelled,' with the
addition of 'for Atheism.' Though greatly shocked
I was not much surprised at the news, having been
led to augur such a close to his collegiate career
from the Syllabus and *The Posthumous Works of Peg
Nicholson* which he had sent me."[1] Medwin adds that
he visited Shelley at his lodgings and took with

---

[1] Medwin's *Life of Shelley*, vol. i. pp. 147–8. I have used Professor
Dowden's copy of this book, corrected from the author's revised copy, in
which he had substituted the last five words for Medwin's original "and
the bold avowal of his scepticism." This correction also appears in Mr.
H. Buxton Forman's new and revised edition of Medwin's *Life of Shelley*.

From a drawing by D. Collins.

15 POLAND STREET, OXFORD STREET

O

him frequent walks in the parks, and on the banks of the Serpentine, where the poet indulged in his recreation of making "ducks and drakes" and sailing paper-boats. He also relates a story (to illustrate Shelley's habit of somnambulism) of being in Leicester Square one morning at five o'clock, when he was attracted by a group of boys collected round a well-dressed person lying near the rails. On coming up to them, his curiosity being excited, he recognised "Shelley, who had unconsciously spent part of the night *sub dio.*" He could give no account how he got there.[1]

Shelley's daily walks with Hogg, which had formed such a pleasurable part of his Oxford days, were resumed. When on these rambles they would dine at any coffee-house wherever they might chance to be at dinner-time, and return for tea at their rooms. Occasionally they would take tea or dine at Bysshe's cousins, the Groves, in Lincoln's Inn Fields, or would visit Medwin at Garden Court, Temple. The Groves often accompanied Bysshe and Hogg on their walks, and John Grove, the surgeon, took them one Sunday morning into Kensington Gardens, where

It is noticeable that Medwin, in the Memoir prefixed to *The Shelley Papers*, 1833, states that Shelley's visit occurred "in the *morning after* his expulsion," and that he had "been led, from the *tenour of his letters*, to anticipate some such end to his collegiate career." The italics are mine.

[1] Medwin's *Life of Shelley*, vol. i. p. 151.

neither Bysshe nor Hogg had been before. "Bysshe was charmed with the sylvan and somewhat neglected aspect of the place, and they soon became a favourite resort. He was especially delighted with the more retired parts of the gardens, and more particularly with one dark nook where there were many old yew trees." [1] Another resort was St. James's Park, where Bysshe used to express great indignation at the sight of the soldiers, as he believed that the maintaining of a standing army was likely to fetter the minds of the people. Charles Grove, at the time, was a medical student, and was attending Mr. Abernethy's anatomy lectures. The study of anatomy, especially after some conversations with John Grove, appealed to Bysshe, and he attended a course of lectures at St. Bartholomew's Hospital with Charles Grove, who, in recalling the incident many years later, thought that Hogg also occasionally went with them. Apparently Bysshe at one time had serious intentions of doing more than merely to study anatomy. In his letter of October 8, 1811, he wrote to Miss Hitchener, "When last I saw you I was about to enter into the profession of physic."

Byron's *English Bards and Scotch Reviewers* had appeared some two years previously and had created a sensation, but neither Bysshe nor Hogg had seen it. One day Bysshe came across the satire in an Oxford

---

[1] Hogg, vol. i. p. 301.

Poland Street

Street bookshop, and having bought it took the volume with him on one of his country walks with Hogg. He read the whole poem aloud "with fervid and exulting energy," and was delighted with the " bitter, wrathful satire." Hogg seemed to think that this was Bysshe's first introduction to the poetry of Byron, but, as some of his lines in *St. Irvyne* plainly show, he must at one time have been familiar with *Hours of Idleness.*[1]

Bad news travels apace, and Mr. Timothy Shelley would have been informed by the College authorities at once of his son's disgrace. Apparently the first step that he took was to write the following note to Hogg, who, as Bysshe's companion in misfortune, was no longer a welcome visitor :

FIELD PLACE, *March* 27, 1811.

SIR,—The invitation, my son wrote me word, that you would accept to spend the Easter vacation at Field Place,—I am sorry to say the late occurrence at University College must of necessity preclude me that pleasure, as I shall have to bear up against the Affliction that such a business has occasioned.—I am, your very humble servant, T. SHELLEY.

[1] " Shades of the dead ! have I not heard your voices
Rise on the night-rolling breath of the gale?"
BYRON'S " Lachin y Gair," *Hours of Idleness,* 1807.

" Ghosts of the dead ! have I not heard your yelling
Rise on the night-rolling breath of the blast ?"
SHELLEY in *St. Irvyne,* 1811.

Shelley in England

Three days had elapsed since his expulsion, while Bysshe must have pondered over the inevitable letter which he would have to write to his father, and on the fourth day he accomplished it.

The letter, which was addressed from the lodgings of his friend Edward Graham at Vine Street, Piccadilly, is a credit to Shelley, who, with perhaps too much frankness, enclosed with it a copy of *The Necessity of Atheism* for his father's perusal. The pamphlet is still in existence, and bears the word " Impious " on the fly-leaf in the bold handwriting of Timothy Shelley.[1]

P. B. Shelley to Timothy Shelley

LONDON, *March* 29, 1811.

MY DEAR FATHER,—You have doubtless heard of my misfortune and that of my friend Mr. Hogg :—it gives me great regret to be deprived of the advantages which Oxford held out to me, but still more when I consider the vivid sympathy which you always have evinced for my errors and distresses and which I now fear must be greatly excited.

The case was this :—You well know that a train of reasoning and not any great profligacy has induced me to disbelieve the scriptures :—this train myself and my friend pursued, we found to our surprise that

[1] An allusion has already been made, on a previous page, to the fact that at one time there was some talk of prosecuting the publisher of *The Necessity*. Bysshe was evidently aware that this step was contemplated, as he wrote on May 15, 1811, to Hogg, " All danger about prosecution is over ; it was *never* more than a hum."

Poland Street

(strange as it may appear) the proofs of an existing Deity were as far as we had observed defective.

We therefore embodied our doubts on the subject and arranged them methodically in the form of " The Necessity of Atheism," thinking thereby to obtain a satisfactory or an unsatisfactory answer from men who had made Divinity the study of their lives.

How then were we treated ? not as our fair, open, candid conduct might demand, no argument was publickly brought forward to disprove our reasoning, and it at once demonstrated the weakness of their cause, and their inveteracy on discovering it, when they publickly expelled myself and my friend. It may be here necessary to mention that at first *I* only was suspected. I was summoned before a common Hall, and refusing to disavow the publication was expelled. My friend Mr. Hogg insisted on sharing the same fate as myself ; the result of their proceedings therefore is, that we are both expelled. I know too well that your feeling mind will sympathise too deeply in my misfortunes, I hope it will alleviate your sorrow to know that for *myself* I am perfectly indifferent to the late tyrannical violent proceedings of Oxford. Will you present my affectionate duty to my Mother, my love to Elizabeth. I will not write to-day but should be happy to hear from them. May I turn your attention to the advertisement which surely deserved an *answer* not expulsion.—Believe me, my dear Father, ever most affectionately, dutifully yours,

PERCY B. SHELLEY.

GRAHAM'S.

As soon as Mr. Shelley received Bysshe's letter he must have bustled up to London, and taken his usual rooms at Miller's Hotel, over Westminster Bridge. From Graham he would have obtained information as to the whereabouts of Bysshe, whom he appears to have seen on Sunday, March 31. Bysshe's ingenuous invitation to his father to discuss the subject of the syllabus by drawing his attention to the advertisement [1] prefixed to *The Necessity of Atheism* was probably not ignored by Mr. Shelley, and he most likely endeavoured to obtain a full account of the expulsion. He attempted to persuade his son to write an apology to the authorities of University College, but in this attempt he failed. Bysshe was evidently sincere in his expressions of sorrow for causing his father pain, but he had confessed himself indifferent to the "late tyrannical proceedings of Oxford," and the idea of being constrained to apologise must have struck him as another attempt at tyranny.

Having meditated on his talk with Bysshe for some days, Mr. Shelley wrote him one of his oddly phrased letters. He was undoubtedly anxious to reclaim his son, but with his passion for laying down the law, he could not forgive him without making conditions.

[1] "*Advertisement. As a love of truth is the only motive which actuates the Author of this little tract, he earnestly entreats that those of his readers who may discover any deficiency in his reasoning, or may be in possession of proofs which his mind could never obtain, would offer them, together with their objections to the Public, as briefly, as methodically, as plainly as he has taken the liberty of doing.* Thro' deficiency of proof.—AN ATHEIST."

Poland Street

Timothy Shelley to P. B. Shelley

MILLER'S HOTEL, *April* 5, 1811.

MY DEAR BOY,—I am unwilling to receive and act on the information you gave me on Sunday, as the ultimate determination of your mind.

The disgrace which hangs over you is most serious, and though I have felt as a father, and sympathized in the misfortune which your criminal opinions and improper acts have begot : yet, you must know, that I have a duty to perform to my own character, as well as to your younger brother and sisters. Above all, my feelings as a Christian require from me a de-cided and firm conduct towards you.

If you shall require aid or assistance from me—or any protection—you must please yourself to me :

1st. To go immediately to Field Place, and to abstain from all communication with Mr. Hogg, for some considerable time.

2nd. That you shall place yourself under the care and society of such gentlemen as I shall appoint, and attend to his instructions and directions he shall give.

These terms are so necessary to your well-being, and to the value, which I cannot but entertain, that you may abandon your errors and present unjustifiable and wicked opinions, that I am resolved to withdraw myself from you, and leave you to the punishment and misery that belongs to the wicked pursuit of an opinion so diabolical and wicked as that which you have dared to declare, if you shall not accept the proposals I shall go home on Thursday.—I am, your affectionate and most afflicted Father,

T. SHELLEY.[1]

[1] From Hogg's *Life of Shelley*.

Shelley in England

It is not unlikely that Bysshe might have agreed to his father's conditions but for the request that he should give up Hogg. This he could not bring himself to do; apart from his regard for Hogg, he was too loyal to throw over the friend who had willingly shared with him the onus of his expulsion from the University. The mere proposal was sufficient to raise Bysshe's hot temper, and it is not difficult to detect the scornful tone which underlies his polite reply to his father's letter.

P. B. Shelley to Timothy Shelley

POLAND STREET (*after April* 5, 1811).

MY DEAR FATHER,—As you do me the honour of requesting to hear the determination of my mind as to the basis of your future acts I feel it my duty, although it gives me pain to wound " the sense of duty to your own character, to that of your family and your feelings as a Christian " decidedly to refuse my assent to both the proposals in your letter and to affirm that similar refusals will always be the fate of similar requests.

With many thanks for your great kindness.—I remain, your affectionate dutiful son,

PERCY B. SHELLEY.[1]

On April 5, the same day that he wrote to Bysshe, Mr. Timothy Shelley addressed a letter to Hogg's

[1] From Dowden's *Life of Shelley*, vol. i. p. 130.

father " on the subject of the unfortunate affair that has happened to my son and yours at University College, Oxford." He went on to say that he had endeavoured to part the young men, by directing Bysshe to return home, and giving the same advice to T. J. Hogg. " Backed up in that opinion by men of rank and influence," he suggested that Mr. Hogg senior should come to London and help him to carry out his purpose. " They are now at No. 15 Poland Street, Oxford Road. . . . These youngsters must be parted and the fathers must exert themselves. The favour of your answer will oblige." Poor Mr. Shelley, who was making a shot in the dark, addressed this letter to Stockton-on-Tees instead of Norton, and being unacquainted with Mr. Hogg's Christian name, he said somewhat bluntly, " I am at a loss now to know whom I address, not being able to get the direction." He then added, by way of postscript, with his characteristic oddity of expression, " Sir James Graham tells me there are several of the name, therefore into whosoever's hands this comes will have the goodness to find out the right person."

After he had sent this letter to the post, with his mind thoroughly absorbed by his mission, and with anxious solicitude, Mr. Shelley discovered someone who was able to supply him with the name and address of Mr. Hogg, and to vouch for his respectability.

Shelley in England

Doubting whether his first letter had reached Mr. Hogg, he wrote again on the following day urging him to get his son to return home. "They want to be in professions together," he said. "If possible they must be parted, for such monstrous opinions that occupy their thoughts are by no means in their favour. I hope you have received my letter of yesterday, and will take immediate means of acting as you think proper. This is a most deplorable case and I fear we shall have much trouble to root it out. Paley's *Natural Theology* I shall recommend my young man to read, it is extremely applicable. I shall read it with him. A father so employed, must impress his mind more sensibly than a stranger. I shall exhort him to divest himself of all prejudice already imbibed from his false reasoning, and to bring a willing mind to a work so essential to his own and his family's happiness. I understand you have more children. God grant they may turn out well, and this young man see his error.—I remain, your obedient and afflicted fellow-sufferer, T. SHELLEY." [1]

Mr. John Hogg entrusted to his friend Mr. R. Clarke (the Earl of Bridgwater's agent) the task of dealing with his son. And Mr. Clarke, who was on the spot in London, with an address in New Bond Street, apparently was soon in a position to throw some light

[1] From Hogg's *Life of Shelley*.

Poland Street

on the expulsion at Oxford. The following letter appears in Hogg's *Life of Shelley* above the signature C. R., which would seem to be Clarke's initials transposed.[1] I think one may assume that Clarke was the writer of the letter.

R. Clarke to John Hogg

April 6, 1811.

B . . . . . J . . . . came to me this morning from Oxford, I have had the whole history from him : and the reason of all this strange conduct in your son and Shelley is what I supposed, a desire to be singular. There is no striking impiety in the pamphlet : but it goes to show, that because a supreme power cannot be seen, such power may be doubted to exist. It is a foolish performance, so far as argument goes, but written in good language. These two young men gave up associating with anybody else some months since, never dined in College, dressed differently from all others, and did everything in their power to show singularity, as much as to say, "We are superior to everybody." They have been writing Novels. Shelley has published his and your son has not. Shelley is son to the Member for Shoreham. He has always been odd, I find, and suspected of insanity : but of great acquirements : so is your son : I mean, as to the latter, he is of high repute in College.

C. R.

To JOHN HOGG,
    Norton.

---

[1] Hogg's exasperating habit of suppressing or altering names and initials in his *Life of Shelley* is sufficiently well known.

Shelley in England

On Sunday, April 7, Hogg accompanied Bysshe to dine with his father, by invitation, at Miller's Hotel. After an early breakfast the two young men went for their usual long walk, and reached the hotel at the appointed hour of five. Bysshe had spoken of his father's strange habits and manner to Hogg, who took the description to be an exaggerated one, but he assured him it was not. Hogg's amusing account of the humorous side of the dinner loses nothing in the telling: it reads like a comic episode out of one of Peacock's fantastic novels, and it was probably highly overdrawn. He says that Mr. Timothy Shelley received him " kindly, but he presently began to talk in an odd unconnected manner ; scolding, crying, swearing, and then weeping again." They dined well, and after the meal, when Bysshe had been sent out on some errand for his father, he said to Hogg :

" You are a very different person, sir, from what I expected to find ; you are a nice, moderate, reasonable, pleasant gentleman. Tell me what you think I ought to do with my poor boy ? He is rather wild, is he not ? If he had married his cousin, he would perhaps have been less so. He would have been steadier. He wants someone to take care of him : a good wife. What if he were married ? "

Hogg admitted the wisdom of this suggestion, but Mr. Shelley declared it impossible, as he feared that

if he were to tell Bysshe to marry he would refuse.
Hogg suggested that it would be better to bring
him into contact with some young lady likely to
make him a suitable wife, without mentioning anything about marriage, and if he did not take a fancy
to her he could try another. Old Mr. Graham, the
father of Mr. Shelley's protégée, who acted as his
factotum, was present. He interposed, and said he
thought the plan an excellent one, and for some time
he and Mr. Shelley conversed in a low tone and went
over a list of young women of their acquaintance.
The conversation, however, was brought to a conclusion by Bysshe's return. Mr. Shelley then proposed some more port—better wine than they had
been drinking—but, no one assenting, the civil and
attentive Mr. Graham made tea.

"After tea our host became characteristic again,"
said Hogg; "he discoursed of himself and his own
affairs ; he cried, laughed, scolded, swore, and praised
himself at great length. He was so highly respected
in the House of Commons: he was respected by the
whole House, and by the Speaker in particular, who
told him that they could not get on without him. He
assured us that he was greatly beloved in Sussex.
Mr. Graham assented to all this. He was an excellent magistrate. He told a very long story how he
had lately committed two poachers : 'You know the

fellows, Graham, you know who they are. . . .' "
Then Mr. Shelley said, "There is certainly a God,
there can be no doubt of the existence of a Deity."
No one expressed any doubt, not even Hogg who was
chiefly addressed. Mr. Shelley declared that he could
prove it in a moment, and consenting to read his argument took from his pocket a sheet of letter paper and
began to read. "Bysshe, leaning forward, listened
with profound attention. ' I have heard this argument
before,' he said." They were Paley's arguments, as
Hogg remarked. Mr. Shelley admitted as much and
observed, turning towards Hogg, "Yes! you are right,
sir, they are Palley's arguments; I copied them out
of Palley's book this morning for myself: but Palley
had them originally from me; almost everything in
Palley's book he had from me."

The time had now arrived for Bysshe and Hogg to
depart. Mr. Shelley shook hands with Hogg in a very
friendly manner, and said, "'I am sorry you would not
have any more wine, I should have liked much to have
drunk a bottle of the old wine with you. Tell me the
truth, I am not such a bad fellow after all, am I ?'

"'By no means.'

"'Well, when you come to see me at Field Place
you will find that I am not.'"

Thus Hogg and Mr. Shelley parted, and they never
met again. Hogg said of Mr. Shelley: "I have some-

times thought that if he had been taken the right way things might have gone better ; but this his son Bysshe could never do, for his course, like that of true love, was not to run smooth." This was, unhappily, only too true, but the blame was not entirely Bysshe's. Had Mr. Shelley been content to trust to his own judgment, wrong-headed as it often was, instead of seeking the advice of his family lawyer, a reconciliation might have been arrived at between father and son. Bysshe as a boy was fond of his father. His sisters remembered on some occasion when Mr. Shelley was ill, " seeing their brother (who was then about fourteen years of age) several times a day watching and listening at the door of the sick-room to try to discover how his father was getting on." [1] And this is not the only indication that we have of the boy's affection for his father. He may have thought him absurd at times, and said so in his letters with boyish priggishness, but he was not always unfilial. They were both eccentric, and, though Mr. Shelley lacked the genius of his son, they would probably have come to an understanding. Eccentric people are seldom entirely devoid of imagination, and Bysshe would have found some vulnerable spot in his father's mind or heart. But the thing became impossible when the older man endeavoured to adopt the hard and fast legal precepts of his solicitor,

[1] Hogg's *Life of Shelley*, vol. i. p. 459.

Shelley in England

Mr. Whitton. Mr. Shelley, suspecting his own weakness, sought the aid of this gentleman, and was thus able to make a show of possessing a hardness of heart which was new and unfamiliar to his son. The process of alienation, though gradual, was unfortunately sure.

On April 8, Mr. Shelley wrote from Miller's Hotel to Mr. Whitton :

"You observe how they are now determined and what materials they are made of—I shall and will be firm, for he begins now to cast off all duty so he did before, and I must make up my mind in affection— your most kind and friendly advice will be acceptable.

"I expect Mr. Hogg, he wrote to me to-day, and will call on me and see me I hope before he sees his Son. I understand he is a very gentlemanly man—and if he agrees with me no doubt but we shall bring these youngsters to reason."

We are not able to say exactly what was Mr. Whitton's advice to Mr. Shelley, but it is evident that they had a consultation ; Mr. Shelley decided henceforth to place the whole business in his lawyer's hands, and he promised to be guided by him and him alone. Declining to communicate with his son he sent on all his letters and those of any others connected with this affair to Mr. Whitton, who received his client's instructions to deal with them. There is, however, a passage in a letter, dated April 11, to Sir Bysshe Shelley which indicates pretty clearly what Mr. Whitton

WILLIAM WHITTON.
From the painting by James Leakey.
By permission of the owner, Dr. W. Shirley Arundell.

thought about the baronet's grandson. He says:
"I lament exceedingly the conduct of Mr. Percy B. Shelley—He is an extraordinary young man, and I greatly fear he will give much cause of uneasiness to his father. His impiety and effrontery in the avowal of it exceeds belief, and if anything can bring him to a sense of his duty it is the firm conduct in my opinion of Mr. Tim Shelley."

There was a Mr. Hurst, a trustee of some of the Shelley estates, to whom Mr. Timothy Shelley's thoughts turned in his perplexity as a suitable person to treat with his son over this delicate matter. He lived at Horsham Park, and was consequently a neighbour of Mr. Shelley, who may have called on him there. Hurst evidently gathered that Mr. Shelley desired him to act, as he speedily approached Bysshe in regard to the proposals contained in his father's letter. The immediate result of this unexpected and unwelcomed intervention was a strong feeling of resentment on the part of Bysshe, who at once addressed an indignant note to his father:

15 POLAND STREET,
Wednesday mor. [April 10].

MY DEAR FATHER,—I am astonished that you should employ such a man as Mr. Hurst as the medium thro' which you may communicate any proposals.— If any change in your intentions should have taken place I shall give respectful attention to their merits if addressed to me, 15 Poland Street.—Yr. affect. dutiful Son, P. B. SHELLEY.

[Addressed]
 T. SHELLEY, Esq.
  Miller's Hotel,
   Westr. Bridge.

" I desired Mr. Hurst," wrote Mr. Shelley to Whitton on April 11, on receiving Bysshe's note of protest, " after I saw you to take no part in the business whatever—by a note left for him and in person as I accidentally saw him." Mr. Shelley added that he had no intention to answer Bysshe's note, and then, by way of postscript, " I have given no authority to Mr. Hurst, but the contrary." In another letter to Whitton of the same date, Mr. Shelley sa'd : " I will, my dear Sir, now leave this young Lunatic to your management, as I shall go home."

Although Mr. Shelley wrote to Whitton in his first letter of this date, " I will thank you from henceforth to be the only person I shall apply to in this business from every idea of doing what is right," he had already discussed the matter with others. Besides Hurst, he had seen during his visit to town his brother-in-law, Robert Parker (husband of his sister Hellen, the eldest daughter of Sir Bysshe Shelley), and discussed his troubles with him ; also with John Grove and R. Clarke, all of whom saw Bysshe under the impression that they were carrying out Mr. Shelley's wishes. Parker's letter which follows was undoubtedly written in good faith, but it is not clear what Mr. Shelley meant by the note which he added, for the benefit of his lawyer: "He is a very intelligent man. I desired him not to call on my son on any account, for I was fix'd and determined. I have the most hopes of Mr. Parker's getting him to retract these opinions." Perhaps he was anxious to keep up the part of the stern parent, but Parker having seen Bysshe he hoped that it would have a satisfactory result.

Robert Parker to Timothy Shelley

OSBORNE'S HOTEL,
Friday afternoon (April 12, 1811).

MY DEAR SHELLEY,—I have seen your son and his friend—Mr. Jno. Grove was there—Our conversation was long and not much gained by it—he expressed great satisfaction at finding you did not send Mr. Hurst to him—a pretty strong desire to be reconciled to his family but an adherence to his own points, and of course very little bending to yours, but an *expression of affection towards his mother and sister,*[1] and he said he should go to Field Place in ten days or a fortnight to see you and them, and try to effect a reconciliation—I engaged nothing for you, but urged abstaining from corresponding together upon that one subject as a duty he owed to your commands, and the reasonableness of it—

[1] The words "never to me" were inserted in ink at this point by Sir Timothy, who is also responsible for the underlining.

He's a very accute [*sic*] reasoner and seems to be very fond of it—I have asked him to write to me, and he seemed pleased—I think a lapse of a fortnight and a visit to Field Place may operate considerably towards bending him to your arrangement, but conviction alone can alter his opinion—

Mr. Hogg said very little—My kind love to Mrs. Shelley and Elizabeth and John.—I am, Yours very affectionately,   R. PARKER.

" I go to Maidstone to-morrow."

It would appear from this letter, and the next from his cousin the surgeon, that Bysshe was already a little home-sick, and that he wanted to see his mother and sisters who were cut off from him.   On the other hand, he was not prepared to give up the fight.

John Grove to Timothy Shelley

[LINCOLN'S INN FIELDS, LONDON]
Thursday night, April 11, 1811.

DEAR SIR,—Since I saw you I have had several conversations with Bysshe. I am convinced that there is nothing he wishes more than to be on terms with you and all his family, but he has got into his head ideas which he will not be prevailed on to relinquish till he is convinced of their being wrong, he is, however, very willing to be put right. I have told him he ought to consider that your and Mrs. Shelley's happiness depend on his conduct, that he ought not to sacrifice everything to his own opinions and be entirely regardless of your feelings, and bid him think what a wretched life he must lead if he forced you to withdraw your support and affection from him, which I assured him you would do if he did not agree to your proposals. Mr. Hogg's father is now in Town and I believe at this minute talking with him, I think if he takes his son out of Town [1] you will find Bysshe inclined to agree to most of your proposals, if not to all. Bysshe considers himself at present bound by honour to remain with Hogg until he is reconciled to his father, if that reconciliation should take place this evening I have great hopes that he would then think of nothing but returning to his duty. I fully intended to have called on you this morning but was prevented by want of time. Bysshe expressed a great wish this morning to go to Field Place but yet he would not prevail on himself to accede to all your terms. His opinions I think may in time be changed ; he appears *to me* to be waivering already. I beg to be remembered to Mrs. Shelley and Elizabeth.—I remain, Yours sincerely,   JOHN GROVE.

The following was added in Timothy's writing :

" Mr. Grove is a Surgeon, his father married Mrs. Shelley's sister. My answer was that I had plac'd the business in your hands to guard my honour and character against Prosecutions in the Courts."

Hogg and Bysshe in the meantime had not been idle, but had put their heads together and had drawn up a paper of " proposals " with a view of coming to

---

[1] The idea that Hogg had influenced Bysshe for the bad seems to have been entertained pretty generally.

terms with their respective fathers. They probably realised that talking the matter over with Mr. Timothy Shelley and his emissaries was unlikely to lead to any definite results. These proposals they submitted first to Mr. Hogg senior, who had now arrived in London, and, having obtained his approbation, Bysshe sent them on to his father with the following note :

P. B. Shelley to Timothy Shelley

Copy.

15 POLAND STREET.

MY DEAR FATHER,—I enclose you a copy of the proposals which were submitted after the joint consideration of myself and my Friend to the latter's Father.

He has done us the honour of expressing his approbation of them with the consent of yours.

I do this with a real and sincere wish for coming to an accommodation which I respectfully hope will not now be refused.—Your obt. affectionate Son,

P. B. SHELLEY.

" The Parties will make to Mr. Faber any apologies that he or his friends may require.

" They will not obtrude Atheistical opinions upon any one whatever, they will refrain from publishing Atheistical Doctrines or even speculations.

" They will return immediately to their respective homes.

" The parties feel it their duty to demand an unrestrained correspondence.

" When Mr. T. J. Hogg enters at the Inns of Court

or commences any other profession, that Mr. P. B. Shelley may be permitted to select that situation in life, which may be consonant with his intentions, to which he may judge his abilities adequate."

The document, which was endorsed by Mr. Shelley "Fine fellows these to presume to offer proposals," is not in Bysshe's handwriting. It was sent through the post to Whitton with the address in the handwriting of Mr. Shelley, who franked and dated it April 14, 1811. The copy of Bysshe's letter, and of the "proposals," are written on the same sheet of foolscap paper which bears a watermark similar to that on the paper used by Mr. Shelley in other correspondence from Field Place. It is headed with the word "copy" in Mr. Shelley's writing, and was evidently made by some member of the household at Field Place.

Besides Clarke, Mr. Hogg also sought the aid of another acquaintance, the Rev. George Stanley Faber, formerly Vicar of Stockton-on-Tees, near Norton where Mr. Hogg resided; he was then Rector of Redmarshall, Durham, four miles from Stockton. Faber had been at University College, Oxford, was at one time a Bampton Lecturer, and the author of some controversial works. His name was already familiar to Bysshe, who had described him, somewhat cynically, in his correspondence with the younger Hogg, as one

233

of the Armageddon heroes who " maintain their posts with all the obstinacy of long-established dogmatism."

Faber wrote a letter on the subject of the expulsion to his friend, Mr. Hogg senior, who placed it in Clarke's hands. That this letter was shown to young Hogg and Bysshe is evident from the fact that they undertook in their " proposals " to apologise to Faber. The epistle was also read to Mr. Shelley, who wrote to Whitton that Clarke was sending him Faber's letter, " which will open more to your view."

In his conversation with Clarke, Mr. Shelley must have blustered out his belief that young Hogg had been the " original corruptor " of Bysshe's principles. The suggestion became known to Bysshe a day or two later when he and Hogg went to call on Clarke. This visit may have been concerned with the " proposals " which the two young men had drawn up and had submitted to Mr. Hogg senior for his approval. Bysshe, however, was determined not to allow his father's accusation to pass unnoticed, and he sent the following letter to Mr. Hogg to exonerate his friend. It was not until long after Shelley's death that Hogg, in looking over his father's old papers, came across, and read for the first time, this letter which contains so fine a proof of Bysshe's loyalty :

P. B. Shelley to John Hogg

SIR,—I accompanied (at his desire) Mr. Jefferson Hogg to Mr. C[larke] who was intrusted with certain propositions to be offered to my friend. I was there extremely surprised: no less hurt than surprised, to find, my father in his interview with Mr. C. had either unadvisedly or inadvertently let fall expressions, which conveyed an idea that Mr. J[efferson] H[ogg] was the "original corruptor" of my principles. That on this subject (notwithstanding his long experience) Mr. T. Shelley must know less than his son, will be conceded, and I feel it but justice, in consequence of your feelings, so natural, what Mr. C[larke] communicated, positively to deny the assertion: I feel this tribute, which I have paid to the just sense of horror you entertain, to be due to you, as a gentleman. I hope my motives stand excused to your candour.

Myself and my friend have offered concessions: painful indeed, they are to myself, but such as on mature consideration, we find due to our high sense of filial duty.

Permit me to request your indulgence for the liberty I have taken in thus addressing you.—I remain your obedient humble servant,   P. B. SHELLEY.[1]

To JOHN HOGG, Esq.

Timothy Shelley to William Whitton

FIELD PLACE, *April* 14, 1811.

DEAR SIR,—I communicated the whole business in regard to my son to my Father.

[1] From Hogg's *Life of Shelley*.

Shelley in England

He very much approved of the decision taken by me and still consider'd I should be firm. As to Mr. Faber I know no more of than hearing his very long letter to Mr. Hogg once read over. I gave Mr. Hogg my letter and my son's disrespectful and undutyful answer and desir'd him to be steady and firm with his son and then they would be brought to reason from the evidence of their own senses. They never think of their offended and injur'd Parents' situation, but endeavour to treat by a flag of Truce, like two contending armies, disagree in some point, and then go to Battle again—I am rous'd into energy and a determined resolution not to give way to his insolent demand of corresponding with Mr. Hogg, or his chusing for himself what would not be admitted with his monstrous opinions at the Inns of Court. Perhaps a correspondence could not be prevented or the word of a person of such dreadful opinions could not be taken. I have enclosed you the letters, not having given authority to any person but yourself to relax from my letter, or even to say they went to him on my account, so that I will now beg the favour of your opinion how I am to act, whether to take no notice or write another letter that you shall think right I should do. I will very much thank you for your advice and anything I should now do for my own and Family's comfort, and you may depend on me. A gentleman just come here from London says he doubts the two . . .[1] articles having been known to . . .[1] excepting Mr. Hogg's Father.

Could you call on my son, or send to Mr. Hogg. Mr. Clark is his friend at No. 38–42, New Bond Street.

[1] Portion of letter missing, caused by removal of seal.

Poland Street

Don't spare my Apostate Son though I know it is only obstinacy. This agitates me so that I cannot act for myself to my own satisfaction, and as my Father is so well pleas'd by your kindness I entreat the following this business up in the best manner you so well know how to act in it.—I remain, Yours very truly,

T. SHELLEY.

[Addressed]
WM. WHITTON, Esq.
No. 10, Great James' St.,
Bedford Row, London.

Mr. Timothy Shelley having, as he says in this letter to Whitton, "communicated the whole business in regard to his son" to Sir Bysshe. The old baronet duly considered the case, and then delivered judgment to Mr. Shelley, and afterwards to the family solicitor in the following characteristic letter written in his trembling, crabbed handwriting, with its old-fashioned contractions :

Sir Bysshe Shelley to W. Whitton

[*Postmark* : HORSHAM, *April* 15, 1811].

DEAR SR,—Agree with you yᵗ *P.B.S.* etc. are extraordinary characters, in my opinion there is but one way to bring them to their senses, not by remonstrance, not by treaty yᵗ cant be with rebels se by *his* letter to his Father he is in a state of High rebellion. No terms but unconditional Submission can be admitted now, and yᵗ is not likely to be the case whilst he is treated with. Now my plain unrefined Opinion is

(I never deceive myself) let these two young men run their career without interruption, this in my opinion will bring them to their senses sooner than any thing.— Very Hble. Servt.,   B. SHELLEY.

[Addressed in Mr. Timothy Shelley's handwriting] :
    WM. WHITTON,
        No. 10, Great James St.
           Bedford Row, London.
T. SHELLEY.

Mr. Shelley also wrote on April 14 to Clarke, informing him that he had received Bysshe's letter with the " proposals." These " proposals " had been submitted by T. J. Hogg to his father, who had given them his approval subject to Mr. Shelley's consent. Timothy Shelley, however, declined to follow Mr. John Hogg's lead, or to be influenced by the letter of the " mild and benevolent " Mr. Faber, and he stated that he had considered it right to place his business in the hands of his lawyer, " to guard his honour and character in case of any prosecutions in the Courts." He thought that Mr. Hogg must be deceived, if he agreed to the proposals. Indeed, what right had " these opinionated youngsters " to dictate terms ? Their demand especially for an unrestrained correspondence with one another was " undutiful and disrespectful to a degree." Mr. Shelley thought that Mr. Hogg could not " agree to such insolence," as he described the young men's stipulation that they should be per-

Poland Street

mitted to choose their own professions. "Desire Mr. Hogg junior to inform you of our conversation last Sunday," Mr. Shelley added by way of postscript.

In replying to the above letter on the following day Clarke said that Mr. Hogg senior had "refrained from stating objections to a correspondence between the young men, because it did not appear to him that it could be prevented from being carried on through the medium of a third person." He assented to their correspondence in the hope that they might either dismiss or moderate their obnoxious opinions. They were recommended to exclude from their letters all religious subjects by Clarke, who took care to read to them from Blackstone and Burn what the penalties are for writing or publishing profane doctrine. Mr. Hogg had not felt himself justified to give or express any opinion with regard to Bysshe's idea of selecting law as a profession, which was plainly a matter for the consideration of Bysshe's family. T. J. Hogg was to be entered at one of the inns of Court, but Clarke, who was evidently himself in the law, did his best to discourage Bysshe from becoming a lawyer. He expressed the opinion that the young men might be led, but were not to be driven. With Hogg he had " endeavoured to apply mild reasoning and mild words : much more than his conduct merits perhaps," and had

239

persuaded him to leave London with him on the following day. Clarke concluded his letter by adding that "your son, will not be supported or countenanced by his friend in standing out against you ; and I should be much inclined to think that some judicious friend might bring him back to you."

Clarke also sent a note to Whitton on April 16, informing him that young Hogg had agreed to go that evening to his friends in the north ; and that it was hoped that they might dissuade him from corresponding with Bysshe.

Hogg said, "I quitted Shelley with mutual regret, leaving him alone in his trellised chamber, where he was to remain, a bright-eyed, restless fox amidst sour grapes, not, as his poetic imagination at first suggested, for ever, but a little while longer. I left London at nine o'clock in the evening by the Holyhead mail, having dined with the grave companion of my journey at a coffee-house in Bond Street." [1]

On April 14, Mr. Shelley also wrote to his lawyer about Hogg's departure. "My son," he said, "will be left, as it were, in solitary confinement. I wish something could be done with the apostate." Bysshe's place at University College was now vacant, and Timothy Shelley's half-brother, John Shelley-Sidney, having given him the nomination to the Leicester

[1] *Life of Shelley*, vol. i. p. 334.

Exhibition at the College, he recommended Christopher Dodson, of Sussex, for the vacant place.

Whitton was by no means disposed to deviate from Mr. Shelley's instructions, and was determined not to spare his client's "apostate son." The lawyer was ill, and he seized the opportunity, while he was taking a few days' rest at his house at Camberwell, to lecture his client. "I saw Mr. Clarke on the proposals," he wrote on April 16 to Mr. Shelley; "I cannot form to myself a reason why you should relinquish your judgment to your inexperienced son and allow him to say what is most fitting for himself as tho' he alone was capable of judging rightly on the subject. Either you must have allowed your son extraordinary liberties or I think he would have hesitated greatly before he had penned such a proposal. Mr. Hogg's son is to do as his father directs him but your son proposes that you should now resign to his pleasure his future conduct in life. As to all the conditions about not writing or publishing Atheistical books, the punishment which attends such a conduct must be an effectual check. . . . In a few days and the first I am able I will use my endeavours to see Mr. P. B. Shelley."

It would appear from the following letter, addressed to Whitton on April 18 by Mr. Shelley, that, after his son's expulsion from Oxford, he had proposed that Bysshe should take a voyage to Greece. The idea,

Shelley in England

suitable enough in any circumstances, was expressly intended to separate him from Hogg, who was regarded as a bad influence, and to divert Bysshe's mind from philosophical studies by new scenes and interests. Mr. Shelley had made the tour of Europe before he settled down to matrimony, and he probably recognised its benefits. It is not possible to say when this proposal was made to Bysshe, but he declined it; perhaps besides the reason given because his father imposed the condition that he should cease to correspond with Hogg. Mr. Shelley endeavoured to explain, in his simple-minded way, that Bysshe's waywardness could not have been the result of his exemplary upbringing.

"I cannot express the great obligations," said Mr. Shelley, "I feel towards your exertions on this unpleasant business of my Son. I can assure you that I never gave him Liberties that from his conduct you have reason to suppose I must have done: from six years of age he has never been kept *one day* from School when he ought to be there, and in his Holydays I read the Classics and other Books with him in the full hopes of making him a good and Gentlemanly Scholar.

"Now in what manner he has got all this Heterodoxy in a place fam'd for Piety and Learning I am at a loss to guess. If he even now expresses the least goodness of Heart, he will be very sorry that he has not seen that whatever a Parent had requir'd that he did not

242

see it was sufficient, whose happyness has been so wounded by his conduct and opinions, which to speak most mildly of them, are not only extremely singular, but abhorent in a Christian Society. He ought therefore to correct them, and not shut his mind against conviction in favour of such abominable opinions merely because he fancies his reasoning powers infallible.

"He cannot long continue in the same erroneous way of thinking, for in studied conversation I had with them on Sunday ye 7th inst. their tongues which obey'd their will in speaking the Fallacy are evidences against it.

"My son threw away the chance he had of going to the Greek Islands because he would not leave Hogg. Travelling would of course dispel the gloomy ideas which he has too long fix'd on objects, tending to produce Temporary Insanity, it would have rais'd his depress'd spirits to a proper height of vivacity, and by placing him constantly in the presence of real dignity, bring him naturally to reflect on his *own*. Such a scheme I am confident would effect what no abstract reasoning can produce, dissipate all despairing doubts, tranquilize his perturb'd imagination 'et se sibi reddet amicum.'

"I am much concern'd for the trouble this occasions to all parties, it is so unpleasant and withal to steer the best course. I will do all I can so that no reasonable pecuniary allowance on my part shall be wanting.

"I shall hope to hear in due time all the success I can desire if possible; Home will not do long, as I must occasionally be away. He or Hogg has a Box which they call their Poison Box that should be burnt."

Whitton kept his promise to Mr. Shelley and wrote to Bysshe, probably on Wednesday, April 17. He said that he had been very unwell for the week past, and was confined to the house, otherwise he would have called on Bysshe or have asked him to come to his chambers at Great James Street. As it was not his intention to go to London until the following Monday, he said that both he and Mrs. Whitton would be very pleased if Bysshe would come to Camberwell on Thursday or Friday and spend a couple of days with them. He added, "we may perhaps qualify the proposals made to your Father in a manner acceptable to him." If it should happen that Bysshe were unable to accept the invitation, Whitton promised to see him at Great James Street on Monday at one o'clock.

Whitton wrote at the same time to Mr. Shelley: "I hope young Hogg has left your son as he will see by it how unsteady the mind is in its first purposes.

Poland Street

. . . I have written to your son and invited him to come to this house and spend a few days. I shall if he accepts my invitation get more possession of his mind and perhaps be able to settle some plan for his future conduct at least for a time."

After Hogg's departure, Bysshe found his lodgings at Poland Street "a little solitary." He missed the society of his friend and his talks and walks with him, but he endeavoured to console himself by writing poetry and, in order to pass the time, he went to bed every evening at eight o'clock. A letter which he had written to Mr. Shelley had been intercepted by his mother, who perhaps thought it was not likely to improve the relations between father and son. Mrs. Shelley sent Bysshe some money and asked him to come home, but he was in no mood to return to Field Place, and he sent back the money. His solitary hours, however, were sometimes cheered by visits from Miss Westbrook and her sister Harriet—another Harriet who was to play an important part in the poet's life.

Bysshe was now losing patience over the negotiations with his father regarding the "proposals." He probably argued with himself that, so long as he continued to be his father's heir, he would have to submit not only to Mr. Shelley's authority, but to that of his grandfather and of the family solicitor. Bysshe's father was an example of what even an elderly man was expected to do who was heir to a wealthy baronet, and the prospect could not have been much to the young man's liking. He wanted to be free to act and live where he pleased, and he was willing to sell his birthright for a mess of pottage, if the pottage meant liberty. Moreover, Godwin, who hated vows and covenants as fiercely as Tolstoy, had pronounced against entails, and his opinion was in itself a sufficient reason for Bysshe's attitude.

Under the will of his great-uncle, John Shelley, Bysshe was tenant-in-tail of certain estates in Sussex, subject to the prior life-interest therein of Sir Bysshe and Timothy Shelley. Bysshe told Hogg, in his letter of April 18, that he had written to say he would "resign all claim to the entail," if his father would allow him two hundred pounds a year and divide the rest among his sisters : "Of course he will not refuse the offer," he remarked. As a matter of fact, Bysshe, being under age, was powerless to relinquish his rights. In the first of the following letters to Whitton, written before he received the lawyer's invitation, Bysshe asked for one, not two hundred pounds a year ; all he wanted was an independent income, and with his inexperience of money matters, he was not emphatic about the amount.

Poland Street

P. B. Shelley to W. Whitton

15 POLAND STREET,
[*Postmark :* 4 *o'clock, April* 17, 1811].

SIR,—As common report and tolerably good authority informs me that part of Sir Bysshe Shelley's
property is entailed upon me ; I am willing by signature to resign all pretensions to such property in case
my father will divide it equally with my ,sisters *and
my Mother*, and allow me now 100£ per an: as an
annuity which will only amount to 2000£, perhaps less.
—Your obt. humble sert.

P. B. SHELLEY.

[Addressed]
WHITTON, Esq.
Bedford Row.

It was not until after he had posted this letter that
he received Whitton's invitation to discuss the " proposals." Although Bysshe was evidently aware that
Whitton's letter was written before he received the
proposal regarding the entail, he deliberately referred to
it in the following note, in order to avoid any misunderstanding, that he was really serious in his offer
to renounce what he believed to be his interests in the
property.

P. B. Shelley to W. Whitton

· 15 POLAND STREET,
[*Postmark :* 4 *o'clock, April* 18, 1811].

DEAR SIR,—I will do myself the pleasure of waiting
on you in Great James Street at the appointed time.

I should have been happy to have accepted your kind invitation [1] were I not confined within by a slight fever, which I calculate will soon be over. I do not exactly see how it is possible to qualify the proposals : I am perfectly willing and not only willing but desirous to give up all claim to the entail.

Pray give my best compts. to Mrs. Whitton, with wishes for your speedy recovery.—I remain, your hum. obt.   P. B. SHELLEY.

[Addressed]
    W. WHITTON, Esq.
        Grove House,
            Camberwell.

The letters that had passed, between Bysshe and Whitton, had crossed so rapidly through the post that the lawyer was obliged to make his position quite clear to the poet. Having received the letter in which Bysshe expressed his desire to renounce the entail, Whitton wrote first the stern reply printed below. Perhaps on reflection he realised that he had been too stern, and therefore followed it by the more or less friendly letter to say that on Monday he would be pleased to meet Bysshe and that his reference to the " proposals " in the letter containing his invitation was not to be taken as relating to the proposal for relinquishing the entail.

---

[1] In Bysshe's letter of April 18, 1811, to Hogg he wrote, " Yesterday I had a letter from Whitton to invite me to his house : of course the answer was in the negative."

Poland Street

W. Whitton to P. B. Shelley

GROVE HOUSE, CAMBERWELL
[*no date, ? April* 18, 1811].

SIR,—I am not a willing instrument by which insult may be offered to your father and I must therefore decline acting in any manner under the paper you have sent to me. I most sincerely wish you to reflect on the tendency of the proposal you have thought proper to make before you offer it to your father's consideration.—Yours, etc.,

W. WHITTON.

Mr. P. B. SHELLEY.

W. Whitton to P. B. Shelley

GROVE HOUSE, CAMBERWELL,
April 18, 1811.

DEAR SIR,—You will perceive by the circumstances that my letter of yesterday was written without reference to the proposals you addressed by letter of yesterday's date. These proposals did not come to my hands until 12 o'clock this day, and I immediately wrote to you the only sentiment which the perusal of them begot. The proposals to which my letter referred were those you some days since sent to your father, and which he forwarded to me. I shall be happy to see you on Monday, and remain, your very obedient W. WHITTON.

P. B. SHELLEY, Esq.
15 Poland Street.

Bysshe had no love for lawyers, and he was not likely to have been prejudiced in favour of his father's solicitor, of whom he may have suspected as influencing Mr. Shelley in regard to the "proposals." Mr. Whitton's letter therefore was the very thing to cause Bysshe to give way to a burst of that violent anger which he was known to possess, and which on rare occasions he was incapable of controlling.

P. B. Shelley to W. Whitton

15 POLAND STREET,
[*Postmark :* 12 *o'clock, April* 19, 1811].

SIR,—I am not a likely person to submit to the imperious manner of address, of which this evening's letter is a specimen ; nor am I inclined to withdraw, nor *ever will* I be inclined to withdraw the proposal which I sent you. As therefore you seem to have much to do in this business on the part of my father, it is your duty either to go through with it, or to give it up. I never *will* withdraw that proposal : It is for my father's or rather my family's interests which ought to be the same that I make it. *Here* is no appeal to mercy, leniency, or favor. I have *not* found nor do I care to find either : but an appeal to justice, reason, humanity if you, if he were deaf to that nothing can be done.—I will not listen to the suggestions of family pride, to interest to fortune I am indifferent and I desire that when I am addressed again, a less authoritative manner be used, or subsequent letters are returned unopened.—Yr. humbl. sert.   P. B. SHELLEY.

[Addressed]
   WM. WHITTON, Esq.
      Grove House,
         Camberwell.

Poland Street

Mr. Whitton was evidently taken aback at the violence of Bysshe's letter. In his reply, while he endeavoured to defend himself against the imputation of having been offensive, he had no intention to let the young man off without a few words of advice. He was at any rate able to convey to Bysshe the intelligence that as a minor he had no independent income and therefore could not relinquish it. Whitton's warning, however, that he would not see Bysshe or receive any more of his letters was no doubt received by the young philosopher with indifference.

W. Whitton to P. B. Shelley

10 GREAT JAMES STREET.

SIR,—I have just received a letter signed by you without a date. It was apparently written in great anger and the only reason I can give for such anger is that you did not understand the plain truth which I wished to communicate by my letter referred to, for I am sure I intended no offence. I have not estimated on situation as it seems you expected, and why you think it is my duty to be an instrument of insult I cannot guess. I know where to begin and how to practise my duties without your instructions, and it would be well if you would consider the duties most called for and now unperformed by yourself.

Why do you suppose that you are the one that can best provide for your father and mother and their families interests. I do not know that you have the value of 6d. to relinquish, and if you had you cannot

251

dispose of it from the legal disability which your infancy creates, for I understand that you are only about 19. I will take a further liberty of telling you that it is your families present greatest misfortune that you think but slightly on subjects on which you think proper to write, and which immediately concern their and your future prosperity. You care not you say for Family Pride. Allow me to tell you that the first part of the Family Pride of a Gent is to observe a propriety of manners and a decency of expression in communication, and your forgetfulness on those qualifications towards me in the letter which I have just received induces me to say that you will postpone your intended call on me on Monday, nor shall I receive any more letters from a pen so unguarded and insulting.—Yours, &c., W. WHITTON.

[Addressed]
   P. B. SHELLEY, Esq.
     15 Poland Street.

Whitton sent on to Mr. Shelley copies of the correspondence that had passed between him and Bysshe, but he withheld, on account of its "indecency," the letter containing the proposal to relinquish the entail. "The Gent is very angry," said the lawyer, "and has thought proper to lecture me on the occasion." In consequence of this letter Whitton had decided not to give Bysshe "a personal conversation" because, he added sententiously, from "his pertinacity of opinion and inclination to insult he may call on me to turn him out of the house, which would hurt my feelings exceedingly." Mr. Whitton thought that if Mr. Shelley allowed Bysshe to direct his future progress in life, that he would prove "an eternal scourge of discomfort" to his father. This letter was not calculated to put anything but the gravest complexion on Bysshe's correspondence. Mr. Shelley was naturally alarmed, and he said, in announcing his intention of coming to London on Tuesday, April 23: "This misguided young man courts persecution, and which to him would be a favor." On reading over the correspondence again, Mr. Shelley sat down and wrote at greater length to his attorney.

Both Mr. Shelley and his solicitor seem to have regarded and treated Bysshe as an *enfant terrible*, an impossible child, bent on destroying the peace of Field Place and its inmates, whose dangerous pranks were feared, enhanced as they were by the consciousness that they could not be restrained.

Timothy Shelley to W. Whitton

FIELD PLACE, *April* 22, 1811.

DEAR SIR,—From my very great surprise I could scarcely sufficiently thank you for the great kindness you was shewing to my unworthy son, and the Friendship towards me. I never felt such a shock in my Life, infinitely more than when I heard of his expulsion, for I could not then have thought it of so hidious [*sic*] a cast. Everything seems worse, for I had hop'd from

253

the seperation [*sic*], that as they could not comfort and support each other in the enthusiasm of their erroneous opinions, each would have been glad to have return'd home obedient to their Parent's Injunctions.

The insulting ungentlemanly letter to you appears the high-ton'd, self-will'd dictate of the Diabolical Publications, which have unluckily fallen in his way, and given this Bias to his mind, that is most singular. To cast off all thoughts of his Maker, to abandon his Parents, to wish to relinquish his Fortune and to court Persecution all seems to arise from the same source. The most mild mode of giving his conduct a thought, it must occur that these sallies of Folly and Madness ought to be restrain'd and kept within bounds. Nothing provokes him so much as civility, he wishes to become what he would term a martyr to his sentiments—nor do I believe he would feel the Horrors of being drawn upon a Hurdle, or the shame of being whirl'd in the Pillory.

I trouble you with this that I may not take up your time in relating it. I hear he has corresponded with Lucien B.[1] and it is thot he did with Finnerty. Perhaps I have not heard half. All these matters make me wish to come to some decision on which I can and ought to act towards a son in such dire disobedience, and act too for the real interests of comfort, and Happiness for the rest of the Family.

I shall be in London to-morrow evg. at Miller's Hotel, Westr. Bridge.—I remain, yr. very obedt. and much oblig'd Hbl. Servt.,   . T. SHELLEY.

[1] Is it possible that Lucien Bonaparte was numbered among Bysshe's correspondents?

Poland Street

Endorsed :

MILLER'S HOTEL, *April* 23, 1811.

" I was too late for the post, therefore send it by the 2d. Post. I will call this morning, but do not stay at home on my account. I will call at any time you will have the goodness to name.

I must attend some Committees on Thursday at 12 o'clk.

I hear he is woefully melancholy.

[Addressed: HORSHAM, *April twenty two*, 1811]
    WM. WHITTON, Esqre.
        No. 10, Great James Street,
            Bedford Row, London.

T. SHELLEY.

CHAPTER XI

HARRIET WESTBROOK

Mr. Shelley's attempt to make Bysshe a politician with the aid of the Duke of Norfolk—Bysshe's speech at the British Forum—His offer to preach for Rowland Hill—Captain Pilfold—Elizabeth Shelley's disaffection—Bysshe's allowance—Meets Harriet Westbrook—Her appearance—His acquaintance with her and her sister—Bysshe's loneliness—Views on marriage—Letter from Eliza Westbrook—Hogg's fears—Bysshe's return to Field Place—His mother and sister—Miss Hitchener—Janetta Philipps—Hogg and Elizabeth Shelley—The Prince Regent's fête—Bysshe visits the Groves at Cwm Elan—He resolves to elope with Harriet—Mr. Shelley's suspicions.

AFTER Bysshe left Oxford the question of inducing him to take up some suitable profession had exercised the mind of his father. Bysshe had shown an inclination, like his friend Hogg, towards entering one of the Inns of Court. The bar, however, did not appeal to Mr. Shelley; the prizes such as had fallen to the Erskines, the Eldons, or the Broughams were few, and those contending for them very numerous.

Bysshe had said in his letter to Leigh Hunt, which is quoted in a previous chapter, that " on attaining twenty-one " he should in all probability fill his father's vacant seat in Parliament. Although the idea, since then, had grown distasteful to him, it had been decided by Mr. Shelley that Bysshe should become a professional politician, apparently without regard to his inclination or possible vocation. In the spring of 1811, therefore, while Mr. Shelley was attending the House of Commons, he endeavoured to persuade his son to give his attention to politics, and the Duke of Norfolk entered into the plan of bringing him in as member for Horsham. The Duke, a "*bon vivant*," as Professor Dowden says, "surrounded by men who kept the table in a roar, and a famous trafficker in boroughs," invited Bysshe to meet his father at dinner at Norfolk House to talk over the matter. In giving an account of the dinner to his cousin, Charles Grove, Bysshe expressed great indignation "at what he considered an effort to shackle his mind, and introduce him into life as a mere follower of the Duke."

He also related the incident to Hogg, who gave an account of the Duke's conversation which, if not exactly representing his words, is probably correct in substance. The Duke told him that he could not direct his attention towards politics too early in this country, and said, "they are the proper career for a young man of ability and of your station." With worldly wisdom his Grace pointed out the advantages of a political career, for, this being a monopoly, a small success would count because of the limited

number of competitors, and those for the most part
without talent, or too indolent to exert themselves.
The Church, the bar, and letters were otherwise,
because the number of rivals is far greater. There
none can win gold, though all may try to gain reputa-
tions, and it is a struggle for glory—the competition
infinite without bounds—"a sea without shores."
The Duke thus talked to Bysshe, said Hogg, many
times, and strongly urged him to devote himself to
politics without delay, but Bysshe was not to be
persuaded. He expressed his unconquerable aversion
from political articles in newspapers and reviews,
and especially from political talk of which he had
heard a good deal. Mr. Shelley had taken him
several times to the House of Commons, and he was
not impressed with what he saw there. "Good
God!" he exclaimed, "what men did we meet about
the House—in the lobbies and passages! and my
father was so civil to them all." [1] When this plan
failed, said Charles Grove, Mr. Shelley was puzzled
what to do. If he had known what were his son's
opinions on religion or politics he would have been
still more puzzled.

Not long after this date Bysshe expressed his views
in a letter to Miss Hitchener. [2] "In *theology*," he said,
"inquiries into our intellect, its eternity or perish-

[1] Hogg's *Life of Shelley*, vol. i. p. 207.   [2] June 25, 1811.

Harriet Westbrook

ability, I advance with caution and circumspection.
I pursue it in the privacy of retired thought, or the
interchange of friendship; but in politics—*here* I am
enthusiastic. I have reasoned, and my reason has
brought me on this subject to the end of my inquiries.
I am no aristocrat, nor any "*crat*" at all; but
vehemently long for the time when man may *dare* to
live in accordance with Nature and Reason, in consonance [1] with Virtue, to which I firmly believe that
Religion, its establishments, Polity, and its establishments, are the formidable, though destructible
barriers."

Although Bysshe eschewed the idea of entering
Parliamentary life, he gave early proofs of his gifts
of oratory. John Grove tells how his brother Charles
went with Bysshe in the spring of 1811 to the British
Forum in the neighbourhood of Covent Garden. "It
was then a spouting club, in which Gale Jones, and
other Radicals abused all existing governments.
Bysshe made so good a speech, complimenting and
differing from the previous orators that, when he left
the room, there was a rush to find out who he was,
and to induce him to attend there again. He gave
them a false name and address, not caring a farthing
about the meeting, or the subjects there discussed." [2]

---

[1] Shelley wrote *consequence*, but he probably meant to write *consonance*.
[2] Hogg's *Life of Shelley*, vol. i. p. 332.

Shelley in England

Shelley, however, had some thoughts, even at that date, of becoming a reformer. One Sunday he went with Medwin to the Surrey Chapel to hear Rowland Hill, and he afterwards wrote, under an assumed name, to that popular preacher offering to address his congregation, but he received no reply to his letter.

When Hogg departed from London he went to Ellesmere in Shropshire to spend a few days with a fellow-collegian before settling down to his legal studies at York. After his separation from his solitary friend in Poland Street, letters began to pass from one to another, and it is possible to give some account of Bysshe's movements from his part of the correspondence.

Bysshe wrote on April 24 that he had called that morning on John Grove: "I met my father in the passage, and politely inquired after his health. He looked as black as a thundercloud, and said, 'Your most humble servant!' I made him a low bow, and, wishing him a very good morning, passed on. He is very irate about my proposals. I cannot resign anything, therefore, till I am twenty-one. I cannot do anything, therefore I have three more years to consider of the matter you mentioned."

Bysshe's uncle, Captain John Pilfold, a retired naval officer, was living at Cuckfield, some ten miles from Field Place, with his wife and children. Captain Pilfold, who had fought with Nelson in the Battle of the Nile, and had commanded a frigate at Trafalgar, seems to have been a good-hearted man with a liking for his nephew, who reciprocated this feeling. Bysshe had received "a very civil letter" from his uncle, whose arrival he awaited in order that he might return with him to Sussex. He said: "I shall go down to Field Place soon." . . . His father ("the old fellow," he calls him) was resolved, however, that Bysshe should not stay at Field Place, "but," said his rebellious son, "if I please—as I shall do for some time —I *will*. This resolution of mine was hinted to him: 'Oh! then I shall take his sister away before he comes.'" Bysshe said that he should follow her, as her retirement could not be kept a secret, and this would probably result in him wandering about for some time. He soon realised, however, that his favourite sister, Elizabeth, could no longer be counted upon as one of the faithful.

"My sister does not come to town, nor will she ever, at least I can see no chance of it," he wrote to Hogg.[1] "I will not deceive myself: she is lost, lost to everything; intolerance has tainted her—she talks cant and twaddle. I would not venture thus to prophesy without being most perfectly convinced in my own

[1] Shelley to Hogg, April 28, 1811.

mind of the truth of what I say. It *may* not be irretrievable; but, yes, it is! A young female, who only once, only for a short time, asserted her claim to a unfettered use of reason, bred up with bigots, having before her eyes examples of the consequences of scepticism, or even of philosophy, which she must now see to lead directly to the former. A mother who is mild and tolerant, yet narrow-minded; how, I ask, is she to be rescued from its influence?"

Mr. Shelley was still unappeased—"Father is as fierce as a lion again"—but the question had been broached to him of making a small provision for Bysshe. John Grove had seen him, and had "succeeded in flattering him into a promise" that he would allow his son £200 a year and leave him alone. Mr. Shelley, however, went home [1] and wrote to withdraw his promise of the income, though Bysshe conjectured that Grove (whom he calls *Gelidum Nemus*), like a flattering courtier, would bring him about again. Mr. Shelley now wanted Bysshe to go to Oxford to apologise to the master, but this suggestion met with a stout refusal.

It was not without a sense of humour that Bysshe wrote to Hogg (May 8): "The estate is *entirely* entailed on me—totally out of the power of the enemy.

[1] In an unpublished note, April 25, 1811, Mr. T. Shelley wrote to Whitton, "I return home on Saturday (that is April 28), leaving the young man to his own imagination."

Harriet Westbrook

He is yet angry beyond measure—pacification is remote; but I will be at peace, *vi et armis*. I will enter his dominions, preserving a Quaker-like carelessness of opposition. I shall manage *à l'Amérique* [*sic*], and seat myself quietly in his mansion, turning a deaf ear to any declamatory objections."

In anticipation of obtaining a fixed allowance from his father, Bysshe told Hogg that he wished to meet him at York, that he might settle pecuniary matters with him. "I am quite well off in that [respect] now," he said. "Remember it is idle to talk of money between us, and little as it may do for politics, with us, you must allow the possession of bullion, chattels, &c., is common. Tell me, then, if you want cash, as I have nearly drained you, and all delicacy, like sisters stripping before each other, is out of the question." Bysshe's ideas of a sufficient income were very moderate; he never cared about money for himself; he gave away to others with liberal hands practically all he ever had. "£200 per annum," he wrote,[1] "is really enough—more than I can want—besides, what is money to me? What does it matter if I cannot even purchase sufficient *genteel clothes?* I still have a shabby greatcoat, and those whose good opinion constitutes my happiness would not regard me the better, or the worse, for this, or any other

[1] Shelley to Hogg, May 12, 1811.

consequence of poverty. £50 per annum would be quite enough."

By the middle of May, when he was at Field Place, the income was arranged with the help of Captain Pilfold, "who settled matters admirably" for Bysshe. "I have come to terms with my father," he announced to Hogg on May 15, "*I* call them very good ones. I am to possess £200 per annum. I shall live very well upon it. . . . I am also to do as I please with respect to the choice of abode. I need not mention what it will be."

Had Mr. Shelley arrived at a reasonable arrangement with his son directly after the expulsion, and carried him off to Field Place instead of leaving him at Poland Street while he pottered with his solicitor over the terms of reconciliation, it is possible that much of the trouble that was in store for them might have been avoided. His acquaintance with the Westbrooks might, for one thing, have been nipped in the bud. Although eighteen and a half is an age when many youths have to shift for themselves and do so quite effectively, it was an unfortunate, and indeed dangerous experiment in the case of Bysshe, with his singular lack of worldly wisdom and experience.

Charles H. Grove spent a part of the Christmas vacation of 1810 with the Shelleys at Field Place, and he returned to London in the following January. He recalled in after years going with Bysshe to Mr. Westbrook's house in Chapel Street, Grosvenor Square ; the object of this visit being to deliver a letter of introduction and a present from Mary Shelley to her schoolfellow, Harriet Westbrook.[1] This, apparently, was Bysshe's first meeting with Harriet, whom, Miss Hellen Shelley said, she well remembered as a very handsome girl, with a complexion quite unknown in those days—" brilliant pink and white, and hair quite like a poet's dream, and Bysshe's peculiar admiration." Harriet Westbrook was at Miss Fenning's school on Clapham Common, where Bysshe's sisters, Mary and Hellen, were also boarders. Both the schoolmistress and teachers used to remark upon Harriet's good looks. They evidently regarded her as the beauty of the school without rival, and on one occasion, when they were discussing together a possible *fête champêtre*, they singled her out for the rôle of Venus.

Such was her appearance as a young girl. Peacock, who knew her later, and was to the last her valiant advocate, tells us that she possessed a good figure, and was light, active, and graceful. Her features

---

[1] The Register of Baptisms in the parish of St. George, Hanover Square, states that Harriet, daughter of John and Ann Westbrook, was born on August 1, 1795, and baptized on August 27 of the same year ; consequently in January 1811 her age was nearly sixteen and a half.

were regular and well-proportioned, her hair light brown, and she " dressed with taste and simplicity." In her dress she was *simplex munditiis*. Her complexion was beautifully transparent, the tint of the blush-rose shining through the lily. The tone of her voice was pleasant ; her speech the essence of frankness and cordiality ; her spirits always cheerful ; her laugh spontaneous, hearty, and joyous." Her beauty easily won Bysshe's admiration ; his sister Hellen suggests that he was attracted to her because she bore the name of Harriet, that of his earlier love, Miss Grove. That she was the daughter of John Westbrook, who had retired on a fortune made in keeping the Mount Coffee House[1]—probably also a club—was no obstacle in Bysshe's eyes. It did not seem to enter into his calculation in cultivating the friendship of the lovely daughter of " Jew " Westbrook, as he was called, some say, on account of his swarthy complexion, but more probably because he may have added money-lending to his regular business. On January 11, 1811, shortly after Bysshe's introductory visit to the Westbrooks' house, he requested his publisher to send Harriet a copy of his recently published novel, *St. Irvyne*. In writing these instructions he erred in the number of her house, which was then evidently unfamiliar to him.

[1] At 78 Lower Grosvenor Street, Grosvenor Square.

23 CHAPEL STREET, GROSVENOR SQUARE

THE RESIDENCE OF JOHN WESTBROOK, SHELLEY'S FATHER-IN-LAW.
THE THOROUGHFARE HAS BEEN REBUILT IN RECENT YEARS,
AND RENAMED ALDFORD STREET.

Harriet Westbrook

From that time both Bysshe and Harriet corresponded with one another. After his expulsion from Oxford, while he was living in Poland Street, he was a frequent visitor at Chapel Street. Cut off from all intercourse with his family, he probably found the society of Harriet and her sister very pleasant, while they were obviously flattered by his attentions. Eliza, the elder Miss Westbrook, was ten or eleven years her sister's senior, had none of her good looks, but resembled her father in possessing dark eyes and a quantity of coarse black hair. Harriet's beauty no doubt attracted more attention than was pleasant to Eliza who, while "mothering" her, may have prompted Mr. Westbrook to keep her at school.

Bysshe told Hogg on April 18 that Miss Westbrook had at that moment called on him with her sister; "it certainly was very kind of her." When at length the younger girl was sent back to school Bysshe wrote:[1] "My little friend, Harriet W., is gone to her prison-house. She is quite well in health; at least so she says, though she looks very much otherwise. I saw her yesterday. I went with her [? and her sister] to Miss H.[2] and walked about Clapham Common with them for two hours. The youngest is a most amiable girl; the eldest is really

[1] Shelley to Hogg, April 24, 1811.
[2] Miss Hawkes, who succeeded Miss Fenning as headmistress to the school.

conceited, but very condescending. I took the Sacrament with her on Sunday."

That Harriet seemed to be setting her cap at Bysshe, Hogg evidently feared, and he accused his friend, perhaps ironically, of talking " philosophically of her kindness " in calling on him. Bysshe, however, thought that she was " very charitable and good," as in paying these visits to a solitary young man, ostracised from his family on account of religious differences, she exposed herself to much possible odium. Bysshe admitted that " to point out to her a road which leads to perfection " would perhaps be scarcely doing her a kindness, and it might induce positive unhappiness, and " not repay the difficulties of the progress." Then he adds, as if on reflection : " If trains of thought, development of mental energies, influence in any degree a future state ; if this is *even* possible—if it stands on *at all* securer ground than mere hypothesis ; then is it not a service ? " Bysshe concluded this letter with the announcement that he was going to Miss Westbrook's to dinner. " Her father is out."

A day or two after Bysshe wrote [1] from the Groves' house at Lincoln's Inn Fields, again with regard to Harriet. At last he seemed to have a vague suspicion that all was not right, that Eliza was playing the part

[1] Shelley to Hogg, April 28, 1811.

of match-maker, and doing her best to secure him for her sister. Women generally discovered pretty soon that Bysshe's heart was his most vulnerable point. " I don't know where I am, where I will be. Future, present, past, is all a mist; it seems as if I had begun existence anew, under auspices so unfavourable. Yet no! That is stupid! My poor little friend has been ill, her sister sent for me the other night. I found her on a couch, pale; her father is civil to me, very strangely; the sister is too civil by half. She began talking about *l'Amour*. I philosophised, and the youngest said she had such a headache that she could not bear conversation. Her sister then went away, and I stayed till half-past twelve. Her father had a large party below. He invited me; I refused. Yes! The fiend,[1] the wretch shall fall! Harriet will do for one of the crushers, and the eldest (Emily),[2] with some taming, will do too. They are both very clever, and the youngest (my friend) is amiable. Yesterday she was better; to-day her father compelled her to go to Clapham, whither I have conducted her, and I am now returned."

Harriet Westbrook, who was much older than the rest of the pupils, disliked returning to school, and Bysshe was only too ready to conclude that she was

[1] Mr. Rossetti suggested that Shelley is here referring to Intolerance.
[2] She was generally known as "Eliza"; this may be a slip of the pen or she may have possessed both names.

a martyr to her father's tyranny. She may have boasted of her acquaintance with Bysshe, who had not only taken her to the school but had paid her attentions when he visited his sisters there, and had walked with her and Eliza Westbrook on Clapham Common. He told Hogg[1] that Harriet's school-fellows would not speak to her, or even reply to her questions. They called her "an abandoned wretch," and she was "universally hated"; she returned this treatment, however, "with the calmest contempt." But Harriet had a champion in little Hellen, Bysshe's third sister, who, "in spite of the *infamy*," was not afraid to speak to her, because she could not see what she had done to incur the dislike of the other pupils. "There are some hopes of this dear little girl," said Bysshe slyly, with reference to Harriet Westbrook. "She would be a divine little scion of infidelity if I could get hold of her. I think my lessons have taken effect."

As a matter of fact, it was with horror that Harriet had learnt that Bysshe was an atheist, for such he was described at the school. She did not at first under-stand the meaning of the word, but when it was explained to her, she was "truly petrified." She could not conceive how it was possible that he could for one moment continue to live after professing such

[1] Shelley to Hogg, (?) May 1, 1811.

principles, and she solemnly declared that he should never change hers. When she wrote to Bysshe, Harriet endeavoured to shake his opinions, but she declined to listen to any of his arguments.[1]

Bysshe found the solitude of Poland Street unbearable, notwithstanding his habit of philosophising. He was rather young to derive much solace from philosophy, and confessed that he could not endure " the horror, the evil which comes to *self* in solitude." He wanted to go home, and said, " I long for the moment to see my sisters." So he spent most of his time at Miss Westbrook's, whose character he thought he had been too hasty in criticising. He now thought her " amiable " because he wished to be charitable, though not perhaps " amiable " in the same degree as her pretty sister. One day he wrote [2] to Hogg from the Westbrook's house in Chapel Street, and while Eliza, no doubt desiring to please him, was reading an odd book for a young woman of those days—none other than Voltaire's *Dictionnaire Philosophique*—Bysshe filled his letter, as usual, with many of the topics that interested him.

Hogg apparently had been discussing in a former letter the prospects of his future income, and something that he had written caused Bysshe to accuse

[1] In a letter to Miss Hitchener (March 14, 1812) Harriet gives this account of her early acquaintance with Shelley.
[2] Shelley to Hogg, (?) May 12, 1811.

him of wishing to be a "grandee." Bysshe computed that "when heaven takes your father," as his eldest son Hogg would probably have some three thousand pounds a year of property, perhaps convertible from three into five per cent. Bysshe confessed that were he in such a position it would puzzle him how to act with such a store, although he himself would not consent to own even half that sum. He believed, however, that he could see why Hogg would not relinquish his inheritance : "You think it would possibly add to the happiness of some being to whom you cherish a remote hope of some approximative union —the indissoluble, sacred union of Love." He was probably thinking of Elizabeth and of his own case when he wrote these words. That he was ready to fall in love seems to be shown in some lines in a poem that he enclosed in this letter to Hogg, with the excuse that his effusion was the result of a "strange momentary mania " :

> "And oh ! when on the blest reviving
> The day-star dawns of love,
> Each energy of soul surviving
> More vivid, soars above.
> Hast thou ne'er felt the rapturous thrill,
> Like June's warm breath, athwart thee fly,
> O'er each idea then to steal
> When other passions die ? "

It was love, not matrimony, for which he yearned. But Hogg was for supporting the marriage bond, and

Harriet Westbrook

Bysshe replied with the following ominous remarks, as if prompted by Miss Westbrook's presence. "Marriage," he said, quoting Godwin, "is hateful, detestable. A kind of ineffable, sickening disgust seizes my mind when I think of this most despotic, most unrequired fetter which prejudice has forged to confine its energies. Yes! this is a superstition, and superstition must perish before this can fall! For men never speak of the author of religion as of what he really was, but as being what the world would have made him. Anti-matrimonialism is as necessarily connected with scepticism as if religion and marriage began their course together. How can we think well of the world? Surely these moralists suppose young men are like young puppies (as, perhaps, *generaliter* they are), not endowed with vision until a certain age."

Still dwelling on this subject, in another letter [1] to Hogg, who had been writing in support of matrimony, he wrote: "I could not endure the bare idea of marriage, even if I had no arguments in favour of my dislike; but I think I have," and then, after discussing the matter as he said, *à la Faber*, he concluded: "For God's sake, if you want more argument, read the marriage service before you *think* of allowing an amiable, beloved female to submit to such degradation."

[1] Shelley to Hogg, (?) May 13, 1811.

Shelley in England

This letter was written from his uncle's place at Cuckfield, and on the eve of his departure for Field Place. "Misses Westbrook are now very well. I have arranged a correspondence with them, when I will impart more of the character of the eldest."

One at least of Eliza Westbrook's letters to Bysshe has been preserved. The following, although unsigned, is sealed with the initial "E," and had fallen into Mr. Shelley's hands, who attested it with his endorsement, "Miss Westbrook." One cannot say exactly what was the nature of Bysshe's "proposition," but it was evidently with regard to removing Harriet from school. Is it possible that he thought of obtaining an invitation for her to visit either Field Place or his uncle's house at Cuckfield ? Eliza's request, however, that Bysshe should not talk about his intimacy with the Westbrooks would have revealed her designs to anyone but the most unsophisticated.

Eliza Westbrook to P. B. Shelley

LONDON, *May*,
[*Postmark, June* 11, 1811].

MY DEAR MR. SHELLEY,—It gives me pleasure to see from the trend of your last letter that your mind has greatly recovered its accustomed cheerfulness, and that you are otherwise amended by a change of residence.

I am obliged to you for your proposition in regard

to Harriett, but I am in hopes she will leave school for good—there has been another little misunderstanding between the friends at Clapham, which has rendered the situation of my sister so completely uncomfortable my Father has now determined upon her not returning there again; he talks of wholly retiring into the country, but not to any distant part. It is so much my wish to leave this busy scene that I shall do all in my power to expedite his plan.

You will not take any notice to your sister Mary, or indeed any of your family, of your intimacy with us; for particular reasons which I will explain to you when next I have the pleasure of seeing you.—Adieu, ever yours obliged.

[Addressed]
    P. B. SHELLEY, ESQ.,
        Capt. Pilfold's, R.N.
            Cuckfield, Sussex.

Hogg realised that the scent of danger was stronger than ever, owing to his friend's unrestricted correspondence with Harriet and her sister, and he again uttered a word of warning. "I cannot so deeply see," said Bysshe, who was disinclined to take the hint, "into the inferences of actions, as to come to the odd conclusion, which you observed in the matter of Miss Westbrook." [1] The elder sister improved upon Bysshe's acquaintance, an acquaintance developed in the course of his correspondence with her. But he was not sure whether she appeared to advantage

[1] Shelley to Hogg, May 19, 1811.

merely by comparison "with surrounding indifference and degradation."

He was, however, no very sure judge of character, and the opinions he formed of his acquaintances too frequently were self-delusory, resulting from the interchange of letters. He admitted Hogg's superiority, as a man of the world, in his estimates of people. Bysshe's unsophisticated little friend Harriet was still kept at school, or "prison," as he calls it. "There is something in *her* more noble, yet not so cultivated as the elder—a larger diamond, yet not so highly polished. Her indifference to, her contempt of surrounding prejudice, are certainly fine. But perhaps the other wants opportunity. I confess that I cannot mark female excellence, or its degrees, by a print of the foot, a waving of vesture, &c., as in your case; but perhaps this criterion only holds good when an *angel*, not a mortal, is in the case."

By May 15 Bysshe was once more under the paternal roof, and for a time able to be with his mother and sister. On his arrival at Field Place he learnt that Elizabeth had been ill with scarlet fever, but she was now getting better, though hardly yet able to speak. Bysshe reproached himself for having misjudged her; and it was with " some emotions of pleasure mingled with those of pain " when he learnt that illness had prevented her from writing to him. Mr. Shelley had forbidden Bysshe to have any conversation with her, but Captain Pilfold had talked him over, and so brother and sister were able to see one another, with restrictions. A part of his time was spent in reading to Elizabeth, but he realised that he no longer had her full confidence. In talking to his mother, whom he found "quite rational," she confessed to no belief either in prayer or thanksgiving, and was of the opinion that a good man, whether philosopher or Christian, "will do very well in whatever future state awaits us." Indeed, he now believed that the mass of mankind were Christians only in name, and that there was no reality in their religion. "Certain members of my family," he said, "are no more Christians than Epicurus himself was." Even Mr. Shelley himself, the advocate of Paley, while with Captain Pilfold, had unburdened himself so far as to say, "To tell you the truth, *I* am a sceptic!" 'Ah! eh!' thought the captain, 'old birds are not to be caught with chaff.' 'Are you, indeed?'" was the cold reply, and no more was got out of him.

Captain Pilfold, who had taken up Bysshe's cause, made him welcome at his house, to which he was glad to return after spending a few days in the gloomy atmosphere of Field Place. "I am now with my uncle," he wrote to Hogg,[1] "he is a very hearty

[1] Shelley to Hogg, May 19, 1811 ; *ib.*, May 26.

fellow, and has behaved very nobly to me, in return for which I have illuminated him. A physician, named Dr. J——, dined with us last night, who is a red-hot saint ; the Captain attacked him, warm from *The Necessity*, and the Doctor went away very much shocked." Still writing from Cuckfield, some days later, he said, "I take the opportunity of the Old Boy's absence in London to persuade my mother and Elizabeth, who is now quite well, to come to Cuckfield, because there they will be three, or more, days absent from this Killjoy, as I name him."

During his visit to Cuckfield, Bysshe made the acquaintance of Miss Elizabeth Hitchener, who kept a school at Hurstpierpoint, and numbered among her pupils two of the Captain's daughters. She was some ten years older than Bysshe, but her views were liberal, and she was quite ready to discuss with him his favourite subjects of religious philosophy and philanthropy. He was at this time exactly in the mood for such an acquaintance to whom he could pour out his soul in long, unrestrained and frequent letters written in his bold flowing hand. Bysshe was charmed with his new friend, whom he soon invested with all the virtues and attributes he most admired, and it was with characteristic enthusiasm that he enlisted her among his correspondents. Miss Hitchener was a worthy woman who had endeavoured to make the best of her opportunities and, as the daughter of humble parents, they were few. Her father, it is said, was formerly a smuggler, a not uncommon occupation in Sussex in his day, but it had its dangers as well as its compensations, and he had abandoned it for the trade of innkeeper, changing his name at the same time from Yorke to that of Hitchener. Shelley began to write to Miss Hitchener shortly after he returned to London, and her letters soon became scarcely less ardent than his.

While at Oxford, Mr. Strong, an acquaintance of Shelley, had shown him the manuscript of some verses by a Miss Janetta Philipps. Shelley much admired the verses, and offered to print them at his own expense, as he stated that in doing so it would " make even some balances " with his printer. Mr. Strong promised to deliver the manuscript for that purpose to Shelley, who, fearing his " intention might shock the delicacy of a noble female mind," was resolved that his assistance should not be made known to the authoress. After Shelley's expulsion Mr. Strong declined to have anything further to do with him. Shelley, however, was still interested in the fate of her poems, and, nothing daunted, addressed a letter to Miss Philipps from Field Place, on May 16, 1811, " wholly unacquainted, unintroduced, except through the medium of " her " exquisite poetry." He explained the circumstances which had prompted him to write to her, and still solicited "the honour" of being allowed to bear the expenses of printing the book.

The poems were subsequently issued in 1811 at Oxford by Collingwood & Co., to subscribers, of whom there is a list in the volume occupying ten pages, and among them are the names of Mr. P. B. Shelley (six copies); Miss Shelley, Field Place; Miss Hellen Shelley; Mrs. Grove, Lincoln's Inn Fields (three copies); Miss H. Westbrook; Thomas Medwin, Esq., Horsham; Mr. Munday, Bookseller, Oxford; Mr. Graham, 29 Vine Street, Piccadilly; and Mr. Philipps (six copies). The last named, who subscribed for the same number of copies as Shelley, was probably a relative of the author, no one else taking as many copies. Miss Philipps seems to have declined Shelley's offer; but the evidence is there that he was active in obtaining subscribers for the volume. The sale of the 525 copies of the book, for which the list of subscribers accounts, would probably have been sufficient to defray the printer's bill. Miss Philipps' relatives and acquaintances, it is stated, were mostly resident in Bridgwater and its neighbourhood, and she does not appear to have been connected with Phillips, the Worthing printer, whose name is spelt differently.

There is little in the poems to justify Shelley's high opinion, but the little volume is interesting as a proof of his generosity to a fellow-poet. He concluded his letter to Miss Philipps by saying that, in the pamphlet which caused his expulsion from Oxford, he had questioned the existence of a Deity. " In justice to myself," he added, " I must also declare that a proof of *his* existence, or even the divine mission of Christ, would in no matter alter one idea on the subject of morality." Miss Philipps replied, and in acknowledging her letter he admitted that it had caused him extreme surprise. One gathers that she declined his offer, and expressed disapproval of his principles, but there is nothing to show whether his request that she would write again was ever granted.

Shelley found that time dragged along wearily enough at Field Place. " I have nothing to tell you which you will like to hear," he wrote to Hogg on June 2nd. " The affected contempt of narrowed intellects for the exertion of mental powers, which they either will not or cannot comprehend, is always a tale of disgust. What must it be when involving a keen disappointment ? I have hesitated for three days on what I should do, what I should say. I am your friend, you acknowledge it. You have chosen me, and we are inseparable ; not the tyranny of idiots can affect it ; not the misrepresentations of the interested."

Hogg, however, was no longer available for personal companionship, and the confidence of his sister Elizabeth, as he said, " even is diminished, that confidence once so unbounded : but it is to be regained." He had written a long letter from Cuckfield, probably one of his appeals that she should " assert her claim to an unfettered use of reason," but her answer was unsympathetic. His letters to Hogg filled a part of his time.

Bysshe had suffered a great disappointment when his father cancelled Hogg's promised visit to Field Place. It was the wish of his heart that his friend should fall in love with his sister Elizabeth, and he had done as much as was possible to further his object by talking about one to the other. Sometimes Bysshe had shown Hogg's letters to Elizabeth, or delivered his messages to her. Since Bysshe's return to Field Place he had found her so changed and unsympathetic that apparently she gave him no encouragement to discuss his friend. But Bysshe, still cherishing the idea of making the match, devised the following plan. Hogg was to be secretly admitted to Field Place : no one except Bysshe was to know of his presence in the house, and he was to occupy a room from the window of which he was to see Elizabeth in the garden and to fall in love with her. The arrangements for this scheme must be given in Bysshe's words : [1] " Come then, my dear friend :

---

[1] Shelley to Hogg, June 23, 1811.

happy, *most* happy shall I be if you will share my little study ; happy that you come on an errand so likely to soothe me, and restore my peace. There are two rooms in this house which I have taken exclusively to myself ; my sister *will* not enter them, and no one else *shall ;* these you shall inhabit with me. You must content yourself to sleep upon a mattress ; and you will be like a State prisoner. You must only walk with me at midnight for fear of discovery. My window commands a view of the lawn, where you will frequently see an object that will amply repay your journey—the object of my fond affections. Time and opportunity must effect that in my [1] favour with him which entreaties cannot. Indeed I do not think it advisable to say too much on the subject; but more when we meet. Do not trouble yourself with any baggage ; I have plenty of clean things for you. The mail will convey you from York to London, whence the Horsham coach will bring you to Horsham ; (news !) there I will meet you at midnight, whence you shall be conveyed to your apartment. Come then, I entreat you; I will return with you to York. *I* almost *insist on your coming*—I shall fully expect you."

In answer to this mad plan Hogg, not unnaturally,

---

[1] Shelley may have written "that in your favour with her," and that this is one of Hogg's altered or careless transcripts. The original is not available for comparison.

accused Bysshe of being unreasonable. Bysshe replied,[1] "I was mad ! You know that very little sets my horrid spirits in motion. I drank a glass or two of wine at my mother's instigation, then began raving. She, to quiet me, gave me pens, ink, and paper, and I wrote to you. Elizabeth is, indeed, an unworthy companion of the Muses. I do not rest much on her poetry now. Miss Philipps betrayed twice the genius : greater amiability, if to affect the feeling is a proof of the latter."

Bysshe did not, however, abandon his project that his sister Elizabeth should make a match with Hogg ; and he also looked forward to the time when he could join his friend. In writing somewhat later (from Cwm Elan towards the end of July) Bysshe said, " I did *execrate* my existence once, when I first discovered that there was no chance of our being united. To enjoy your society and that of my sister has now for some months been my aim. She is not what she was : you continue the same, and may you ever be so." Bysshe, who had at one time so much admired Elizabeth's verses, was disappointed, and he now thought that Miss F. D. Browne [2] ("certainly a tigress ") surpassed his sister " in poetical talents."

[1] Hogg to Shelley, (?) June 27, 1811.
[2] Felicia Dorothea Browne, afterwards Mrs. Hemans (1796-1835), whose " Poems" were printed in 1808, when the youthful authoress was twelve years old.

Harriet Westbrook

A fortnight later he wrote [1] from London to tell Hogg that he had a rival in his sister's affections, in the person of John Grove, whose chances of success, he thought, were equal to Hogg's. It was difficult to see how this could be the case when Grove had the opportunity of frequently seeing and conversing with Miss Shelley, whereas Hogg had never seen her. But, according to Bysshe, Grove was not a favoured lover, nor ever could be. She feared she would "lose an entertaining acquaintance who sometimes enlivened her solitude by his conversation, by his conversion into the more serious character of a lover." She seems to have rejected the advances of John Grove, whose attachment was "that of a cool, unimpassioned selector of a companion for life." Bysshe, however, was not able to give Hogg much hope, as he had no reason to suppose that her rejection "proceeded from any augmented leniency for another."

Nor did Bysshe find his mother very companionable. "I am a perfect hermit : not a being to speak with ! I sometimes exchange a word with my mother on the subject of the weather, upon which she is irresistibly

[1] Shelley to Hogg, from London, Aug. 15, 1811. This letter, like many others printed by Hogg in his *Life of Shelley*, contains some passages which are not easy of explanation. The late Lady Shelley, however, had an opportunity of correcting this and some other letters of Shelley with the originals, and her copy (in Lord Abinger's hands) was printed by M. Koszul in *La Jeunesse de Shelley*, and in the Appendix to the new edition of *Shelley's Letters*, 1912 and 1915.

eloquent; otherwise all is deep silence! I wander about this place, walking all over the grounds, with no particular object in view." He was too unsettled in mind to do any writing except now and then a letter to Hogg or the Miss Westbrooks, and he confessed himself "tired and ennuied." He found little to read except Miss Owenson's *Missionary*, which he described as "a divine thing; Luxima, the Indian, is an angel. What a pity that we cannot incorporate these creations of fancy; the very thoughts of them thrill the soul!" Another book that had excited Shelley's interest at this time was Southey's *Curse of Kehama*, which he described to his newly-made friend, Miss Elizabeth Hitchener, as his "most favourite poem." He was already a reader of the poetry of Scott and Campbell, for neither of which he seems to have cared. Southey's poetry was his first experience of the new influence in letters, and it remained Shelley's ideal until he later became acquainted with, and learnt to appreciate, the work of his two great contemporaries, Wordsworth and Coleridge.

Hogg asserted that a newspaper never found its place into Shelley's rooms at Oxford, but he did not disdain them at Field Place. His fancy was diverted by reading about the Prince Regent's *fête* at Carlton House on June 19, 1811, described by a journalist of the day as on a "scale of unprecedented magnificence." The *Morning Chronicle*, which came out with a long account of the banquet, contains the following passages : " His Royal Highness the Prince Regent entered the State apartments about a quarter past nine o'clock, dressed in a scarlet coat, most richly and elegantly ornamented in a very novel style with gold lace, with a brilliant star of the Order of the Garter. . . . The conservatory presented the fine effect of a lofty aisle in an ancient cathedral. . . . The grand table extended the whole length of the conservatory and across Carlton House to the length of 200 feet. . . . Along the centre of the table, about six inches above the surface, a canal of pure water continued flowing from a silver fountain, beautifully constructed, at the head of the table. Its faintly waving, artificial banks were covered with green moss and aquatic flowers ; gold and silver fish, gudgeons, &c., were seen to swim and sport through the bubbling current, which produced a pleasing murmur when it fell, and formed a cascade at the outlet. At the head of the table above the fountain sat his Royal Highness the Prince Regent on a throne of crimson velvet trimmed with gold. The throne commanded a view of the company, consisting of, among other distinguished guests, the Bourbon Princes." "What think you," wrote Shelley [1] on June 20, " of the bubbling *brooks* and

[1] To Elizabeth Hitchener.

mossy banks at Carlton House—the *allées vertes*, &c. ?
It is said that this entertainment will cost £120,000.
Nor will it be the last bauble which the nation
must buy to amuse this overgrown bantling of
Regency. How admirably this growing spirit of
ludicrous magnificence tallies with the disgusting
splendours of the stage of the Roman Empire which
preceded its destruction. Yet here are a people
advanced in intellectual improvement wilfully rushing
to a revolution, the natural death of all commercial
empires, which must plunge them in the barbarisms
from which they are slowly rising."

But the ludicrous side of the banquet also appealed
to Shelley, who wrote to Edward Fergus Graham,
above the signature of Philobasileus, a burlesque letter,
calling upon him to join in a " loyal endeavour to mag-
nify, if magnification be possible, our Noble Royal
Family. . . . In fine, Græme, thou hast an harp of
fire and I a pen of honey. Let, then, the song roll—
wide let it roll.—Take thou thy tuning-fork—for the
ode is coming—lo ! Fargy, thou art as the bard of
old, I as the poet of the other times. When kings
murdered men ; then was the lay of praise poured
upon their ears—when adulation fled afar, and
truth, white-robed seraph, descended to whisper into
royal ears. . . . They were not so rude as to say,
' Thou Tyrant.' No ! Nor will I . . . see if I do."

Harriet Westbrook

On the back of the sheet he wrote out this stanza of his version of the " Marseillaise " :

> "Tremble, Kings, despised of man !
> Ye traitors to your Country,
> Tremble ! Your parricidal plan
> At length shall meet its destiny . . .
>
> We are all soldiers fit to fight,
> But if we sink in glory's night,
> Our mother EARTH will give ye new
> The brilliant pathway to pursue
> Which leads to DEATH or VICTORY." [1]

Charles Grove mentions the Regent's *fête* at Carlton House as being much commented on in the papers ; it was disapproved of and laughed at by the Opposition, of which Bysshe was one.   He also states that Bysshe " wrote a poem on the subject of about fifty lines, which he published immediately, wherein he apostrophised the Prince as sitting on the bank of his tiny river ; and he amused himself with throwing copies into the carriages of persons going to Carlton House after the *fête*."   No copy of this satire has as yet been discovered ; but Grove recalled the following fragment :

> " By the mossy brink
> With me the Prince shall sit and think ;
> Shall muse in visioned Regency,
> Rapt in bright dreams of dawning Royalty."

---

[1] This letter was first printed by M. H. Buxton Forman in *The Shelley Library*, p. 24.   The MS. of Shelley's complete translation of the " Marseillaise " is in the possession of his grandson, Mr. Charles Esdaile, who allowed M. A. Koszul to print it in his work *La Jeunesse de Shelley*, where it appears in the appendix.

291

Shelley in England

While Bysshe was in London he had renewed acquaintance with his cousin, Thomas Grove, and his wife, who were on a visit to Lincoln's Inn Fields. Thomas Grove, the eldest son of the family, lived at Cwm Elan, a fine estate, comprising many thousands of acres, in the heart of Wales, within a few miles of Rhayader in Radnorshire. Bysshe was anxious to see the place after having heard Harriet Grove extol its beauties, and when Grove sent him an invitation early in July to visit Cwm Elan he gladly accepted it. Mr. Shelley also welcomed the idea of getting his son away, as he thought the change of scene might have a happy result. Mr. Whitton, who heard of the proposed visit, wrote to Mr. Shelley on July 10 in a hopeful frame of mind :

" I trust with you that different scenes and habits will create different feelings in your son. He is very young, and time will, I cannot doubt, bring different reflections to his mind and beget different opinions. The course you have taken is, I think, the one best calculated to promote that end and his ultimate good. You have placed him in a situation that necessarily calls forth thought for himself, and his apparent independence is more likely to affect his mind than any restraint under which you could have placed him. Besides the general ridicule which the world would give to his doctrines will correct better than restraint.

Harriet Westbrook

I trust and hope that you and Mrs. Shelley will yet find comfort instead of pain in the progress of your son in life."

Bysshe was at Cwm Elan by July 15,[1] and, in an undated note to Hogg, he wrote to announce his arrival at that place. It had been his intention to take York on his way in order to see his friend. He had written previously asking Hogg to procure lodgings for him in that city, but his plan was discovered by Mr. Shelley, who promptly made its execution impossible. "I had a letter from my father; all is found out about my inviting you to Horsham, and my proposed journey to York, which is thereby for a while prevented. God send he does not write to your father; it would annoy him. I threw cold water on the rage of the old buck. I question whether he has let the family into the secret of his discovery, which must have been *magically* effected."

Bysshe was anxious to enlist his mother's sympathy in Hogg, whose letters he passed on to her. "She feels a warm interest in you," Bysshe wrote to him, "as every woman must, and I am well assured that she will do nothing prejudicial to our interests. She is a good, worthy woman; and although she may in some cases resemble the fish and pheasant ladies,

---

[1] Shelley's first letter to Miss Hitchener from Cwm Elan bears the postmark date of July 15.

honoured with your animadversions of this morning,
yet there is one altitude which they have attained, to
which, I think, she cannot soar—Intolerance. I have
heard frequently from her since my arrival here ; she
is of opinion that my father could not, by ordinary
means, have become acquainted with the proposed
visit. I regard the whole as a finesse, to which I had
supposed the Honourable Member's headpiece unequal.
But the servants may— No, they do not even know
your name." [1]

In accepting his cousin's invitation to Cwm Elan,
Bysshe had intended also visiting the Westbrooks, who
were staying at Aberystwith. He then changed his
mind in order to go to York. He had made no secret
of his intended visit to Hogg in writing to his father
from London, perhaps when he was on his way to
Wales ; Mr. Shelley, however, replied that he might
go, but he should have no money from him if he did.
" The case, therefore," said Bysshe, " became one of
extreme necessity ; I was forced to submit, and I am
now here. Do not think, however, but that I shall
come to see you long before you come to reside in
London ; but open warfare will never do, and Mr.
Peyton will easily swallow up Mr. Shelley. I shall
keep quiet here for a few weeks." He had no alternative but to remain at Cwm Elan, as he did not possess

---

[1] Shelley to Hogg, from Rhayader, (?) August 1, 1811.

the money to pay his fare to York. " I am what the sailors call banyaning. I do not see a soul; all is gloomy and desolate." He seemed to derive little amusement from his chief occupations of climbing rocks, exploring the scenery, and reading the poetry of Erasmus Darwin. But he did luxuriate in the scenery, and was more astonished at its grandeur than he had expected; although he was conscious that other things prevented him from admiring it as it deserved. He found all else stale and unprofitable : " indeed, this place is a great bore."

But, nevertheless, he tried to convey to Miss Hitchener some idea of the natural beauties of the place. " Nature is here marked with the most impressive characters of loveliness and grandeur, once I was tremulously alive to tones and scenes; the habit of analysing feelings, I fear, does not agree with this. It is spontaneous, and, when it becomes subject to consideration, ceases to exist. . . . This valley is covered with trees, so are partly the mountains that surround it. Rocks, piled on each other to an immense height, and clouds intersecting them—in other places, waterfalls 'midst the umbrage of a thousand shadowy trees, form the principal features of the scenery. I am not wholly uninfluenced by its magic in my lonely walks, but I long for a thunderstorm." [1]

[1] July 29, 1811.

Shelley in England

His hosts tried to make Bysshe happy; we read of him acting as Mrs. Grove's cavalier in a ride with her to Rhayader. He spoke of having been to church, where he listened to a sermon in Welsh, and was present at a christening, which "was performed out of an old broken slop-basin." He found some consolation in writing and receiving letters, though he lamented the loss of certain epistles from Hogg, which had gone astray owing to the pillage of the mail.

Bysshe had heard from the Westbrooks, and towards the last week in July he still contemplated visiting them at Aberystwith. But his frequent references to them in his correspondence had caused Hogg to employ some banter at Harriet's expense. Bysshe, however, was apparently not very well pleased with his friend's humour, and remarked, somewhat stiffly, probably on the last day of July, "Your jokes on Harriet Westbrook amuse me : it is a common error for people to fancy others in their own situation, but · if I know anything about love, I am *not* in love." Still, a few days later, he had made up his mind with regard to her, and he wrote to tell Hogg, who was still at York:[1] "You will perhaps see me before you can answer this ; perhaps not, Heaven knows ! I shall certainly come to York, but *Harriet Westbrook* will

[1] The letter bears the Rhayader postmark ; there is no date, but it was probably written in the first week of August.

decide whether now or in three weeks. Her father
has persecuted her in a most horrible way, by endeavouring to compel her to go to school. She asked
my advice : resistance was the answer, at the same
time that I essayed to mollify Mr. W. in vain ! And
in consequence of my advice *she* has thrown herself
upon *my* protection. I set off for London on Monday.
How flattering a distinction !—I am thinking of ten
million things at once. What have I said ? I declare,
quite *ludicrous*.[1] I advised her to resist. She wrote
to say that resistance was useless, but that she would
fly with me, and threw herself upon my protection.
We shall have £200 a year ; when we find it run short
we must live, I suppose, upon love ! Gratitude and
admiration all demand that I should love her *for ever*.
We shall see you at York. I will hear your arguments
for matrimonialism, by which I am now almost convinced. I can get lodgings at York, I suppose. Your
enclosure of £10 has arrived ; I am now indebted to
you £30. In spite of philosophy, I am rather ashamed
of this unceremonious exsiccation of your financial
river. But, indeed, my dear friend, the gratitude
which I owe you for your society and attachment
ought so far to overbalance this consideration as to

---

[1] Professor Dowden says, "The 'ludicrous' thing is that Harriet should
have chosen as a protector a youth of nineteen, expelled from College,
estranged in some degree from his family, and at the present moment in
want of money " (*Life of Shelley*, vol. i. p. 174).

leave me nothing but that. I must, however, pay you when I can. . . . I am thinking at once of ten million things. I shall come to live near you as Mr. Peyton. I shall be at 18 Sackville Street; at least direct there. Do not send any more cash; I shall raise supplies in London."

From this statement one gathers that Shelley had advised Harriet to resist her father's decision to send her back to school, but that, fearing she was not strong enough to defy her parent's wishes, she had offered to elope with Bysshe. We should remember that he had been in constant communication with Harriet since he first met her in January 1811, a matter of some seven months.[1] In a letter to Hogg, probably written about July 28, he had spoken of " a dis-interested appreciation for what is in itself excellent," evidently with reference to Harriet, though he seemed to imply that for he · he had no feelings of passion. But his correspondence with her and his general attitude may have encouraged her to confess her love. That he had paid her a good deal of attention was certainly known to her sister, and probably to her father. Bysshe's interest in Harriet, for instance, had shown itself in his attempt to move Mr. Westbrook in his determination that she should return to school.

---

[1] Hogg says, " The wooing continued for half a year at least " (*Life of Shelley*, vol. i. p. 422).

Harriet Westbrook

Hogg's timely loan had made it possible for Bysshe to escape from the solitude of Cwm Elan. "Particular business has occasioned my sudden return," he wrote from London on August 10 to Miss Hitchener, but he did not tell her the nature of his business, namely that he had come to town to await Harriet Westbrook's final decision. To Hogg, who was in his confidence, he wrote on August 15, with less reserve: "The late perplexing occurrence which called me to town occupies my time, engrosses my thoughts. I shall tell you more of it when we meet, which I hope will be soon. . . . I am now returned to London; direct to me, as usual, at Graham's. My father is here, wondering, possibly, at my London business. He will be more surprised soon, possibly! My unfortunate friend, Harriet, is yet undecided ; not with respect to me, but herself. How much, my dear friend, have I to tell you! In my leisure moments for thought, which since I wrote have been few, I have considered the important point on which you reprobated my hasty decision. The ties of love and honour are doubtless indissoluble, but by the brutish force of power they are delicate and satisfactory. Yet the arguments of impracticability, and, what is even worse, the disproportionate sacrifice which the female is called upon to make—these arguments, which you have urged in a manner immediately irresistible, I cannot withstand. Not that I suppose it to be likely that *I* shall directly be called upon to evince my attachment to either theory. I am become a perfect convert to matrimony, not from temporising, but from *your* arguments ; nor, much as I wish to emulate your virtues and liken myself to you, do I regret the prejudices of anti-matrimonialism from your example of assertion. No. The *one* argument, which you have urged so often with so much energy : the sacrifice made by the woman, so disproportioned to any which the man can give—this alone may exculpate me, were it a fault, from uninquiring submission to your superior intellect."

So Hogg's simple argument had won Shelley over to regard marriage at least as a measure of expediency. Harriet would have been aware of this change in Bysshe's views, and it may have decided her to take the final step.

Charles H. Grove, in his recollections of Shelley, said that his cousin's continued correspondence with Harriet Westbrook during his visit to Wales led to his return to London and subsequent elopement with her. In one of Bysshe's letters to Grove, belonging to this period, he spoke of "his summons to link his fate with another, closing his communication thus " in adapting the words of Macbeth :

> " Hear it not, Percy, for it is a knell
> Which summons thee to heaven or to hell ! "

Harriet Westbrook

After leaving Wales Bysshe paid a short visit to Field Place ;[1] and while he was there he saw Tom Medwin's father, the Horsham lawyer, from whom he borrowed twenty-five guineas, but without informing him that he required the money to help him with the expenses of his forthcoming journey to Edinburgh. He also probably called on his uncle, Captain Pilfold.

On his return to town he went as usual to Lincoln's Inn Fields, and Charles Grove accompanied him when he called on Harriet at Chapel Street.[2] Mr. Shelley was now no longer blind to the fact that something was going on between Bysshe and the younger Miss Westbrook, as he evidently instructed Whitton to call on Mr. Grove (apparently John Grove), and to find out the exact state of affairs. The good lawyer was puzzled what to do, and how to prevent, if possible, such an awful calamity as a misalliance between Sir Bysshe's heir and the daughter of the retired coffee-house keeper. He may not have relished the prospect of encountering Bysshe, but from the following letter, dated August 26, the day after the birds had flown, he was evidently prepared to do anything at the bidding of his client—even to calling on Mr. Westbrook, or at

[1] Shelley to Miss Hitchener, from London, August 10, 1811, " I shall be at Field Place to-morrow, and shall probably see you before September."
[2] Professor Dowden says that Bysshe had arranged his plans at John Grove's house without his knowledge, but with his cousin Charles as his aider and abettor (*Life of Shelley*, vol. i. p. 172).

Carlton House. He was zealous enough to have gone to the Vatican if Mr. Shelley had so desired it.

"Mr. Grove is out of town or I should have seen him. I fear that by knowing so much of your son's conduct as you must possess by his residing with you will cause you and Mrs. Shelley much additional anxiety, and you will no doubt do well to let him go elsewhere. An inquiry by me into his pursuits in this place must, as you know, be very difficult, and it is highly probable that the father [Mr. Westbrook] may be at least passive if not aiding in the intercourse between the young persons. Your authority alone can influence your son, and whether that influence will be sufficient to protect him against the extreme folly of his present pursuit I am led to doubt, but if you shall think proper to authorise me to call at the Prince of Wales and on your son and on Mr. Westbrook I will do so, but I have no hope of effecting your wish or of inducing your son to avoid any act of indiscretion—his will alone governs and leads his conduct."

Sir Bysshe had been told of his grandson's doings, as Whitton wrote to him on the same date as the above letter that he feared Mr. Shelley would have trouble with his son, who seems to be "ungovernable, and to have no will but his passions. I have offered," he said, "to see him and others about him if his father shall authorise me to do so, but without his authority I shall not like to meddle with such a chicken, for he has much confidence, and I am not in the habit of receiving from young persons their indelicate conduct."

In his letter of October 11, 1811, to Miss Hitchener, Shelley gave her an account of the circumstances that led him to marry Harriet Westbrook. He was at that period attentively watching over his sister Elizabeth, " designing, if possible, to add her to the list of the good, the disinterested, and free." He therefore desired to learn something of the character of her friend Harriet, whom he asked to correspond with him. She complied, and, while he was in Wales, her frequent letters interested him, but he became alarmed at their despondent tone and her constant allusions to suicide. One letter, more despairing than the rest, caused Shelley to come to London. Her altered looks shocked him, and when he learnt the cause, that " she had become violently attached " to him and feared that he " should not return the attachment," he promised to unite his fate with hers. Her spirits revived while he was in London, and, on leaving her, he promised to return to town at her bidding. When, shortly afterwards, her father wanted her to go back to school, she wrote to Shelley, who came to London and proposed marriage.

CHAPTER XII

THE ELOPEMENT, AND AFTER

Shelley elopes with Harriet Westbrook to Edinburgh—Their marriage—Appeals to his father—Hogg's arrival—His account of their life in Edinburgh—Captain Pilfold's friendliness and help—Mr. Shelley learns of the marriage, and stops supplies—Bysshe's letters to his father—Leaves Edinburgh for York—Mr. Shelley's correspondence with Hogg, senior—His reckless conclusions—Bysshe leaves York for Sussex—He reproves his father—Correspondence with Whitton—Graham and Elizabeth Shelley—The Duke of Norfolk's interest in Bysshe—Mr. Shelley frightened.

ONE evening, late in August 1811, probably Saturday, the 24th of that month, Bysshe made his way to a small coffee-house in Mount Street, near Mr. Westbrook's house in Chapel Street, and despatched a note to Harriet in which he named the hour on the following day that a hackney coach would be in waiting at the coffee-house to receive her. On Sunday morning, August 25, Charles Grove and Bysshe arrived at Mount Street some time before Harriet was expected. Breakfast was ordered and ended, and yet Harriet did not appear. While Bysshe waited, he amused himself by flinging across the street the shells of the oysters on which they had breakfasted, and said, " Grove, this is a *Shelley* business." Harriet at length appeared,

The Elopement, and After

and the three were soon on their way to the Bull and Mouth Tavern in the city, from whence the coaches started for Edinburgh by way of York. But, as the mails did not leave till the evening, there were some hours of waiting before Charles Grove had bidden farewell to Bysshe and his bride.[1] They travelled from London to Edinburgh without breaking the journey, but at York Bysshe wrote a hasty note which was brought to Hogg's lodgings the next morning:

P. B. Shelley to T. J. Hogg

MY DEAREST FRIEND,—Direct to the Edinburgh post office—my own name. I passed to-night with the Mail. Harriet is with me. We are in a slight pecuniary distress. We shall have seventy-five pounds on Sunday; until when can you send £10 ? Divide it in two.—Yours, PERCY SHELLEY.

Whether Bysshe had decided to go to Edinburgh when he left London is not quite clear from the following letter to his father, which may have been written before he left town. Did he intend to go to York and from thence to Ireland via Holyhead ? If this were so, he probably altered his determination in the coach. His travelling companion a part of the way was a young Scotch advocate, to whom Bysshe con-

---

[1] This account of Bysshe's departure is derived from Professor Dowden's *Life of Shelley*, vol. i. pp. 172-174.

fided the object of his journey. The young lawyer told them how to get married according to the law of Scotland, and, if Bysshe had ever seriously intended going to Ireland, he changed his mind and continued on his way to Edinburgh.

P. B. Shelley to Timothy Shelley

[*Postmark :* HOUGHTON, *Aug.* 26, 1811.]

MY DEAR FATHER,—Doubtless you will be surprised at my sudden departure ; you will be more surprised at its finish ; but it is little worth the while of its inhabitants to be affected at the occurrences of this world.

I have always considered my clothes, papers, gun, &c., as my own property.

I cannot think, altho' I confess it has been hinted to me, that you will condescend to the pitiful revenge for the uneasiness which I may have occasioned, of detaining these. Will you direct them to Charles Grove, Esqr., Lincoln's Inn Fields.

At present I have little time.

You will hear from me at Holyhead more fully and particularly.—With sincerest respect, your ever affect. son,   P. B. SHELLEY.

[Addressed]
   T. SHELLEY, Esq., M.P.,
      Field Place,
         Horsham,
            Sussex.

Bysshe had made a good way on his journey when he despatched this letter, and, as the postmark of

The Elopement, and After

Houghton-le-Spring shows, he was in the neighbourhood of Durham. Mr. Shelley endorsed it, as was
his habit: "Sunday morning, ye 25th Aug., he
borrowed £10 of Mr. Dunn, saying he was just come
from Wales, and was going home directly he had paid
his fare. Recd. this letter Aug. 27, by post."

As soon as this letter reached Mr. Shelley, he has-
tened up to London and summoned his lawyer to
confer with him on its contents and Bysshe's elopement with Harriet. Perhaps he talked of disinheriting
his son, for the abstract of the settlements of the
Sussex estates and other deeds were got out and carefully scrutinised by Mr. Whitton, with the result that
he found that Bysshe " was tenant in tail in remainder
under both settlements, and that there was not any
power of revocation and new appointment." Mr.
Shelley, accompanied by Whitton, then proceeded
to Chapel Street, and had a lengthy talk with Mr.
Westbrook and his daughter Eliza, and obtained from
them the circumstances of Harriet's elopement. On
the following day, August 28, there was a further
conference on the same subject, at which Mr. Shelley,
Mr. Westbrook, Whitton, Grove (probably John),
and Desse—Mr. Westbrook's solicitor—attended.[1]
These meetings must have been far from pleasant:

[1] From information in Whitton's minute-book : August 27 and 28,
1811.

the only decision Mr. Shelley arrived at, of which we are sure, was a determination to stop Bysshe's allowance and to leave his letters unanswered.

Acting on the advice of his travelling companion, as soon as Bysshe arrived in Edinburgh, he took the preliminary steps for his marriage with Harriet. It was necessary, according to the law, first to obtain a proclamation of banns, entailing a residence of six weeks in the parish, and afterwards for the marriage to be solemnised by a minister of religion. In the absence of personal knowledge on the part of the session clerk that the parties had resided in the parish for the required time, or that they were unmarried, they were required to bring a certificate signed by two householders and an elder. Such a certificate, evidently falsified, was discovered some years ago.[1] It is contained in a register of certificates for the proclamation of banns of marriage " of soldiers, carters, smiths, and labourers," and is signed by " Percy Bysshe Shelley, as well by William Cumming and Patr. Murray." The certificate was afterwards entered in the books of the Register House, Edinburgh, on August 28, 1811.[2] Hitherto no evidence has been

---

[1] By Mr. James G. Ferguson, City Session Clerk at Edinburgh, among the city archives. See *Chambers's Journal*, March 31, 1900, for an interesting side-light on the subject.

[2] Shelley lost no time, as he could hardly have arrived at Edinburgh until the evening of August 27.

The Elopement, and After

published that Shelley was actually married in Edinburgh. It is possible, however, now for the first time to give proof in the following certificate ; the date of the ceremony is unfortunately not stated.

In a document, however, connected with his re-marriage in 1814, the date is given as August 29 (the day after that on the certificate), when he was " joined in holy matrimony by the Rev. — Robertson, minister of the Church of Scotland, at his dwelling-house in the city of Edinburgh." From this wording it is not clear whether the minister's or Shelley's house was the place of marriage.[1] The following certificate of marriage is practically in the same words as the certificate of banns, but with the endorsement of the minister.

Marriage.

EDINBURGH, *August* 28, 1811.

That Mr. Percy Bysshe Shelley, Farmer, and Miss Harriet Westbrook, St. Andrew's Church Parish, Daughter of Mr. John Westbrook, London.

That the parties are free, unmarried, of legal age, and not within the forbidden Degrees, and she has resided in Edinburgh upwards of six weeks preceding the proclamation of Banns is certified to me, for which I shall be answerable. And are orderly proclaimed in several Churches in this City in order to marriage,

---

[1] This document is given in full under 1814, where his re-marriage is described.

and no objections made why the same may not be solemnised, is certified by

J. FETTES, D.S. Clerk.

Certified by Mr. Patrick Murray, Teacher, and Mr. William Cumming, both of Edinburgh.

Endorsed as follows:

The within designed Parties were married before Witnesses by me, JOSEPH ROBERTSON, Minister.

Bysshe had found lodgings at a handsome house in George Street. Peacock tells us that the journey had absorbed Shelley's stock of money, but he " immediately told his landlord who they were and what they had come for, and the exhaustion of their resources, and asked him if he would take them in and advance them money to get married, and carry them on till they could get a remittance. This the man agreed to do on condition that Shelley would treat him and his friends to a supper in honour of the occasion." It was therefore arranged accordingly. But, notwithstanding the landlord's assistance, Shelley had to repay him, and now his funds were very low. His bride could not be expected to subsist on the poet's meagre fare of bread and raisins, and no course remained to him but to apply in advance to his father for his quarterly allowance of £50.

The Elopement, and After

P. B. Shelley to Timothy Shelley

EDINBURGH, *Aug.* 30, 1811.

MY DEAR FATHER,—I know of no one to whom I can apply with greater certainty of success when in distress than you. I must own that I am not so frugal as could be wished, but I know you are kind to forgive youthful errors, and will perhaps be good enough to enclose me a Dft. for £50. Mr. Graham will take care to forward your letter. There is not a creature in Edinburgh, 'tis as dull as London in the dog days . . . there is, however, much worth seeing; it rains now, but a friend of mine promises if it holds up to lionize me. Holyrood, Arthur's Seat, and the Castle will, of course, be objects of my attention.

If I move I shall continue to write, but as I remain here until the reciept of your answer, in consequence of having incurred a slight debt, all letters may be forwarded by Graham.

I hope Mother, Sister, and all are well; my love to them.—With great respect, your aff. Son,

P. B. SHELLEY.

[Addressed]	[Readdressed]
T. SHELLEY, Esq.,	Horsham,
Miller's Hotel,	Sussex.
Westr. Bridge,	
London.	

If not there, to be immediately forwarded.

Mr. Shelley paid not the slightest heed to his son's appeal; Captain Pilfold, however, was ready with some words of sympathy for his nephew. "To be confoundedly angry is all very well," wrote the bluff old

Captain, "but to stop supplies is a great deal too bad."
Mr. Westbrook was not any more accommodating
than Mr. Shelley, for he also declined to help the
young couple, with whom he made a show of being
exceedingly angry.

It is noticeable that Bysshe does not mention a
word about his marriage in this letter, but he speaks
of a friend who promised to show him the wonders of
Auld Reekie. Perhaps this friend was the young
Scotch lawyer with whom he had struck up an
acquaintance in the coach from London.

The long vacation had commenced, and Hogg was
endeavouring to make up his mind where to spend it
when Shelley's letter, announcing his flight to Edinburgh with Harriet, was put into his hands. Hogg
wrote at once to his friend, promising to join him
immediately, and a few days later—in the first week
of September—he started out on his journey north.
On arriving at Edinburgh, Hogg set about finding
Shelley, whose address he obtained from the post
office, and at length discovered him in the handsome
front parlour of his lodgings in George Street. "He
looked just as he used to look at Oxford," said Hogg,
"and as he looked when I saw him last in April, in
our trellised apartment, but now joyous at meeting
again, not as then sad at parting." Hogg also met,
for the first time, Shelley's "lovely young bride,

bright as the morning—as the morning of that bright day on which we first met ; bright, blooming, radiant with youth, health, and beauty. . . . She was always pretty . . . smart, usually plain in her neatness ; without a spot, without a wrinkle, not a hair out of its place." The newly-married couple gave their guest a warm welcome ; they had received his letter, and his arrival had been awaited eagerly. Shelley exclaimed, "We have met at last once more, and we will never part again ! " He insisted that Hogg should have a bed in the house, and one was accordingly provided.

A walk was proposed, and, as Harriet wished first to see the palace of "the unfortunate Queen Mary," they went to look at Holyrood House, which Hogg described as "a beggarly palace in truth." Bysshe had to go home to write letters, and he left Harriet in the charge of Hogg, who was to take her to the summit of Arthur's Seat, where she was unsuccessful in persuading her cavalier to wait for Bysshe, who, she thought, might join them when he had finished his writing. Hogg tells us, among other things connected with these days in Edinburgh, of Bysshe's morbid sensibility to strange discordant sounds : how he shrank from the unmusical voice of the lodging-house servant—a Caledonian maiden—and how Hogg and Harriet took a mischievous delight in tormenting him by making the girl speak in his presence. When Shelley went every morning to the post office for his letters, " of which he received a prodigious number," he returned with supplies of fine honey, and still possessing his " sweet tooth " he much relished it. Hogg teased him, saying, " It approaches cannibalism to feed on it; indeed, it is too like eating Harriet! I think you could eat Harriet herself! " " So I would," replied Bysshe, "if she were as good to eat, and I could replace her as easily! "

One Sunday, while they were taking a harmless stroll in Princes Street, Bysshe had an experience of the mirthless character of Scottish Puritanism. He happened to laugh aloud at some remark of Hogg, when he was reproved by a passer-by, who said, " You must not laugh openly, in that fashion, young man. If you do you will most certainly be convened." Hogg tried to scare his friend by explaining that he was in danger of being " cast into prison, and eventually banished from Scotland, for laughing in the public streets and ways on the Christian Sabbath." He was, however, tempted one Sunday to attend worship at a kirk, but the lengthy discourse of the preacher resulted in thoroughly depressing Shelley, and his friend never saw him so dejected, desponding, or despairing. On another occasion, when they attended the meeting of a Catechist, Shelley was affected differently.

The Elopement, and After

The good man had asked " Wha was Adam ? " and, receiving no answer, he angrily inquired "Wha's the Deel ? " at which Shelley burst forth into a shrieking laugh, and rushed wildly out of doors.

Shelley obtained plenty of books, some of these possibly from a public library with the aid of the young advocate, his fellow passenger on his journey to Edinburgh. Among these books was a treatise of Buffon, which so charmed him that he made a careful translation of it with a view to its publication. While he was busy in the mornings with this work, Harriet set herself the task of translating a story from the French of Madame Cottin, and having completed two volumes she copied them out in "her neat, flowing, and legible feminine hand." As Hogg remarks, this feat proves that Harriet was far from being illiterate, as she has sometimes been represented. He adds that he had seldom, if ever, met a girl who had read so much for her years. But he never heard her speak on the subject of religion, in which he thought she was entirely uninstructed. Her chief delight was reading aloud, of which exercise she was never weary, and Hogg found it agreeable to listen to her. Bysshe, however, was not so attentive, and when, overcome with his fits of drowsiness, he fell off to sleep, his neglect was fiercely resented by his studious young wife.

While this happy trio were spending their days in

315

conversation, walks, and study, Captain Pilfold sent his "peccant" nephew "cheerful, friendly, hearty letters," and what is more, supplies of money. Mr. Shelley, who had perhaps received by September 8 but scanty information respecting his son's elopement with Harriet, addressed the following letter on that date to Hogg's father: "I wrote to you from London by the advice of a gentleman in the law, who I had advised with respecting my son having withdrawn himself from my protection, and set off for Scotland with a young female, though at that time it was conjectured he might make York in his way.

"This morning I have a letter from a gentleman, who had heard from him, that he was at Edinburgh, and that H. had joined him there. I think it right to give you the information, as from one parent to another, both of whom have experienced so much affliction and anxiety. God only knows what can be the end of all this disobedience."

Mr. Hogg replied that he had learnt that his son had left his lodgings in York, stating that he would be absent for a few days, without saying when he would return, or where he was going. He concluded that he had gone to Edinburgh to join Bysshe, but that, as he was only allowing him such money as was necessary for his expenses, he expected that he would shortly return to York.

The Elopement, and After

The news of Bysshe's marriage had evidently thrown Mr. Shelley into a violent state of agitation, and had caused him to seek the advice of his friends. He naturally found them very willing to listen attentively to all that he had to tell them about his son's elopement, but his want of reserve had given rise to a good deal of idle gossip which, so far from helping him, had tended to increase his troubles. Some of these rumours must have reached Mr. Whitton, who was taking the waters at Cheltenham, as he wrote from that place to his client on September 16, and offered him some sound advice. He said: " Very few indeed among our friends who, though they will talk a great deal about our family concerns, and particularly such a circumstance as has occurred in yours, will take the trouble of acting for our relief, and repeated conversations and letters about it makes a source of eternal agitation to your mind and feelings, and it cannot heal your wound. Do let me entreat of you to cease correspondence and conversation on the topic unless in the moment of privacy with Mrs. Shelley. Be assured that I say this with the sincerest wish to add stability to your resolution and strengthen your confidence in the propriety of that determination which you state you are come to. Your correspondence with him, and his with you and your family, produce great discomfort and renew all the feelings of disquiet and disgust."

Notwithstanding Captain Pilford's helping hand, Bysshe was now feeling the pinch of poverty. It was to him a new and painful experience. He had learnt either from his uncle or from Hogg that his father was aware of his elopement, and that he was justly angry. He realised that it was not the time to apply for his allowance, but that he owed his father an apology.

P. B. Shelley to Timothy Shelley

EDINBURGH, *Septr.* 15, 1811.

MY DEAR FATHER,—As some time has now elapsed since I did myself the pleasure of last addressing you, forgive me, if presuming on the inaccuracy of the post, or your own engagements of importance, that I repeat the request contained in my last.

Yet pardon me if the sincerity with which I am ever desirous to distinguish our communications compels me to unfold to you the doubts which perhaps I insult your kindness by harbouring. It has been insinuated, altho' I cannot for a moment cherish the idea, that your displeasure concerning my late proceedings has been awakened.

I can well imagine that you were surprised, nay, am willing to admit that I perhaps acted with impoliteness in quitting you without previous information, yet you surely will not regard this when you well know that business of importance superseded the attention due to these considerations.

The Elopement, and After

Proceeding on the idea suggested the vague information above alluded to that you were displeased with me, permit me with the utmost humility to deprecate any anger on your part, perhaps also I may succeed in pointing out its inutility and inadequacy to the happiness of anyone whom it may concern. . . . To distrust your own mind (the first consideration) which the duties of legislation demand to be unruffled, which the happiness of your family requires calm, which your own peace needs to be unaffected by the base passion of anger, is certainly as wrong as it is inconsistent with the Christian forbearance and forgiveness with which you are so eminently adorned. The world too, which considers marriage as so venial a failing, would think the punishment of a father's anger infinitely disproportioned to the offence committed.

That two beings who like each other's society should live together by the law of the land, is too conformable to the opinion of the world for its approbation to justify any resentment on your part. My mother, also, and sisters, in whose eyes the very venerable institution cannot fail to be regarded as at least innocent, cannot fail to be sorry if deprived (excuse the vanity) of my society. These points of consideration I offer, more abstractedly considered and as general remarks rather than as applicable to you, who doubtlessly have long percieved thier truth; you, who are the best and kindest of fathers, and as such posess the most dutiful and aff. Son,   PERCY B. SHELLEY.

This letter was duly sent to Whitton, who, after reading it, wrote to Mr. Shelley: "I return you the extraordinary production of your son. How lost are his feelings towards you and his mother and sisters, and how much does he forget the duties of that situation which he fills, after the education he has received."

In the letter that follows Bysshe endeavoured to argue his case from what he imagined should be the point of view of a person professing a belief in Christianity. It shows us the simple-minded side of Shelley's character to suppose that a plea for forgiveness on such a basis would have any weight with his father. Bysshe admitted that he had given his father cause for anger, but, had Mr. Shelley been in any degree discerning, he might have detected the pathos underlying the appeal, or even the comicality of the circumstance, that the author of *The Necessity of Atheism* should lecture him for neglecting to act up to his religious belief.

Bysshe feared that on seeing his direction on the letter his father might decide to send it unopened to Whitton. The very personal nature of its contents was such that he would have much disliked the idea of its falling into the unsympathetic hands of the family lawyer. He therefore resorted to the pardonable subterfuge of getting the letter addressed in Hogg's handwriting, which he supposed was not known to Mr. Shelley. Whether the trick succeeded it is not possible to say, but Mr. Shelley endorsed the letter in pencil, " Hogg's direction."

The Elopement, and After

P. B. Shelley to Timothy Shelley

EDINBURGH, *Septr.* 27, 1811.

MY DEAR FATHER,—You have not condescended to answer either of my letters altho' the subject of them was such as demanded at least your acknowledgement of their arrival. I can no longer profess ignorance as to the cause of this silence, nor refrain from making remarks as to the cause of it ; on the supposition of its bare possibility I offered a few in my last, they were respectful, and such as you have no right to be offended with, considering that the event has turned out as my suspicions anticipated. I am married—this is a circumstance which you have no right to see with regret. It ought to be the ambition of a real parent to see his son honorably established; you dare not assert the contrary of my present situation, it is such as the laws of my country sanction, such as the very religion which you profess regards as necessary to the true state of its votaries. I have availed myself of my civil rights in obtaining to myself the legal sanction of this proceeding; I have neither transgressed custom, policy, nor even received notions of religion. My conduct in this respect will bear the severest scrutiny, nor do I suppose you will find one bold enough in paradox to assert that what I have done is criminal. . . . That I did not consult you on the subject is because you could not have placed yourself in my situation, nor however well calculated you may be to judge in other respects, as I suppose you neither aspire to infallibility or intuition, it would be next to impossible to calculate on the meer question of the taste of another, particularly, as your general tastes

are diametrically opposed to his. Let us admit even
that it is an injury that I have done; let us admit that
I have wilfully inflicted pain on you, and no moral
considerations can palliate the heinousness of my
offence. Father, are you a Christian? it is perhaps
too late to appeal to your love for me. I appeal to
your duty to the God whose worship you profess, I
appeal to the terrors of that day which you believe
to seal the doom of mortals, then clothed with immortality—Father, are you a Christian? Judge not,
then, lest you be judged. Remember the forgiveness
of injuries which Christians profess and if my crime
were even deadlier than parricide, forgiveness is your
duty. What! will you not forgive? How then
can your boasted professions of Christianity appear
to the world, since if you forgive not you can be no
Christian—do not rather these hyprocritical assump-
tions of the Christian character lower you in real
virtue beneath the *libertine* atheist, for a moral one
would practise what you preach, and quietly put in
practise that forgiveness which all your vauntings
cannot make you exert. Forgive, then! and let me
see that at least your professions do not bely your
practise, rather let the world see it: for if you fear not
God as your Judge, this tribunal will sit in judgement
on your actions. I have done nothing but what is
right and natural. Nothing is more common than
elopements between young people, the unforgiving
spirit of fathers is now become banished to antiquated
farces and silly novels, you hope perhaps to set the
fashion, but I have much hope that the world rather
than imitating, would laugh at your precedent. But
by forgiveness I do not mean that barren exertion
which contents itself with saying, " I forgive," and then

sits down contented as having discharged its duty. Nor did Jesus Christ mean this, you must bring forth fruits meet for repentance; you must treat me as a son, and by the common institutions of society your superfluites ought to go towards my support. I have no right not to expect it.

What I have said here which appears severe applies to nothing but your unforgivingness. No son can be so dutiful so respectful as me, and the above remarks are merely urged as what would be my opinion in case you act differently from that mild character which you have hitherto supported.

Adeu. Love to Mother, Sisters, &c.—I remain Your aff. dut.   P. B. SHELLEY.

Will you be so kind as to send me this quarter's due, to Edinburgh post office, immediately, £50.

[Addressed]
   For TIMOTHY SHELLEY, Esq.,
      Field Place,
         Horsham, Sussex.
  M.P.

It had now become necessary for Hogg to return to York. He spoke of having been absent for six weeks, which would have meant the end of October, but it was in the first week of that month that he left Edinburgh. Bysshe and Harriet decided to go with him, and remain in York during the year that he was to pass in that city, and when he was free, they were all to remove to London. He and his friend Hogg already considered their property " as common."

Shelley in England

Edinburgh had already grown distasteful to Bysshe. He disliked the grime of the city as much as he scorned the commercialism of its citizens, and he was anxious to get away from the place. It would not, however, have been possible to accompany Hogg on his journey south, but for the timely help of Captain Pilfold. " My uncle is a most generous fellow," he wrote to Miss Hitchener,[1] " had he not assisted us, we should have been chained to the filth and commerce of Edinburgh. Vile as aristocracy is, commerce—purse-proud ignorance and illiterateness—is more contemptible."

Notwithstanding that Shelley's resources were much reduced, and Hogg's could not have been much better, they decided for the comfort of Harriet to perform the journey to York by post-chaise. They passed the first night at Belford, and the second at Darlington, and on the third day they reached York. Bysshe chafed at the narrow confinement of the chaise and the bother of changing horses every post, " and at Berwick, when Harriet had taken her seat and all was ready he was missing." He was captured, however, by Hogg, who found him " standing on the walls in a drizzling rain, gazing mournfully on the wild dreary sea, with looks not less wild and dreary." Harriet's occupation in the chaise was to read aloud incessantly one of

[1] Shelley to Miss Hitchener, from York, October 10, 1811.

324

The Elopement, and After

Holcroft's novels. Bysshe, who found it tedious, sometimes sighed deeply and inquired, " Is it necessary to read all that, Harriet dear ? " but she was inexorable, and declined to skip.

The narrow, crooked old streets of York, as seen at the close of a dull autumnal day, did not, as Hogg tells us, impress Bysshe favourably, and the dingy lodgings in Coney Street, which they found at the house of two needy mantua-makers, completed his dismal first impression of the city.

Apparently as soon as they arrived Bysshe deemed the opportunity a favourable one to inform his father of his change of address. It was natural that he should show some resentment at the parental silence, especially in his not heeding Bysshe's request that his clothes and other things might be sent to him. The letter, as in the case of his last from Edinburgh, was addressed by Hogg, a fact which is attested by Mr. Shelley, " Hogg's direction. Received Oct. 6."

P. B. Shelley to Timothy Shelley

MISS DANCER'S, CONEY STREET, YORK,
Thursday even. [*Postmark, Oct.* 5, 1811.]

MY DEAR FATHER,—Having changed my residence I beg leave to inform you of it ; I have not heard from you in answer to my last. I do not at present endeavor to account for it. You may suppose that I am in want of the clothes which I left at Field Place, may I beg you to send them, as also the books and papers, which can be of little use to any other. Even supposing that you are offended, do not permit me to suppose you so meanly revengeful as to inflict the pitiful inconvenience of detaining these things. I expected long before this to have heard from you. Your silence has occasioned considerable derangement of my plans. I have not long arrived at York, but take the earliest opportunity of informing you of it. This will afford excuse for my brevity. Love to Mother, Sisters, &c.—Your aff. dut. Son,

P. B. SHELLEY.

[Addressed in Hogg's handwriting]
   For TIMOTHY SHELLEY, Esq.,
      Field Place,
         Horsham, Sussex.
  M.P.

Mr. Shelley received other tidings of Bysshe's arrival at York, for Mr. Hogg wrote on Oct. 8 to tell him of his son's return after the sojourn in Edinburgh with Bysshe. Young Hogg accounted for his prolonged absence by his receiving no remittances from England, but how at last he obtained the money necessary for his travelling expenses Mr. Hogg was not able to explain, as neither he nor his friends had supplied him with any. He was not aware that the young people had spared themselves no expense, and had performed the journey in comfort by post-chaise in easy stages. "My son," he said, "makes no mention of a female being of their party. Whether your son

The Elopement, and After

is now at York or in its vicinity I have not yet heard, though I have made inquiry—perhaps you have heard of the place of his abode. My son has the impudence to write for money, which I have at present denied, for his behaviour in this last business has been such that I shall only allow him what will be necessary to keep him at York in the strictest manner. Oh, my dear Sir! we have been truly unfortunate in our Sons. May our children who are now dutiful by the Grace of God continue so, and be a comfort to us!"

Bysshe now wrote to Miss Hitchener [1] to tell her of his marriage. He guessed that the news would have reached her from the local gossips, but he felt that he owed her an explanation that he, a professed atheist, should choose to subject himself to the ceremony of marriage. He admitted that it was "useless to attempt by singular examples to renovate the face of society, until reasoning has made so comprehensive a change as to emancipate the experimentalist from the resulting evils, and the prejudice with which his opinion (which ought to have weight, for the sake of virtue) would be heard by the immense majority." Would his marriage, of which he had not given Miss Hitchener a hint in his letters, put an end to his correspondence with her? He enjoyed writing to her,

[1] From York, October 8, 1811.

as she was probably the one correspondent to whom
he could unburden his soul without restraint. "Will
you write to me?" he asked. "Shall we proceed
in our discussion of Nature and morality? Nay,
more—will you be my friend, may I be yours? The
shadow of worldly impropriety is effaced by *my*
situation, our strictest intercourse would excite none
of those disgusting remarks with which *females* of
the present day think right to load the friendships
of the opposite sexes. Nothing would be transgressed
by your even living with us. Could you not pay us a
visit? My dear friend Hogg, that noble being, is
with me, and will be always, but my wife will
abstract from our intercourse the shadow of impropriety."

Miss Hitchener did not accept the invitation, but
she consented to pursue the correspondence. Bysshe
wrote again at once, addressing her as "My dearest
friend (for I will call you so), *you* who understand my
motives to action which I flatter myself unisonise
with your own. . . ." He told her that he intended
to be at Cuckfield on Friday night, and added, "That
mistaken man, my father, has refused us money, and
commanded that our names should never be mentioned. Sophisticated by falsehood as society is I
had thought that this blind resentment had long been
banished to the regions of dulness, comedies, and

farces, or was used merely to augment the difficulties, and consequently the attachment of the hero and heroine of a modern novel. I have written frequently to this thoughtless man, and am now determined to visit him, in order to try the force of truth, tho' I must confess I consider it nearly as hyperbolical as ' music rending the knotted oak.' "

Bysshe's belongings were at length sent off from Field Place; perhaps his mother had heard from Mr. Shelley that he was in want of his clothes, and she arranged for them to be despatched. But neither she nor Mr. Shelley sent him a word to say that his request had been complied with; this office was left for the waggoner to perform. It is characteristic of Bysshe that these letters to his father are singularly wanting in tact, and that they become less and less tactful. He made the mistake of judging Mr. Shelley by his correspondence and his actions, which were often very foolish. But he could only recognise his own point of view; otherwise he would have remembered his father's high opinion of his own dignity, and his obstinacy. Bysshe undoubtedly wished to be forgiven, but he could hardly have chosen a more unfortunate way of addressing his father than by criticising his actions.

Shelley in England

P. B. Shelley to Timothy Shelley

[*Postmark :* YORK, *Oct.* 12, 1811.]

DEAR FATHER,—The waggoner has written to inform me that my property is sent . . but does it not look as if your resentment was not to be supported by reason that you have declined to write yourself ?

I cannot avoid thinking thus, nor expressing my opinion ; but silence, especially on so important a subject as I urged, looks as if you confessed the erroneousness of your proceedings, at the same time that your passions impel you to persist in them. I do not say this is illiberal, a person who can once persuade himself as you have done that every opinion adopted by the majority is correct, must be nearly indifferent to this charge ; I do not say it is immoral, as illiberality involves a portion of immorality, but it is emphatically hostile to your own interest, to the opinion which the world will form of your virtues. *If* you are a professor of Christianity, which I am not, I need not recal to your recollection " Judge not lest thou shouldst be judged."

I confess I write this more to discharge a duty of telling you what I think, than hoping that my representations will be effectual. We have taken widely different views of the subject in question. *Obedience* is in my opinion a word which should have no existence . . . you regard it as necessary. . .

Yes, you can command it. The institutions of society have made you, tho' liable to be misled by passion and prejudice like others, the *Head of a family;* and I confess it is almost natural for minds not of the highest order to value even the errors whence they derive thier importance.

330

The Elopement, and After

Adeiu, answer this.—I would be your aff. dut.
Son,   PERCY B. SHELLEY.

In his father's handwriting at foot :

Recd. the 15th Oct. 1811.

[Addressed]
T. SHELLEY, Esq., M.P.,
Field Place,
Horsham, Sussex.
[*Postmark :* York, *Oct.* 12, 1811.]

Shelley's departure from York was delayed for some days, but before he left for Sussex he decided to appeal to his grandfather, to whom he had never before written. For that reason he hoped that the old baronet might induce his father to forgive him. Sir Bysshe, who had eloped with his first bride, might have shown some sympathy for his grandson. But Bysshe was mistaken in thinking that his grandfather, with all his wealth, would be willing to spare him something. He was evidently unaware that the old gentleman had already been consulted by Mr. Shelley with regard to the sequel to the Oxford misfortune, and had advised a course that amounted to starving the culprit into submission.

P. B. Shelley to Sir Bysshe Shelley

MISS DANCER'S,
CONEY STREET, YORK,
Oct. 13, 1811.

SIR,—Excuse me, if never having addressed you before, I appeal in time of misfortune to your benevolence. I have forfeited I think unjustly my father's esteem, for having consulted my own taste in marriage. If there is a question important to happiness it is this; certainly *he* whom the question most nearly concerns has the best right to decide upon its merits. Obedience in this case is misplaced, inasmuch as morality can be nothing but a means of high happiness, and whenever an advanced opinion on it militates with this essential principle, reason justly questions its correctness. I am accustomed to speak my opinion unreservedly; this has occasioned me some misfortunes, but I do not therefore cease to speak as I think. Language is given us to express ideas . . he who fetters it is a BIGOT and a TYRANT, from these have my misfortunes arisen. . . .

I expect from your liberality and justice no unfavorable construction of what fools in power would denominate *insolence*.

This is not the spirit in which I write. I write in the spirit of truth and candor. If you will send me some money to help me and my wife (and I know you are not ungenerous) I will add to my respect for a grandfather my love for a preserver.

Adeiu [*sic*].—Most respectfully yours,

PERCY BYSSHE SHELLEY.

[Addressed]
   Sir BYSSHE SHELLEY, Bart.,
      Horsham,
        Sussex.

Three days after Bysshe left York he arrived at his uncle's house at Cuckfield. He performed the journey on the outside of the coach, and, as he told Miss

The Elopement, and After

Hitchener,[1] he did not sleep because his mind was so full of projects for "accumulating money," not for selfish motives, as he explained, but for the leisure that it would give for its employment in the forwarding of truth. He also probably found plenty of time to think of ways and means for approaching his father.

Mr. Shelley's letter of September 8 to Mr. Hogg had naturally given him cause for alarm when he read that Bysshe had gone off to Edinburgh in the company of "a young female," and that young Hogg had joined him. But Mr. Shelley had foolishly added in another letter that he would not be surprised if Bysshe left the young woman on young Hogg's hands. Mr. Hogg evidently wrote to warn his son of the danger that he ran in associating with Bysshe, who soon heard from his friend in the matter. The fact that Bysshe had left Harriet in the care of Hogg during his temporary absence from York added some point to Mr. Shelley's base suggestion, and had other unhappy results. He had blundered badly, and, as it seemed to Bysshe, from his next letter, it was the last of many spiteful acts of persecution.

We will now, however, for the sake of continuity,

[1] Shelley to Elizabeth Hitchener, October 10 and October 12 (?), 1811. The latter letter was undated, and it is now obvious, in the light of this new correspondence, that it was written some days subsequent to the conjectured date of October 12.

give Mr. John Hogg's letter, which was written three days after Bysshe's passionate remonstrance.

John Hogg to Timothy Shelley

NORTON HOUSE, *Oct.* 21, 1811.

DEAR SIR,—I return you my most grateful thanks for your very kind letter of to-day, and I think it proper to inform you that I received a letter from York, stating that your son left that place (it is supposed for London) about the 18th, leaving his lady to the protection of my son, saying he should return in about a week or ten days. Mrs. Hogg and I were greatly alarmed at this information, thinking it highly improper that they should be left together, and remembering what you said in a former letter, that you should not be surprised at your son's leaving his lady on my son's hands.

Mrs. Hogg thought it proper to write to her, telling her how very imprudent it was for her to be left with our son, and also informing her that he had no money to support her in Mr. Shelley's absence, that she hoped she would by no means continue with him, and pitying her situation, offer'd to write to her friends. To this she wrote a very civil answer, much in the stile. of a Gentlewoman, thanking Mrs. H. for her kindness, but declining her service for the present. I am sorry to say I had a letter from your son about a week since declaring that it was his firm resolution never to part from my son—and my son declares he will not give up your son's friendship on any account. How this business is to end God only knows. I really know not how to act. I find they are in debt at York.

I did all I could to get them once separated, and was

334

The Elopement, and After

happy in succeeding, and was at much expense in placing my son at York with a Barrister for a year, hoping that absence would dissolve our son's unfortunate friendship before I entered him of Lincoln's Inn. I have been disappointed, and all my hopes are banished !!! Oh, my dear Sir! I am almost heartbroken, and so is my wife! We flattered ourselves that one day we should have seen him an ornament to his profession, and no expense from my moderate fortune should have been spared to have made him so—he was well and religiously brought up I can assure you; every person here and in the neighbourhood loved and esteemed him! I can add no more! I shall say with the Psalmist : " It is good for me that I have been in trouble, that I may learn thy Statutes ! "

Mrs. Hogg begs to unite with me in wishing every consolation to you and yours.—I am, dear Sir, your obliged humble st.,   JOHN HOGG.

[Addressed]
    T. SHELLEY, Esq., M.P.,
        Field Place,
           Near Horsham,
             Sussex.

P. B. Shelley to Timothy Shelley

[Endorsed by Mr. Shelley, " Received *Oct.* 18, 1811."]

DEAR FATHER,—I understand you have written to Mr. Hogg of Stockton. I know not what your letter contained, but by some ill effects resulting from it I discover that you have said something which has greatly prejudiced the relations of my friend against me.

This is a cowardly, base, contemptible expedient

of persecution : is it not enough that you have deprived me of the means of subsistence (which means, recollect, you *unequivocally* promised), but that you must take advantage of the defencelessness which *our* relation entails upon me, to *libel* me. Have you forgotten what a libel is ? or is memory *so very treacherous* that it does not tell you the danger you stood in from your misrepresentations of Stockdale the bookseller . . . the mere laws of your country then defend others against your injuries, to these I cannot have recourse. You have treated me *ill, vilely*. When I was expelled for Atheism you wished I had been killed in Spain. The desire of its consummation is very like the crime, perhaps it is well for me that the laws of England punish murder, and that *cowardice* shrinks from thier animadversion.

I shall take the first opportunity of seeing you ; if *you* will not hear my name *I* will pronounce it. Think not I am an insect whom injuries destroy . . . had I money enough I would meet you in London and hollow in your ears Bysshe, Bysshe, Bysshe . . . aye, Bysshe till you're deaf.

[Addressed]
T. SHELLEY, Esq., M.P.,
Field Place,
Horsham, Sussex.

Bysshe was as good as his word, and called on his father on Sunday, October 20, and learnt that it was only possible to discuss the question of his allowance through Mr. Whitton, to whom he therefore wrote for an appointment.

The Elopement, and After

But in the meantime, on Monday, Oct. 21, the day after Bysshe called at Field Place, Mr. Shelley wrote the following note to Captain Pilford :

"FIELD PLACE, *Oct.* 21, 1811.

" Mr. Shelley understands his son is with Captain Pilfold. Mr. S. begs to apprise Captain P. that his son's irrational notions, and the absence of all sentiment of Duty and affection, and the unusual spirit of Resistance to any controul has determined Mr. S. not to admit him, but to place everything respecting him into the hands of Mr. Whitton, that no other person may interfere."

[Addressed]
  TO CAPTAIN PILFOLD, R.N.,
    Cuckfield.

P. B. Shelley to W. Whitton

CAPT. PILFORD'S, R.N.,
CUCKFIELD, SUSSEX,
October 20, 1811.

SIR,—Understanding that pecuniary matters which concern me are entrusted to you, I beg to know, *by return of post*, where I can see you in Town. I intend to bring a friend with me.—Sir, yours' hum. servt.,

P. B. SHELLEY.

[Addressed]
  WHITTON, Esq.,
    Grove House,
      Camberwell, Surrey.

[*Postmark : Oct.* 21, 1811.]

While Bysshe was in Sussex he went to see Sir Bysshe ; it would be interesting to have details of the conversation between the boy and his old grandfather, but such can only be supplied by the imagination. Mr. Shelley, however, in writing to Whitton on October 23 briefly referred to the visit :

"The youngster call'd on him and behav'd very well. He told him to be dutyful and obedient and he would be receiv'd when he properly conducted himself, thank'd him for his advice and went away."

Although Bysshe was now an outcast from his father's house, and not worth sixpence, as Whitton had bluntly put it, he concluded that, in order to "obviate future difficulties," he should make marriage settlements. Accordingly, before he left Cuckfield, he wrote to ask Mr. Medwin, senior, to undertake this business for him. He had evidently seen the Horsham lawyer a day or so before, and sought his advice in regard to the negotiations with his father. As a precaution he intended to be re-married. He said, "I wish the sum settled on my wife in case of my death to be £700 per annum. The maiden name is Harriett Westbrook with two T's. You will be so good as to address me at Mr. Westbrook's, 23 Chapel Street, Grosvenor Square. We most probably go to London to-morrow. We shall see Whitton, when I shall neither forget your advice nor cease to be grateful for it." Captain Pilfold had consented to accompany Bysshe to town, and he may have intended while he was there to make an attempt at conciliating his father-in-law.

Whitton, however, declined Shelley's request to see him, and he gave his reason in a letter to Sir Bysshe bearing the date of October 22 ; he said, " The tenour and manner of his letter bespeaks his consequence, so I have desired him not to take the trouble of the journey from Captain Pilfold's, Cuckfield, but to communicate his sentiments in writing." [1]

So Bysshe at once complied with the lawyer's request, and addressed to him the following brief note :

P. B. Shelley to William Whitton

TURK'S COFFEE HOUSE,
Tuesday evening,
[*October* 22, 1811.]

" Mr. P. B. Shelley being referred to Mr. Whitton on application for an allowance of £200 per an. promised by his father, begs to know in what manner its arrangement is made. Mr. P. B. S. being in haste to quit Town for a remote part of the Kingdom begs the favour of an immediate answer."

Whitton replied on the following day, and told him that his father's communications had been of a very painful nature, resulting from Bysshe's correspondence and the manner in which he had treated him. Mr.

---

[1] Shelley wrote to Miss Hitchener when he returned to York : " We did not call on Whitton as we passed. We find he means absolutely nothing ; he talks of disrespect, duty, &c."

Shelley in England

Shelley was determined to stop supplies until he could be satisfied that Bysshe's "future conduct will be directed by a judgment consonant to his duty to him as a parent." It remained for him to consider the serious question of his father's injured feelings, and to seek a restoration of his confidence.

While Bysshe was at York, he seems to have formed the impression, whether rightly or wrongly, that his mother was contriving a match between his sister Elizabeth and Edward Fergus Graham. How he got this impression it is impossible to say, unless Captain Pilfold had repeated in a letter to his nephew some idle local gossip. Bysshe told his mother, perhaps when he was at Field Place on Sunday, October 20, that he did not come from York on his own business, but to inform her of this rumour. He may also have had some conversation with Elizabeth on the subject, that confirmed him in his impression.

Young Graham's father, who had been in the army, was employed in some capacity by Mr. Shelley, and acted as his factotum. Hogg remembered old Mr. Graham making tea, when he and Bysshe dined with Mr. Shelley at his hotel during their stay at Poland Street. Edward Graham had been brought up in Mr. Shelley's house, and he and Bysshe, according to the statement of one who knew them both, were like brothers. When Graham, later, gave proofs of a talent

The Elopement, and After

for music, Mr. Shelley bore the expenses of his training, and he went to London to become a pupil of Joseph Woelff, a well-known German musician of the day. Bysshe wrote songs to be set to music by Graham, who made himself useful to his patron's son when he was in town during his Eton and Oxford days. "Direct me to Graham's," is a frequent request in Shelley's earlier letters, which likewise contained numerous commissions for his friend. Bysshe could not resist the opportunity of referring, in the following request, to his father's note to Captain Pilfold, which, as Mr. Shelley subsequently observed, remained un-answered.

P. B. Shelley to Timothy Shelley

CUCKFIELD, *Oct.* 22, 1811.

DR. SIR,—I would thank you to deliver the enclosed to my mother; *very* much obliged for this morn's intimation to my uncle.—Yours, &c.,

P. B. SHELLEY.

[Addressed]
    T. SHELLEY, Esq., M.P.,
        Field Place,
            Horsham, Sussex.

P. B. Shelley to Mrs. Timothy Shelley

CAPT. PILFOLD'S,
[*Undated. Oct.* 22, 1811.]

DEAR MOTHER,—I had expected before this, to have heard from you on a subject so important as that of my late communication. I now expect to hear from you, unless you desire the publicity of my sister's intended marriage with Graham. . . . You tell me that you care not for the opinion of the world; this contempt for its consideration is noble if accompanied by consciousness of rectitude; if the contrary, it is the last resort of unvieled misconduct, is the daringness of despair, not the calmness of fortitude. You ask me if *I* suspect you . . . I do; my suspicions of your motives are strong, and such as I insist upon should be either confirmed or refuted.

I suspect your motives for *so violently*, so *persecutingly* desiring to unite my sister Elizabeth to the music master Graham. I suspect that it was intended to shield *yourself* from that suspicion which at length has fallen on you. If it is unjust, prove it. I give you a fair opportunity—it depends on yourself to avail yourself of it. Write to me [at Mr. Westbrook's, 23 Chapel Street, Grosvenor Square.] [1]—Your son,

P. B. SHELLEY.

You had better acquaint my Father with the debt with Mrs. Bowley, *he* is the proper person to do away with the obligation.

[Addressed]
MRS. SHELLEY.

P. B. Shelley to Elizabeth Shelley

CUCKFIELD, *Oct.* 22, 1811.

I write to inform you that my mother has recieved a letter from me, on the subject of Graham's projected

---

[1] The words within square brackets have been struck out.

union with you. My mother may shew the letter to my father . . . in this case do you speak truth.—
Your brother,   PERCY SHELLEY.

> [Addressed]
>   MISS SHELLEY,
>   Field Place, Horsham.

Nothing came of this affair ; but Shelley appears to have been convinced that something was wrong. He seems to have talked the matter over with Miss Hitchener at Captain Pilfold's, for he wrote to her, after his return to York,[1] the following obscure remarks : "I observed that you were much shocked at my mother's depravity. I have heard some reasons (and as mere reasons they are satisfactory) that there is no such thing as moral depravity. But it does not prove the non-existence of a thing that is not discoverable by reason ; *feeling* here affords us sufficient proofs." [2]

Neither Mrs. Shelley nor her daughter saw Bysshe's letters, because Mr. Shelley sent them on to Whitton unopened. It was due to the lawyer that the matter rested where it was ; for he certainly displayed discretion in dealing with the letters. He did not return them to Mr. Shelley, but merely told him that they

---

[1] October 26, 1811.

[2] Miss Elizabeth Shelley died, unmarried, in 1832. Graham, who made no public mark as a musician, survived probably till the early fifties. Mr. W. M. Rossetti, who remembered meeting him in his boyhood, contributed some interesting reminiscences of this early friend of Shelley to the present writer's edition of *Shelley's Letters*.

contained "matter of reflection on Mrs. Shelley and admonition to Miss Shelley too trifling and absurd to be repeated." He then informed Bysshe that he had received the letters, unopened, for his perusal, and asked for leave to destroy them. This was not only well-meant advice, but Whitton's way of letting Bysshe know that no one save himself had read the letters.

The Duke of Norfolk, who had no doubt heard of Bysshe's marriage, had not forgotten his talks with him earlier in the year on the profession of politics. Mr. Shelley dined with the Duke at the Bailiff's feast on Oct. 22. No doubt he was glad of the opportunity of talking about his son to the Duke, who "asked very civilly about this unpleasant business." Mr. Shelley said that the matter was entirely in Whitton's hands, whereupon the Duke asked for his address in order to talk with him on the subject. Writing to Mr. Shelley on Oct. 24, Whitton said, "His Grace of Norfolk has just called." The subject of his conversation is given in Whitton's next letter to Bysshe.

W. Whitton to P. B. Shelley

10 GREAT JAMES ST.,
Oct. 24, 1811.

SIR,—From the tendency and stile of your late communications to your father, he has resolved not again to open a letter from you, and I mention this to save the time which the passage to and from Horsham will occasion of any communication or letter you may make or send. If, therefore, you shall think proper to address your father, and will send the paper to me, I will forward it to him, as I trust it will be conceived in terms that will justify my so doing. Your letter to your mother, which I opened and read this morning, is not proper, and I beg you will allow me to destroy it, as also that to your sister. You forget what is due from you, when you commit such harsh and unfeeling sentiments to writing.

His Grace the Duke of Norfolk, out of respect to your family, called on me just now to learn your address at York ; and I told his Grace you were in Town. He sayed he left Town to-morrow for 8 or 9 days, or that he would endeavour to see you. His Grace will not leave town until to-morrow 12, and perhaps you will take the opportunity of waiting on him in Saint James Square before that hour.—I am, Sir, yours, &c.,

WM. WHITTON.

[Addressed]
   P. B. SHELLEY, Esq.,
      Turk's Head Coffee House,
        Strand.

Bysshe left London for York immediately after this letter reached the Turk's Head, as it was forwarded to him with the address added : " Mr. Stricklands, Blake Street, York." He read the letter with indignation, and wrote across the outside page, which bears Whitton's addressing, the following angry note :

P. B. Shelley to W. Whitton

" William Whitton's letter is concieved in terms which justify Mr. P. Shelley's returning it for his cool reperusal. Mr. S. commends Mr. W. when he deals with gentlemen (which opportunity perhaps may not often occur) to refrain from opening private letters, or impudence may draw down chastisement upon contemptibility.

" York," &c.

Bysshe then despatched the letter with this re-direction :

" MR. W. WHITTON,
    10 Gt. James Street,
        Bedford Row, London."

The postmark is dated *Nov.* 1, 1811.

Referring to this matter, as a topic of local interest, in a letter [1] to his kinsman, the elder Medwin, who lived at Horsham, Bysshe said : " Whitton has written to me to state the impropriety of my letters to my mother and sisters ; this letter I have returned with a passing remark on the back of it. I find that affair on which those letters spoke is become the general gossip of the idle newsmongers of Horsham. They give *me* the credit of having invented it. They do my imagination much honour, but greatly discredit their own penetration."

Whitton also commented on Shelley's note, in writing to Sir Bysshe on November 2, the day following its receipt : " I have had from P. B. Shelley the most scurrilous letter that a mad viper could dictate."

[1] November 26, 1811.

The Elopement, and After

The amenities of correspondence being in abeyance, the writers of these letters were not sparing in invective. In his letters to Whitton Mr. Shelley's language was unrestrained, and he showed himself to be thoroughly frightened. Writing on October 25 he informed Whitton that he had advised Mr. Hogg, senior, to delegate the business of dealing with his son to " some experienced gentleman," as he had done in the case of Bysshe.

" From the present perturbed state of P. B.'s mind, which will not suffer it to rest until it has completely and entirely disordered his whole spiritual past, I will not open a letter from him, and be cautious how I open any in other handwriting for fear he should endeavour to deceive.

" I shall most decidedly keep my resolution with him, and had he stay'd in Sussex I would have sworn in Especial Constables around me. He frightened his mother and sister exceedingly, and now if they hear a Dog Bark they run up stairs. He has nothing to say but the £200 a year.

" He has withdrawn himself from me and my Protection. He forgets his own promise, that he was not to be Idle, but place himself in some Gentlemanly situation long before this. He always varied, and now for the first time he is placed in a situation that he must be humbl'd, for I never before oppos'd or closely pursued him.

" The Duke of Norfolk is most kind towards me upon all occasions. But this young man must manifest to the world his abhorrence of such monstrous opinions as he has sent forth, and also demonstrate by Acts of respect, Duty, and contrite Heart, before I can receive him upon his knees. No doubt his letters were of the most mischievous kind. He would not regard any language against his mother or sister. He accuses me of Libel and the thought of everything that could be bad, nor would he stick at any infamous language in his writing.

" Pray, my dear Sir, don't spare him in his absurdities, for I shall submit to your judgment, and I hope assisted by His Grace the Duke of Norfolk's Influence on P. B.'s mind. . . .

" *N.B.*—I can only guess at the seven deadly sins. He is capable of any mischief, particularly in the Family. He has no regard to character himself. Father, Mother, Sisters and Brother all alike."

On October 27 Mr. Shelley again wrote to Whitton :

. . . " The Duke of Norfolk felt much and wished something might be settled, but His Grace, said Mr. S., you cannot do it. I told His Grace that I had left it to you, and depended on you in every respect. P. B. forgets that I consider you an experienc'd Friend, and lucky for him to have the advice of such a Gentleman. I only wish it had to operate on an Ingenuous Heart and a Sound understanding, but he is such a Pupil of Godwin that I can scarcely hope he will be persuaded that he owes any sort of obedience or compliance to the wishes or directions of his Parents.

The Elopement, and After

He will contest every point, for youth is not the Season for admissions.

"Had Captn. Pilfold informed me when P. B. came to him, or advis'd him differently, and not taken him into his House in his Disobedience, I should have been better satisfied. I hear he was in London with him. P. B. told his mother that he did not come from York on his own business but to inform her what was said of her. Too absurd and ridiculous for a thought. I wish he may continue 100 miles off and not come near me, and I wish he may not work his disorder'd mind up to such a Pitch as to do mischief to himself or some others.

"I have been led on to write more than I had intended, for I am best satisfied when out of sight and out of mind. . . . I will not trouble you unnecessarily because I know you will manage best. We are all well, but often in sad frights with the Ladies' fancies."

END OF VOLUME I

Lightning Source UK Ltd.
Milton Keynes UK
UKHW022001090519
342426UK00008B/223/P